Second Editi

The Social Context of Law

Sheryl J. Grana
University of Minnesota, Duluth

Jane C. Ollenburger
California State Polytechnic University, Pomona

Mark Nicholas

Upper Saddle River, New Jersey 07458

Library of Congress Cataloging-in-Publication Data

Grana, Sheryl J.
The social context of law / Sheryl J. Grana, Jane C. Ollenburger, Mark Nicholas.—2nd ed.
p. cm.
Includes bibliographical references and index.
ISBN 0-13-041374-7 (paper)
1. Sociological jurisprudence. 2. Law—Philosophy. 3. Law—United States. I. Ollenburger, Jane C. II. Nicholas, Mark, (date)

K370 .G72 2002
340'.1—dc21

2001036169

VP, Editorial Director: Laura Pearson
AVP, Publisher: Nancy Roberts
Managing Editor: Sharon Chambliss
Editorial/production supervision
and interior design: Mary Araneo
Marketing Manager: Chris Barker
Prepress and Manufacturing Buyer: Mary Ann Gloriande
Cover Art Director: Jayne Conte
Cover Designer: Bruce Kenselaar

This book was set in 10/12 Palatino by A & A Publishing Services, Inc., and was printed and bound by Courier Companies, Inc. The cover was printed by Jaguar Graphics.

Printed in the United States of America

10 9 8 7

ISBN 0-13-041374-7

Pearson Education LTD., London
Pearson Education Australia PTY, Limited, Sydney
Pearson Education Singapore, Pte. Ltd
Pearson Education North Asia Ltd, Hong Kong
Pearson Education Canada, Ltd., Toronto
Pearson Educación de Mexico, S.A. de C.V.
Pearson Education -- Japan, Tokyo
Pearson Education Malaysia, Pte. Ltd
Pearson Education, Upper Saddle River, New Jersey

Contents

5 SYSTEMS OF LAW 96

6 PRACTITIONERS OF LAW 127

Preface

We are *structural* sociologists. We believe in the tradition of sociology and the idea that the structure of society explains many patterns of social behavior and opportunities in society. This book elucidates for readers the importance of law on and in the structure of society. We emphasize the relationship between law and a set of entities: people, social conditions, and ideas. These realities, as we refer to them, are the variables that most clearly affect and define the social world within which we operate as social beings. The ongoing interplay between law and these realities places all of us in legal positions which we may like and/or dislike; yet the interplay is a dance in which we all participate, whether we realize it or not.

This book was written for undergraduate courses in disciplines such as sociology, criminology, and political science, and for individuals entertaining ideas about entering the legal professions. We include in this list prelaw, paralegal, corrections, and similar studies. But any reader who desires an understanding of the significant bearing law has on contemporary life may find it useful. We are not lawyers, but we do believe that an understanding of the intimate and affective role of law is important to our understanding of society.

We received significant support from a variety of sources, for this edition as well as the first. As always, we would like to thank Nancy Roberts of Prentice Hall. For the first edition, she gave us the time we needed to put this project together, and we are grateful to her for that understanding. In addition to Nancy, Rob DeGeorge, our Production Editor, was very helpful and always available when we needed him. We were fortunate to have two able research assistants, Cori Barrera and Jan Cannata, whose work was funded by the Office of Research Administration at Boise State University. Kathleen Maguire, co-editor of the *Sourcebook of Criminal Justice Statistics*, gave us useful and timely assistance with tables, data, and sources. We would also like to thank the following reviewers: Phillip W. Davis, Georgia State University; Ali Gheissari, University of California at San Diego; Steve B. McConnell, University of Toledo; and Eric Rise, University of Delaware. In addition, the following reviewers provided us with recommendations and insight for the second edition: Matt Lee, University of Delaware; Zoann K. Snyder, Western Michigan University; and Gloria A. Whittico, Hampton University. Mary Araneo and her colleagues from A & A Publishing Services, Inc., did an exceptional job in the copyediting and production of the second edition.

This second edition of *The Social Context of Law* expands on the idea that drove the first, that neither law nor society functions independently of the other. Further case studies and discussions of law as it affects American tribal members as well as persons under U.S. military jurisdiction are presented to illustrate the symbiotic relationship between the two. Data tables and graphs have been updated, where possible, with the most recent information available. Our intent, of course, is to make the information as accessible as possible, and to that end we have added an author. Mark Nicholas is a professional writer whose straightforward prose contributed to improving the readability of the text.

Once again, our thanks to our families and friends for their support and understanding during this process. We couldn't have done it without them. And finally to each other: Cheers!

S.J.G. , J.C.O., M.N.

Introduction

1. Freedom of religion, press, speech, and assembly.
2. Right to maintain a state militia and to keep and bear arms.
3. Right to refuse to house soldiers in private homes.
4. Protection against unreasonable searches and seizures.
5. Right to refuse to testify against oneself.
6. Right to a speedy public trial before an impartial jury; to be told the nature and cause of the accusation; to have legal counsel.
7. Right to a jury in civil cases.
8. Protection against cruel and unusual punishment.
9. Individual rights not limited to those listed in the amendments.
10. Powers not given to the federal government or prohibited to states retained by states or by the people.

Above is a paraphrased list of the first ten amendments to the U.S. Constitution. The Bill of Rights[1] was developed during a specific era in history by a specific group of people and was inspired by a certain set of ideas. It is the cornerstone of many laws in the United States and was written within a particular social context—the struggle to break with Great Britain.

This book is about the *social* context of law, the relationship between law and society. As sociologists, we write this text from our disciplinary bias. We believe it is important to understand the ways in which society and law interact. Law is social. Human beings create laws and do so within the context of their times and societies. Sociology, the study of society, is the perfect vehicle for an investigation of the legal system. As Stimpson and Stimpson (1987) state, two of the "promises" of sociology are its creation of a new awareness of the social world and its ability to help us find our way through the often confusing maze of societal norms, roles, and obligations. By creating a new awareness and helping us to understand the maze, sociology can show us how legal systems are developed and how they work. Charon (1996) reminds us that we are all prisoners of the social organization of society and that the world we live in is often not as it appears. As social beings, we must understand that we never can be released from society or its legalities and must study society without the blinders many of us wear. Because it is sociology that helps us do so, we use sociology as the tool for our investigation into law and society.

A society is a group of individuals who are bound together by territorial, political, and economic ties. All societies have a "culture," which is "the total way of life shared by members of a society" (Brinkerhoff, White, and Ortega, 1995:32). Culture permeates all areas of our social life and is passed down from generation to generation. As individuals, we use the framework of our culture to assist us in solving problems and fulfilling basic human needs. Culture is composed of three interrelated components: the cognitive component, which defines how we think and communicate; the normative component, which defines our beliefs and values; and the material component, which includes all the material possessions used in a society. Figure I–1 illustrates the intersection of these three components.

All of daily life in a society is influenced by cultural components, including language; ways of thinking, feeling, and acting; tools and technologies; eating patterns; sleeping habits; types and styles of communication; and the law. Culture varies around the world and is modified over

FIGURE I-1 Three Interrelated Components of Culture

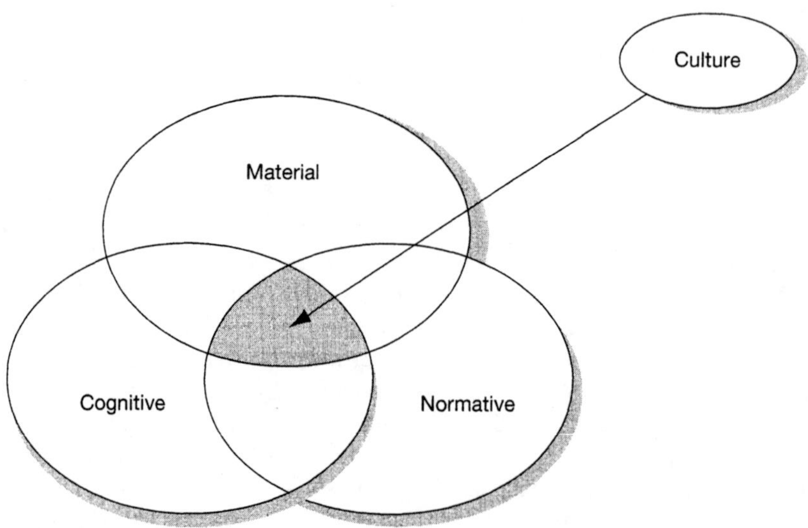

time; it is dependent on the ideas of the people and the social conditions that exist during a given time period.

Just as societies and cultures are fluid and shifting in nature, so is the law, since culture and society shape the law. As cultures experience transition, so do laws, although many critics argue that laws change more slowly. As law evolves, it in turn affects culture. The fact that culture influences law and that law effects a corresponding shift in culture demonstrates an interdependence between societies and their legal systems.

This interdependence will be discussed in the following pages as we examine the many ways in which culture and society affect law and vice versa. We begin our discussion by specifically identifying the three realities that influence the social context of law: people and groups, ideas, and social conditions (Chapter 1). We also include in Chapter 1 a discussion of the components and sources of law, as well as the definition of law that we will use in this text. In Chapter 2, we introduce the various theorists who have discussed law, and we illustrate and clarify the points each of these theorists suggests. We also attempt to illustrate how the three social realities influence the ideas of theorists as they write about law.

Chapter 3 provides an introduction to the diverse legal families that exist around the world. Through this discussion we demonstrate how people, social conditions, and ideas influence the development and evolution of legal systems. Chapter 4 focuses on the different types of law, with special emphasis on criminal law, and also discusses the foundation of law in the United States, the Constitution. We examine systems of law in Chapter 5 by looking at the U.S. court system, including the Supreme Court, and such issues as case attrition and the flow of litigation. Chapter 5 also includes two conceptual models that social scientists use to explain the legal system.

In Chapter 6 we look at law professionals, lawyers, legislators, police, judges, and correctional officers, and we examine how they are trained, their work environments, and the interactions of their jobs with social conditions and ideas. Chapter 7 discusses the purposes and usefulness of law as a social control mechanism, as a conflict resolution mechanism, as a punishment and remedy, and as a form of public policy. Finally, in Chapter 8 we examine the relationship between the law and race and ethnicity, social class, gender, and age, and illustrate the interrelationship of these topics through a discussion of the death penalty.

This book will discuss a variety of topics to help us understand the interaction of law and society. Sociology is our tool for investigation; law is our focus.

NOTE

1. The first ten amendments to the U.S. Constitution, the Bill of Rights, were adopted in 1791. See Appendix for the full text of the Constitution.

1 The Social Context of Law

In order to examine the relationship between law and society we first must realize that societies and cultures are bound to law by three cultural realities: social conditions, societal ideas, and the input of people (singularly and in groups). All three realities are connected across time and in a constant state of transition. The following discussion will highlight the relationship among these three realities that create the social context of law.

SOCIAL CONDITIONS

The social, economic, and cultural conditions of any society determine the *variety* of laws that are created and implemented. The social conditions determine whether or not courts exist and whether there is such a thing as a *legal professional* (lawyers, judges, and police personnel). Democratic industrial societies typically make distinctions between civil and criminal law, substantive and procedural law, and other varieties of law (differences that will be discussed later in the chapter). Hunting and gathering societies have little use for an extensive body of law, a formal legal system, or a complex variety of legal personnel. Societies evolve over time, however, and new social conditions necessitate social change. These cultural shifts dictate a negotiated establishment (or renewal) of the legal system and associated roles within it.

Social conditions affect not only the type of laws that are constructed but also their content, or substance. Rules that govern simple horticultural systems are quite different from the complex codifications produced by postindustrialist societies. In the context of the nontechnical nature of horticultural societies with uncomplicated gender roles, there is little concern about sexual harassment or carjacking, for example. In emerging industrial, capitalistic systems, laws concerning economic monopolies are created by necessity. For example, the social conditions that would lead to the creation of monopolies do not exist in traditional horticultural societies, so that sophisticated economic regulation would be unnecessary. (For a detailed description of various societal types, see Table 2–1.)

SOCIAL IDEAS

The ideas current in a society at any given time affect both the laws that are enacted and the nature of the justice system. For example, in the United States during the 1860s and 1870s, the idea that women could be admitted to the bar, a requirement to practice law, was almost unthinkable. Social ideas dominant at that time placed women in the home in subservient, domestic positions, not arguing cases in a courtroom. When these assumptions were challenged by Myra Bradwell [*Bradwell v. Illinois*, 16 Wall 130 (1872)],[1] the Supreme Court of the United States decided that her rights as an individual were not denied. Bradwell had petitioned the Illinois Supreme Court to admit her to the bar. Although she met all the usual criteria (education, testing on the law, good moral character), the Illinois Supreme Court predicated its decision on laws that precluded women from entering contracts independent of their husbands. If Bradwell were to make a *lawyerly* act that might prompt a lawsuit, her husband would be sued. This was a prospect the court held to be radical and ludicrous. That was the legal rationale, but the decision actually reflected the prevailing social ideas on gender roles. On appeal to the U.S. Supreme Court, the official ruling was once more enveloped in legal rhetoric. The social reality is revealed in Justice Bradley's concurring opinion, which is often quoted to illustrate the unbridled sexism of the time:

> The natural and proper timidity and delicacy which belongs to the female sex evidently unfits it for many of the occupations of civil life. The constitution of the family . . . founded in divine ordinance, as well as in the nature of things, indicates the domestic sphere as . . . the domain and functions of womanhood. *Bradwell v. Illinois*, 83 U.S. (16 Wall) 130 (1872).

Myra Bradwell's attempt to enter the legal profession came at a pivotal time in American history, the immediate post–Civil War, or Reconstruction, period. The South was subject to enforced compliance with and adaptation to the notion of African Americans[2] as free men and women. The passage of the Civil War amendments to the U.S. Constitution[3] crystallized highly charged and complex issues that tested social, economic, political, and legal ideologies and institutions in a deeply fractured society. Bradwell's challenge to limitations on women's ability to enter professions reserved for men (law and medicine) created an unforeseen dilemma for the U.S. Supreme Court justices. Every conceivable public forum in America was scrambling to incorporate the directives of the Civil War amendments and concomitant federal mandates to extend all rights, liberties, and privileges of citizens to African-American males. Political tension was at a fevered pitch, with a great deal of postwar resentment and reticence attached to these radical notions of civil rights for a class of people so recently enslaved. The parallel development in race- and gender-based equity issues will become clearer by considering a more extensive analysis of Myra Bradwell's case and the underlying social and legal phenomena.

Social Ideas: A Note on Constitutional Case Law

As you read the following summary, or *brief*, of Myra Bradwell's case, the role of the U.S. Supreme Court in clarifying and shaping social ideas, even to the extent of mandating sociolegal policy, will become readily apparent. In a subsequent section on constitutional law, we will consider more fully the implications of the Supreme Court's selection of cases and controversies (granting certiorari) for review. Case analysis generally reveals a sociopolitical subtext to the Court's decision making, which extends beyond purely legal questions. Once a case is chosen, the justices select and interpret previously decided cases, which, based on precedent (founded on the principle of stare decisis—to stand by the decision), provide a trail of legal legitimacy back to the Constitution. The Supreme Court, also called the High Court, either reiterates the logic used in deciding earlier cases, adapting to the present issue, or refutes the decisions as being no longer applicable to current realities in society. The *majority* opinion is usually written by one justice and is the expression of the decision reached. It presents the principles of law behind the decision and expounds the legal reasoning that led to it. A majority decision has the most value as precedent. Other justices may write *separate* opinions of the case, either to concur with or dissent from the majority view. *Concurring* opinions agree with the result reached by the majority, but disagree with the precise reasoning used to arrive at the result. *Dissenting* or *minority* opinions disagree with the result, and therefore with the reasoning and/or principles of law behind it. A *plurality* opinion is issued when a

Bradwell v. Illinois
83 U.S. (16 Wall) 130 (1872)

Myra Bradwell, a resident of the state of Illinois, made an application to the Supreme Court of Illinois for a license to practice law. The Supreme Court of Illinois refused to grant her a license on the grounds that women are not allowed to practice law in that state. Bradwell appealed to the U.S. Supreme Court, arguing that the Fourteenth Amendment should protect her from this form of discrimination.

While the Supreme Court recognized problems with the rationale used by the Illinois Supreme Court to deny Bradwell's application to the bar, it did not find fault with the final decision, just with the blatancy of excluding an identifiable class of persons, namely, women.

Bradwell's lawyer, Matthew Hale Carpenter, crystallized the issue before the Supreme Court, in essence challenging the granting of privileges of citizenship regardless of race, while denying the same guarantees on the basis of gender.

> If the legislature, under pretense of fixing qualifications, declares that no female citizen shall be permitted to practice law, it may as well declare that no colored citizens shall practice law; for the only provision in the Constitution of the United States which secures to colored male citizens the privilege of admission to the bar . . . is that "no State shall make or enforce any law which shall abridge the privileges or immunities of a citizen." And if this provision does protect the colored citizen, then it protects every citizen, black or white, male or female. (135–136)

In countering this logic, the Court held that the issues raised under the Fourteenth Amendment were not applicable to this case. It held that the provisions of the Fourteenth Amendment were designed to specifically address only abrogations of citizens' rights, afforded by their home state, by the laws of another state.

> The right to admission to practice in the courts of a State . . . in no sense depends on citizenship of the United States . . . the right to control and regulate the granting of licenses to practice law in the courts of a State . . . are not transferred . . . to the Federal government, and its exercise is in no manner governed or controlled . . . by citizenship in the United States. (139)

JUDGMENT AFFIRMED

majority of justices agree on a result, but fewer than a majority agree on principles and/or reasoning. Justices may refine and communicate their individual opinions of a decision in the form of *obiter dicta* (singular, *obiter dictum*). These *by the way* opinions are entirely unnecessary to the decision of the case, but may lay the sociolegal foundation for later reconsideration of the decision.

Although such dicta are not binding as precedent, they can be indicative of social attitudes and legal policy as they undergo transition. Whether as a result of an evolving collective societal consciousness or perhaps the appointment of a new justice that affects the ideological composition of the Court, the law is constantly in flux. This evolution in case law on a given issue can, and often does, span decades. In considering any case important enough to be adjudicated by the U.S. Supreme Court, we do well to remember that multiple and complex social and legal issues are the norm, not the exception.

In 1872, the Supreme Court upheld the Illinois decision to prevent Myra Bradwell from practicing law. The social ideas of the time were the foundation for Justice Bradley's opinion—ideas that remained relatively immutable until the ratification of the Nineteenth Amendment in 1920, which gave women the right to vote.

In sum, three social ideas helped shape the Supreme Court's refutation of Myra Bradwell's *right* to practice law:

1. Women were not "designed by God" for any significant function beyond that of wife and mother.
2. Defining interaction between races was a volatile concern at the time and was to be explored only with great caution.
3. Postwar tensions transcended race issues, encompassing a very entrenched states' rights agenda that sought to nullify the intrusive federal question inherent in the Fourteenth Amendment.

Beyond the gender issues raised by the Bradwell case, it would take an additional twenty-five years to fully resolve the matter of admitting African Americans to the bar. The Supreme Court facilitated the perpetuation and extension of racially based exclusion in 1896 in *Plessy v. Ferguson*. This case gave constitutional legitimacy to the "separate but equal" doctrine, which will be discussed more fully later in this chapter in the context of *Brown v. Board of Education of Topeka, Kansas* (1954–1955). The legal loophole used to circumvent the Civil War amendments was this rationalization: although the Fourteenth Amendment clearly forbade denying rights of citizenship, it didn't specify that those rights had to occur within "white" contexts as long as "equal" provisions were made. The small motivation to fund "equal" facilities for African Americans, coupled with a very real agenda not to encourage significant changes in status or opportunity, created inequities that would not be modified in actual practice until the civil rights movement of the 1960s.

The influence of social ideas can be seen in a more contemporary example. The ideas of Ronald Reagan about drug use (and Nancy Reagan's "just say no" campaign) influenced federal policies made during his administration, including longer sentences for drug convictions and a renewed interest in law enforcement. Just as with the social ideas that affected Bradwell's life, Reagan's ideas did not surface or operate in a vacuum; they were part of the social environment of the time and were reflected in the laws that were enacted.

PEOPLE

Both individuals and groups influence and promote social change. The previous section mentioned two people, Myra Bradwell and Ronald Reagan. Their presence was significant, given the ideas and social conditions of their times. People and groups promote social ideas that simultaneously affect and are affected by social conditions. As a response to these ideas and social conditions, laws are created.

Various groups and individuals in society attempt to influence the judicial process through a number of specific avenues. They may lobby legislatures to enact laws that reflect their values and beliefs. For example, MADD (Mothers Against Drunk Drivers) has maintained a very aggressive and successful legislative agenda to toughen laws against drinking and driving. In addition, it has worked at a grassroots level to raise awareness in communities and to garner public support to assist in legislative actions. Although pioneered by Candy Lightner in 1980 after the death of her thirteen-year-old daughter by a hit-and-run driver, no one single person can ultimately be identified as the person responsible for the dramatic social change that has occurred as a result of the proactive actions of MADD. A group of people brought together by an issue shaped the opinions and laws related to drinking and driving.

INTERWOVEN NATURE OF THE THREE REALITY CONSTRUCTS

It is perhaps obvious at this point that all three of these realities are interwoven with each other. While they are each individually significant and important, their interdependence highlights the connectedness of culture (see Figure 1–1).

In addition to their interconnectedness, the process is dynamic. As legal outcomes result from the influence of social conditions, ideas, people, and groups, they themselves have an impact on the culture. As the process continues, new legal outcomes result (see Figure 1–2).

Ideas do not exist without people, and social conditions do not change without people. These realities of social and cultural life will be a continuous

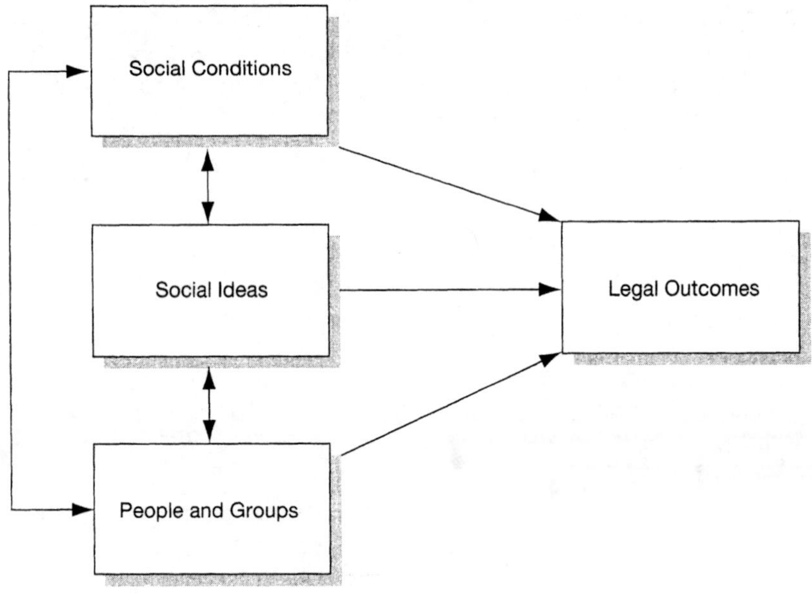

FIGURE 1–1 Interconnections

theme throughout this book. To better understand their importance to the legal cultural environment, Table 1–1 displays some examples.

The interdependent relationship that exists between these reality constructs and the law cannot be stressed enough. The people of a given time, the ideas they have, the social conditions in which they live, and the laws they enact, are inextricably joined in a reciprocal cause and effect. Laws are socially created phenomena; there is no way to study law without recognizing the influence of human lives on the genesis and evolution of laws.

TABLE 1–1 Interrelationship among Law, Social Realities, and Society

REALITIES:	EXAMPLE I	EXAMPLE II
Social conditions	The Great Depression	Children being killed by repeat drunk drivers
Social ideas	The New Deal	Crime victims' rights
People	President Franklin D. Roosevelt	Mothers Against Drunk Drivers (MADD)
Legal result	Social Security Act of 1935	More severe drunk-driving penalties/"designated driver" normalized

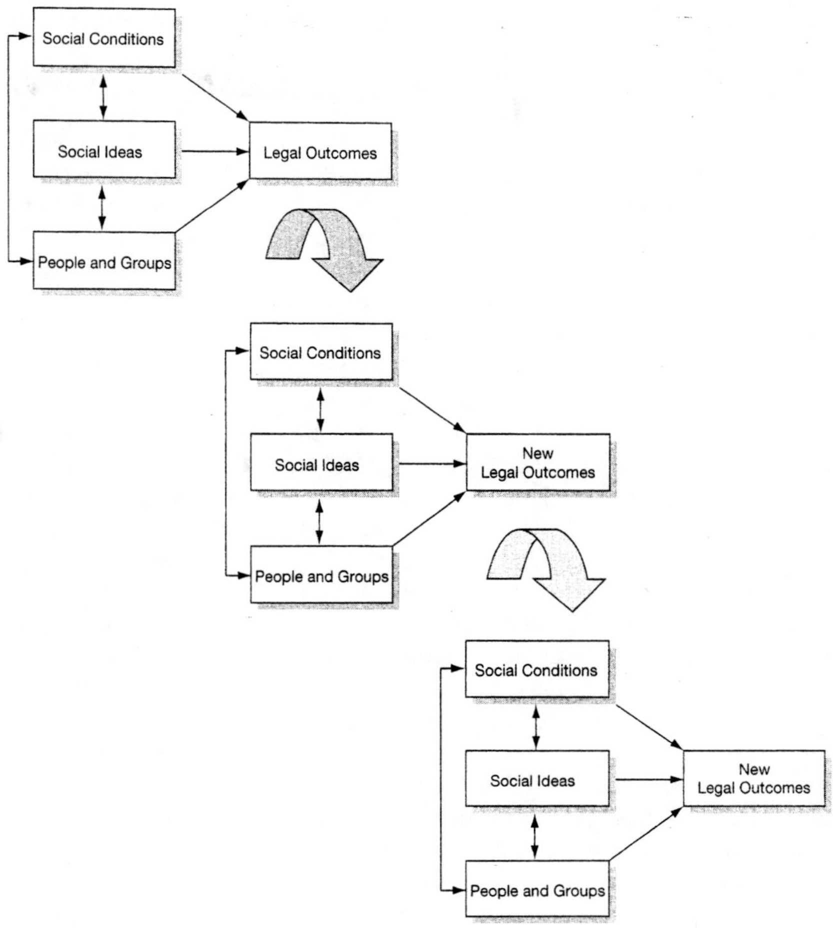

FIGURE 1–2 Nature of Interconnections

LEGAL CULTURE

Legal culture refers to both the structural and the functional components of the legal process. This includes the organization of law and the practice of law and justice in a given place (like Boise or Duluth). The people of a society (individuals, groups, and their institutions) initially specify what they want in their legal codes. Legal culture also refers to professional standards of conduct and ethics for police officers, judges, attorneys, and correctional officers, and it shapes the laws through judicial decisions such as that made in *Bradwell v. Illinois* (1872). We stressed the undeniable role contemporary social ideas and realities played in Myra Bradwell's efforts to effect personal and social change. But no case in the history of American jurisprudence has been more inextricably intertwined in the social fabric and the legal culture than the case we will now consider, *Brown v. Board of Education of Topeka, Kansas* [347 U.S. 483, 495 (1954)]. This case[4] often is associated with superlatives, such as the greatest equity case in our history or the case that generated the greatest number of amicus curiae briefs.[5] *Brown v. Board of Education* is an excellent example of the interaction between law and social conditions. The U.S. Supreme Court wrestled with the realities of the *separate but equal* doctrine, a principle established in the post–Civil War case of *Plessy v. Ferguson* [163 U.S. 537 (1896)]. We cannot adequately consider *Brown* without first discussing the context of the *separate but equal* principle.

In 1896, U.S. society was still in a state of upheaval, as social, economic, legal, and political agendas that resulted from the end of slavery were reconciled. As mentioned in the context of the Bradwell case, the Civil War amendments (thirteenth, fourteenth, and fifteenth) mandated radical changes in every social and legal dimension. The collective social ideology, with respect to the freed African Americans, was a confused mix of agendas. Recognizing this reality, the Supreme Court ruling in *Plessy v. Ferguson* affirmed the status quo, extending the policy that kept the two races apart. The decision validated the constitutionality of Jim Crow laws and provided for separate (and purportedly equal) public facilities for African Americans. In reality, separate but equal treatment was far from equitable. The term *Jim Crow laws* originated with the use of Jim Crow cars on the railroads in some southern states. These were separate rail cars for African-American passengers. Plessy, a "person of color," was charged with violating the Jim Crow statutes in Louisiana when he refused to move from a car reserved for whites. When South Carolina considered adoption of the Jim Crow laws in 1898, the editor of the *Charleston News and Courier* wrote the following editorial:

> If there are to be Jim Crow cars, moreover, there should be Jim Crow waiting saloons at all stations, and Jim Crow eating houses. . . . There should be Jim Crow sections of the jury box, and a separate Jim Crow dock and witness stand in every court and a Jim Crow Bible for colored witnesses to kiss. It would be advisable also to have a Jim Crow section in county auditors' and treasurers' offices for the accommodation of colored taxpayers. . . . Perhaps, the best plan would be, after all, to take the short cut to the general end . . . by establishing two or three Jim Crow counties at once, and turning them over to our colored citizens for their special and exclusive accommodation. (Berman and Greiner, 1972:842–843).

The editor's *reductio ad absurdum* attempted to ridicule the Jim Crow laws. But that which was considered absurd in the beginning became reality for many of the states in the South. With the exception of Jim Crow counties and Jim Crow witness stands, all the other absurdities became realities.

Generally, the laws allowed for segregation in all aspects of social life, and individuals were required to use only "race-appropriate" facilities, live in certain neighborhoods, and attend designated schools. This often meant inferior schools and hospitals for African-American citizens, and higher education and advanced medical care were simply nonexistent. In *Brown v. Board of Education,* the High Court contemplated this inequity and, in rare unanimity (9–0), declared unconstitutional the separate-but-equal policy in public schools. The *Brown* case, which had seemingly innocuous origins, resulted in a sweeping change of public policies related to education and eventually to other public accommodation.

As the following brief on *Brown* illustrates, while the Supreme Court gave legitimacy to the highly charged issue of school desegregation, the actual implementation of the *Brown* decision was resisted. For example, Governor Orval Faubus of Arkansas defied a federal district court order when he prevented African-American students from entering Little Rock High School in 1957. A mob assembled in front of the school, and President Eisenhower was forced to deploy the Arkansas National Guard and the U.S. Army's 101st "Screaming Eagles" Airborne Division. The conflict continued, particularly in the southern states, which resulted in the civil rights movement of the 1960s. The legal culture is a reflection of societal issues; no legal process operates in a vacuum. In addition, all places have their own legal culture, which can and does vary from one city, county, and state to the next.

Law permeates all forms of social behavior, and regulates virtually everything we do, down to our daily routines. The "do not remove under penalty of federal law" tag on our mattress, the level of pesticides allowed in our cereals, the manufacturing standards for the cars we drive, as well as the manner in which we operate our vehicles (driver's license, registration, insurance, gas taxes, rate of speed, and traffic regulations) are governed by laws.

Generally, laws maintain the status quo, but they also provide for necessary changes in society. The purposes of law are dictated by a society and its members as they weigh the useful aspects of law against its intrusiveness. For example, unrestricted access to television programming (First Amendment, free speech; Fourth Amendment, right to privacy) has, at times, competed with Federal Communications Commission (FCC) regulatory policy. The FCC regulates standards concerning the use of profanity and nudity on radio and television. As members of society, we ultimately determine the degree of protection from objectionable content we want through participation in the political and legal processes, by communicating our desires to commercial advertisers, or by changing channels.

The structural components of the legal system (such as laws, adjudicatory bodies, institutions, and their personnel) are also shaped by and should conform to a negotiated social ideology. Not all societies *use* law to the same degree. As illustrated earlier, traditional societies rely more on *custom* than formalized law. The growth of heterogeneity in a society inevitably necessitates a concomitant increase in the role that formal law plays because the potential for conflict is greater. Therefore, any analysis of a society's legal culture must take into account its sociological context.

A DEFINITION OF *LAW*

Language is one of the more important sources of unity or division in the identity of societies and cultures, as well as the life blood of law. We have used the term *law* several times already. Perhaps we mention it so offhandedly because it is a common term with a working definition we all share. But what is law really? Sociological knowledge, perspectives, and theories are all helpful in answering this question. However, it will become clear that there is no consensus on the answer.

According to *Webster's New World College Dictionary* (1995 edition), the word *law* originated in Old English more than 1,000 years ago. Currently, the dictionary posits twenty-four distinct definitions of the term, which seems a bit daunting for a book about the social context of law. For our purposes, we will begin with Webster's first definition: "The principles and regulations established by a government or other authority and applicable to a people, whether by legislation or by custom enforced by judicial decision." The second definition is "any written or positive rule or collection of rules prescribed under the authority of the state or nation, as by the people in its constitution."

Since language is the medium of law, we turn to *Black's Law Dictionary* (1990 edition) in pursuit of a more precise legal construction. Definitions on or about the law span four pages.[6] *Black's* cites forty-one court cases, three code sections, and one gubernatorial proclamation to define adequately the word *law* for legal purposes. Each citation is context-sensitive and gives a particular jurist's interpretation of the word. For example, "The word [law] *may mean* or *embrace*: [a] body of principles, standards and rules promulgated by government." Following Black's directive to "*see 'Laws,'*" we find a reasonably straightforward assignment of meaning. Laws are "rules promulgated by government as a means to an ordered society."

The field of sociology provides yet another definition of law: "Laws are rules that are enforced and sanctioned by the authority of government. They may or may not be norms." Further, norms are "shared rules of conduct that specify how people ought to think and act" (Brinkerhoff, White, and Ortega, 1995:39). Therefore, within a society the standards of appropriate and inappropriate behavior are sanctioned through a variety of mechanisms. Essential *mores*, that is, norms "associated with strong feelings of right and wrong" (p. 39), are often defined and sanctioned by law. Laws, then, become the "formal standards of conduct, enforced by public agencies" (p. 40).

Brown v. Board of Education of Topeka, Kansas
347 U.S. 483 (1954)

Linda Carol Brown (eight years old) had to cross a potentially lethal railroad in Topeka, Kansas, to reach the school bus that transported her to a "colored" school twenty-one blocks away. A "whites only" school was five blocks from her home, with no intervening train yard. Her father, Oliver Brown, appealed to the federal courts and was denied, based on the separate-but-equal doctrine of *Plessy v. Ferguson*. The NAACP (National Association for the Advancement of Colored People) supported Brown's appeal to the U.S. Supreme Court, where it was joined with cases from Delaware, South Carolina, Virginia, and the District of Columbia. The case caused massive societal polarization on interrace relations, which had been growing since the Civil War.

The Court was inundated with amicus curiae briefs from individuals, groups, and organizations that attempted to legitimize the opposing positions, one that favored segregation and the other that felt segregation was inherently unequal. Additionally, the Court entertained oral arguments over a four-day period. This was an unusually long period of time, as the normal outside limit was generally thirty minutes per side. Thurgood Marshall, who in 1967 would become the first African American on the U.S. Supreme Court, eloquently and forcefully challenged the status quo. The justices considered literally hundreds of previous cases, searching for relevant precedent, as well as the due process and equal protection guarantees embodied in the Constitution, Bill of Rights, and Civil War amendments. In an understandably lengthy and legally rigorous ruling, the Supreme Court mandated a radical new ideology of racial equity in public education, totally abrogating the separate-but-equal doctrine. In an unheard of supplemental opinion (he had already written the majority opinion), Chief Justice Earl Warren recognized the social consequences of the Court's holding but reiterated the Court's firm stance.

> While giving weight to these public and private considerations, the courts will require that the defendants make a prompt and reasonable start toward full compliance with our May 17, 1954, ruling. (75)

The question before the court in each of the four cases was whether or not the application of the separate-but-equal rule used by the public schools to justify segregation was in violation of the equal protection clause of the Fourteenth Amendment. The Court found that segregation in public schools violated the Fourteenth Amendment.

> We conclude that in the field of public education the doctrine of "separate but equal" has no place. Separate educational facilities are inherently unequal. Therefore, we hold that the plaintiffs and others similarly situated for whom the actions have been brought are, by reason of the segregation complained of, deprived of the equal protection of the laws guaranteed by the Fourteenth Amendment. This disposition makes unnecessary any discussion whether such segregation also violates the Due Process Clause of the Fourteenth Amendment. (74)

JUDGMENT REVERSED

Cross-disciplinary definitions of laws are basically congruent, with the common denominators of rules, government roles, and the goal of social order, yet defining *the law* is problematic.

WHAT IS LAW?

We have established a beginning definition for the word *law* but have yet to address the fundamental question, "What is law?" Two schools of thought have arisen around this question, the conventionalists and the essentialists (Weinberg and Weinberg, 1980). The conventionalists maintain that it is not possible to come to a correct definition of *law*, a theory supported on its face by our consideration of *Black's*. The essentialists argue that the law has an essence of its own. They advance the theory that it is possible to specify the conditions that must be met for a society to assert that law, as well as its legal system, exists.

COMPONENTS OF LAW

For the law to function in society, it must incorporate a number of components. These include a system of societal norms; a legitimate system of enforcement; a group empowered to enforce the laws; and a system for defining, clarifying, and encoding them. The first of these factors includes the normative structure of a given society. Norms, based on societal values, define appropriate and inappropriate behavior. These norms are enforced through various formal and informal sanctions. If a behavior is deemed unacceptable, sanctions are used to try to prevent it from occurring. Laws provide sanctions for serious violations of societal norms. Authorized persons, such as law enforcement personnel, ensure compliance with the law. Lawmaking bodies, usually legislatures, define and encode the law. Because of the common law legacy of the U.S. judicial system, court decisions can also define legal and illegal behavior through precedent. All of these components are influenced by current societal attitudes and ideas.

SOURCES OF LAW IN THE UNITED STATES

In the United States, law originates from a diverse variety of sources, which we usually call lawmaking bodies. The law of the land is the Constitution. All laws are affected by the Constitution and its ongoing interpretation by the judiciary. Other federal statutes, rules and regulations, some appellate court rulings, and all Supreme Court decisions are also sources of law. Treaties written by the federal government are another, if rare, form of law.

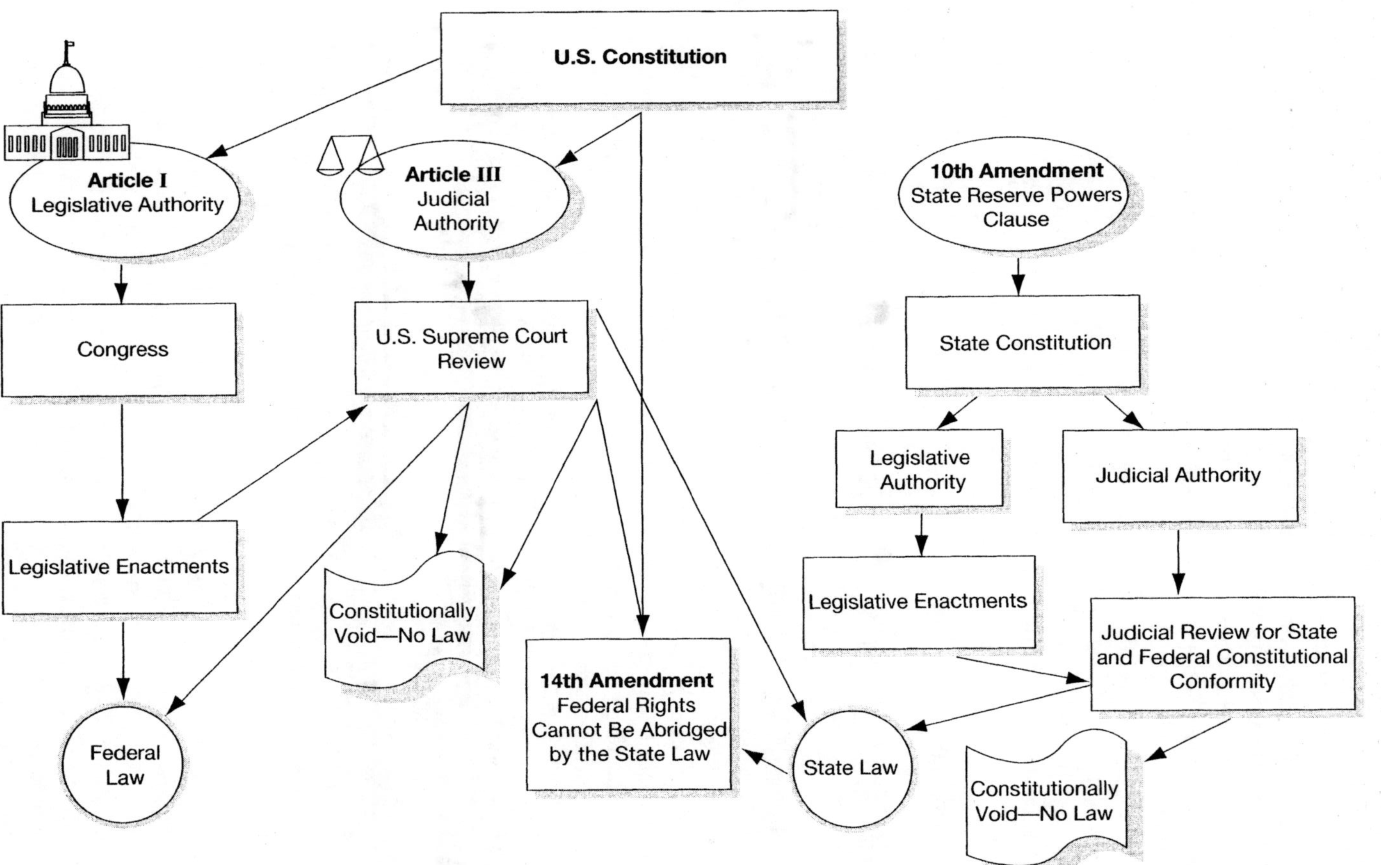

FIGURE 1–3 Sources of Law

This is one of the few forms of law that can be originated by the executive branch, with Senate approval.

States and cities also have their own laws. State constitutions, statutes, and rules and regulations guide the behavior of individuals at the state level. Decisions made by state supreme courts are another source of law specific to that state. And of course, decisions made by local lawmaking bodies (such as city councils and county commissions) are also legitimate sources of law. Figure 1–3 illustrates which articles of the Constitution empower various branches of the government to define both state and federal laws.

TYPES OF LAW

Common law is the *family of law* in the United States. There are several families of law in the world, which will be discussed in more detail in Chapter 3, but at this time, we shall point out that the term *families of law* refers to fundamentally different philosophical ideas about how to create and implement law. The guiding principle behind common law is the use of precedent, that is, using previous legal decisions as a guide for present legal decisions.

The common law system is the least common of all legal families of the world, although aspects of it have been adapted to form a collateral mechanism for judicial review in many legal families. Countries using a pure common law tradition are increasingly rare.

As illustrated in Figure 1–3, Articles I, III, X, and XIV of the U.S. Constitution empower various legislative, judicial, and state entities to enact laws. Article I empowers legislative bodies to enact statutory (written) laws, and Article III empowers judicial bodies to establish case (precedent) law and constitutional law.

In both statutory and case law there are two divisions, substantive law and procedural law, and each of these is divided into civil and criminal law (see Figure 1–4). In general, substantive law refers to the definition of the behavior that is in violation of a civil or criminal code, and procedural law refers to the process one must follow to charge, prosecute, or seek redress against someone who has violated the criminal or civil codes. Substantive criminal law defines what is involved in a crime and the corresponding penalties attached to that behavior. The definition of murder, and its punishment, is an example of substantive criminal law, which consists of the rights and duties each individual in a society must accept (Rembar, 1980). Substantive civil law defines such things as the appropriate rules of conduct for driving a car on the road. While these rules can be very confusing to visitors, they are adaptive and functional for local citizens.

Procedural criminal law describes the manner in which the substantive law is carried out and includes the precepts that define the process, the rules of evidence, and the guidelines for prescribed punishments. Procedural civil

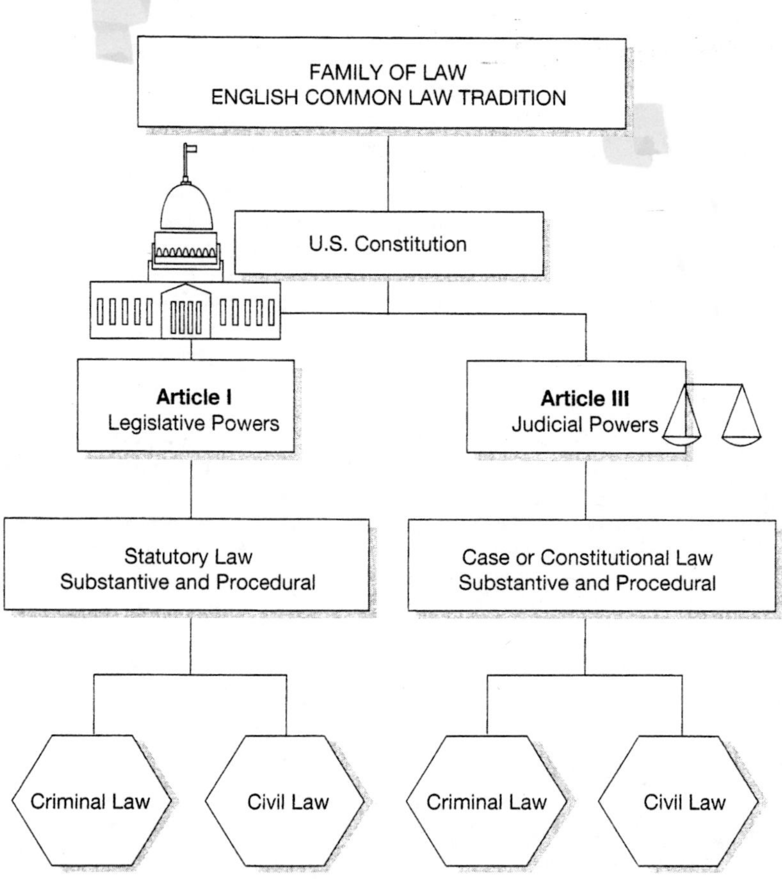

FIGURE 1–4 Types of Law

law is the set of instructions that defines how we carry out civil redresses in such cases as civil rights violations and sexual harassment charges (see Table 1–2, page 20).

Other kinds of law include the distinction between public law and private law. Public law refers to those laws that define and guide the structure of the government and the responsibilities of this structure. Private laws are those substantive and procedural laws that are concerned with individuals.

DEFINING LAW AND SOCIETY

There are many ideas and meanings, both complementary and competing, that are intrinsic to the nature of the sociology of law. We will posit an operational definition in an effort to synthesize the concepts addressed so far:

TABLE 1–2 Types of Law in the United States

TYPES OF LAW:	DEFINITION OF:
Substantive criminal	Defines the elements which constitute criminal behavior (premeditation, malice, criminal intent)
Substantive civil	Defines the rights and duties of citizens (driving a car, restraining-order directions)
Procedural criminal	Defines how to carry out substantive criminal law (procedural rules, evidence rules, and due process)
Procedural civil	Defines how to carry out civil redresses (sexual harassment, civil rights violations)

The sociology of law is the study of the reciprocal relationship of the law and all other factors that make up the social condition; that is, how law affects and is affected by the reality constructs of a society. This interdependence is both directly and inversely proportional, in a constantly evolving process of dialectical cause and effect. The underlying premise, as we consider the social context of law, is that society cannot exist without the law, nor the law without society.

CONCLUSION

This chapter has clearly outlined the themes of this text: the interwoven nature of the three reality constructs, social conditions, ideas, and people, with the law. We have discussed the notion of legal culture; the difficulties inherent in defining law; and the components, sources, and types of law in the United States. In the next chapter, we will consider the ideas of theorists. These ideas vary from notions of how to define law to those about the origin of law, the purpose of law, and the structure of law.

NOTES

1. The case citation method is distinct from that used in the social sciences. The names indicate the parties to the case (Bradwell, the *appellant* has stated a cause of action against the State of Illinois, which is the *respondent* or *appellee*). The first number (16 in this case) refers to the volume number of the *reporter* in which the case is published (*Wall* stands for *Wallace*, a now extinct reporter). The number immediately following the name of the reporter indicates the page in this volume where the case begins. If a second number appears (130 in this example), it specifies the pagination for quoted or paraphrased material. The number in parentheses is the year in which the court made its decision.
2. Any *label* used here to describe an identifiable group of people will inevitably become dated, even insensitive and inappropriate, as language and self-perceptions evolve. Any group-specific language in direct quotations will remain unaltered and reflective of the common usage *at that point in history*, while recognizing and respecting the ongoing efforts of many groups to effect changes in the perceptions of others through a continuing shift in preferred nomenclature.

3. The Civil War Articles of Amendment to the U.S. Constitution are the thirteenth (1865), prohibiting slavery or involuntary servitude (except as punishment for a crime); the fourteenth (1868), extending due process and equal protection prohibitions to nullify any state law abridging the constitutional privileges or immunities of any U.S. citizen; and the fifteenth (1870), in which the right to vote could not be denied on the basis of race, color, or previous condition of servitude. Gender is notably absent; the right to vote was not extended to women until ratification of the Nineteenth Amendment in 1920.
4. More accurately, there were two *Brown* decisions, the first in 1954 [347 U.S. 483 (1954)], and the second in 1955 [349 U.S. 294 (1955)].
5. These are briefs from people and groups other than the litigants themselves. The Latin phrase translates, "friends of the court."
6. To achieve a legally rigorous definition of *law, Black's* also directs the reader to consider the law in its different aspects. "**See:** Absolute law; Adjective law; Administrative law; Arms, law of; Bankruptcy Code; Canon law; Case law; Citations, law of; Civil law; Commercial law; Common law; Conclusion of law; Conflicts of law; Custom and usage; Ecclesiastical law; Edict; Enabling statute; Equity; Evidence, law of; Flags, law of; Foreign laws; Forest law; General law; International law; Local law; Maritime; Maritime law; Marque, law of; Martial law; Mercantile law; Military law; Moral law; Municipal law; Natural law; Oleron, laws of; Ordinance; Oranic law; Parliamentary law; Penal laws; Positive law; Private law; Probate; Procedural law; Prospective law; Public law; Remedial laws and statutes; Retrospective law; Revenue law or measure; Road (*Law of the Road*); Roman law; Special law; Staple (*Law of the staple*); Statute; Substantive law; Unwritten law; War; Wisby, law of; Written law.

2 The Theoretical Context of Law

THE USES OF THEORY

Theory helps us predict behavior. A theoretical understanding of a subject allows inferences to be made, such as, "If A happens, then B should happen." Such hypothesizing is part of the theoretical process.

Theory provides an explanation for the past, the present, and the future. Table 2–1 illustrates the socioeconomic and legal characteristics of different types of societies. Different societal conditions produce different sociological, economic, and legal features. Using the same societal typology format, the table illustrates the ideas of several of the theorists discussed in this chapter. This is important because it helps us to show that theorists themselves are influenced by the societies in which they live (that is, the present), by what they know about the past, and by what they think about the future. Theorists attempt to provide a means of understanding, in this case, of law and the legal system.

INFLUENCES FROM LEGAL PHILOSOPHY

To understand the theoretical context of law, we outline the philosophical background in the study of law and society. There are two basic approaches

TABLE 2–1 Socioeconomic and Legal Characteristics of Societal Typologies

SOCIETAL TYPE	HUNTING/GATHERING	HORTICULTURAL	AGRARIAN	INDUSTRIAL	POSTINDUSTRIAL
Period of dominance	10,000 years ago →	6,000 years ago →	5,000 years ago →	Mid-eighteenth century →	(Since World War II) →
SOCIOLOGICAL FEATURES					
Organizational unit	Kinship ties; small (<50) bands	Kinship ties; some extrafamilial institutions	Well-developed socio/political/religious/military institutions	Complex interdependent institutions	Complex interdependent institutions
Social identity	Homogenous	Homogenous	Homogenous (in transition→)	Heterogenous "melting pot"	Heterogenous "salad bowl"
Settlements	Nomadic/seminomadic	Semipermanent villages	Permanent towns; Some cities	Permanent; urban living predominates	Permanent; urban and suburban living predominate
ECONOMIC FEATURES					
Economic base	Subsistence—no surplus; natural resources	Some surplus/some exchange; simple crop cultivation	Much surplus (market economy); substantial trade/money largely as production	Fully developed market economy	Dual economy; corporate capitalism; small business periphery
Division of labor	Simple (age/sex based)	Simple (age/sex based)	Simple (skill/status based)	Complex (skill/status based)	Complex (largely skill based)
Technology	Very simple (fire, arrows, baskets)	Simple (some blade tools)	Irrigation, fertilization, metallurgy, animal power	New energy sources (coal, gas, electricity); mechanization of production	Self-perpetuating technological expansion; "computer age"
Dominant system	Communism	Communism	Feudalism	Capitalism	Transnational capitalism

TABLE 2–1 (Continued)

SOCIETAL TYPE	HUNTING/GATHERING	HORTICULTURAL	AGRARIAN	INDUSTRIAL				POSTINDUSTRIAL		
Period of dominance	10,000 years ago →	6,000 years ago →	5,000 years ago →	Mid-eighteenth Century →				(Since (World War II)		
Distribution of production[1]				1790	1820	1880	1920	1956	1976	2000
Primary (1)	100%	100%	>95%	>90%	72%	50%	28%	14%	4%	2%
Secondary (2)	0	0	<5%	>10%	28%	36%	58%	37%	29%	22%
Tertiary (3)	0	0	0	0	0	14%	19%	49%	67%	76%
LEGAL FEATURES										
Source of authority	Norms/folkways assigned to government	Values/mores/rules/ laws	Law of sovereign	Assigned to government				Assigned to government		
Decision making	Tribal elder/chief	Elder/chief/counsel	Monarch/feudal government	Formal institutions				Formal institutions		
Focus of law (purpose underlying)	Protect group (conformity)	Protect group (conformity)	Protect monarch (conformity to status quo)	Protect property rights (protect production)				Protect individual rights (protect citizens/ corporations)		
Type of law	Informal	Informal	Formal substantive; criminal	Formal substantive/ procedural civil and criminal				Formal substantive/ procedural civil and criminal		
Sanctions	Group disapproval, ostracism (death)	Group disapproval, ostracism (death)	Harsh corporal/ penal (death)	Economic and penal				Economic and penal		
Underlying philosophy	Deterrence-repression	Deterrence-repression	Deterrence-retribution	Deterrence-retribution (rehabilitation)				Deterrence-retribution (rehabilitation)		

TABLE 2–1 (Continued)

SOCIETAL TYPE	HUNTING/GATHERING	HORTICULTURAL	AGRARIAN	INDUSTRIAL	POSTINDUSTRIAL
Period of dominance	10,000 years ago →	6,000 years ago →	5,000 years ago →	Mid-eighteenth Century →	(Since (World War II)
THEORETICAL MODELS					
Henry Sumner Maine	Status (ascribed)	Status (ascribed)	Status (ascribed/ achieved)	Contract	Contract
Emile Durkheim	Mechanical solidarity	Mechanical solidarity	Mechanical solidarity (in transition)	Organic solidarity	Organic solidarity
Max Weber					
Type of law	Repressive	Repressive	Repressive	Restitutive	Restitutive
Legal decision making	Substantive; irrational	Substantive; irrational	Formal→substantive; Irrational→rational	Formal; rational	Formal; rational
Examples	Plains Indians	Mayans; Incas	Feudal Europe; Chinese Empire	Pre–World War II United States, western Europe; Japan	Contemporary U.S.; European nation-state; Japan

[1]Raw materials; tertiary production = production of service.

Adapted from D. Brinkerhoff, L. White, and S. Ortega, *Essentials of Sociology*, 2nd ed. (St. Paul: West Publishing, 1992).

to the study of the philosophy of law: the natural law approach and the legal positivist approach (see Figure 2–1). Both of these perspectives are concerned with how a rule or custom becomes a valid law.

FIGURE 2–1 Legal Philosophy Perspectives

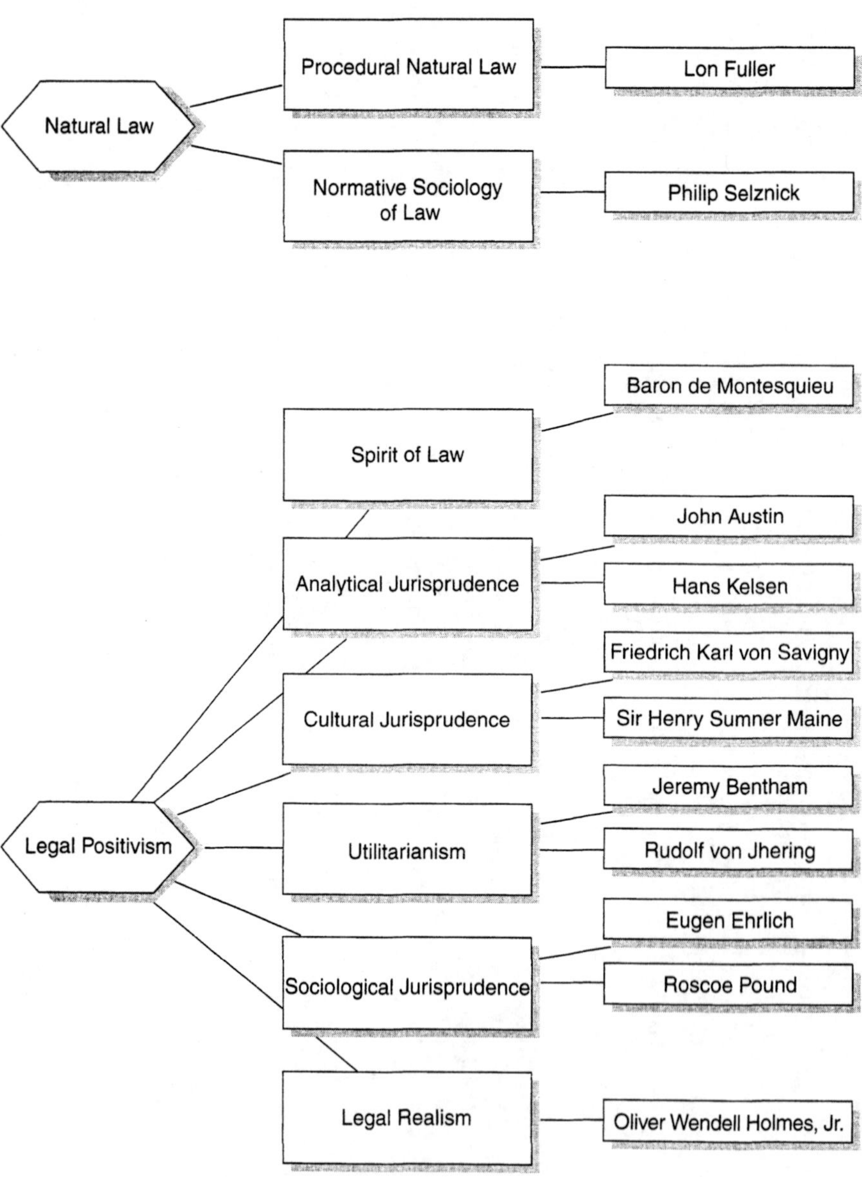

In the natural law approach, the validity of a law is measured against some higher standard. A moral ideal is present to which laws are compared. St. Thomas Aquinas argued that "human laws are means to ends and that they should be reasonable means to those ends. Whether a purported law has the 'force of law' depends on its being a reasonable direction toward the attainment of a given end" (Golding, 1975). Therefore, the ends or pursuit of a law must not violate the higher law, or what could be called the natural law. Early European philosophers believed that through reason, the nature of human beings can be determined (Vago, 1994). In contemporary terms, an abortion protester would argue that the law put in place by *Roe v. Wade*,[1] which legalizes abortion in the United States, is not a valid law since it violates a higher law, that which is defined by a higher moral standard.

The legal positivist approach, in contrast, views the source of the law in determining its validity rather than its content. If, for example, a legislative body elected by the people has been empowered to make laws, the laws that it enacts are considered to be valid. A legal positivist is not concerned with the right or wrong, good or bad, of the law's legal content, simply its source. A valid law is one that is made by a party empowered to make laws. Therefore, laws arising from *Roe v. Wade* would be viewed by a legal positivist as valid since they were enacted by legislatures in response to a finding by a branch of the U.S. government, that is, the judicial branch, which is rightfully empowered to interpret the law. Many early legal philosophers believed that it was necessary to separate the legal and moral realms in the study of law, and eventually the belief in a natural law was replaced by legal positivist beliefs.

NATURAL LAW

Lon Fuller—Procedural Natural Law

In *Anatomy of the Law*, Lon Fuller (1968) suggests that a fundamental element of validity in law is its source. He moderates the debate between the proponents of the natural law perspective and the positivist perspective by proposing a hybrid philosophy of law, which he terms "procedural natural law." As the name indicates, Fuller's model of valid law combines the substantive "inner morality" of law, as proposed by St. Thomas Aquinas (the validity of law has its origin in a higher authority), with an assumption about the inherent procedural validity arising from the integrity of the legal system that enacted the law. Rather than perpetuating the debate between the natural and positivist perspectives, Fuller advocates a synthesis. He observes that the valid sources of law used in legal decision making are a mix of statutes, precedent, societal customs, expert opinions, equity, and morality: "Our interest is not so much in sources of *laws* as in sources of law.

Table 2–2 Characteristics of "Implicit" and "Made" Law

IMPLICIT OR CUSTOMARY LAW	MADE (EXPLICIT) OR STATUTORY LAW
Adopted standard of conduct incorporated by a group; no identifiable author to praise or blame	Derived from a determinate human source, e.g., a legislature or sovereign; can praise or blame if law deemed good or bad
Grows or develops through time; no definitive date of enactment	Becomes effective on definite date; terms contained in statute itself
Purpose can only be inferred to the extent one understands the social context	Statute states purpose of law—to accomplish "good" or abrogate "evil"

From whence does the law generally draw not only its content but its force in men's lives?" (p. 43).

Fuller maintains that the essential issue in the study of law is not the natural-positivist dichotomy but rather the distinctions between "made law" and "implicit law." He establishes statutory law and customary law as the respective models of made (or explicit) law and implicit law, while noting that the two systems are intertwined in practical application. Table 2–2 presents distinctions considered to be fundamental by Fuller (1968:44–46).

In his book *The Morality of Law*, Fuller (1969:46–94) argues that if rules, whether enacted by a legislature or directed by a sovereign, do not have an "inner morality," they are not valid laws. He proposes eight guidelines to test the validity of law, which are shown in Table 2–3.

Fuller (1969) warns that efforts to create and maintain a system of legal rules without any one of these eight criteria can fail. Certainly there can be no rational ground for asserting that a person can have a moral obligation to obey a legal rule that does not exist, that is kept secret from him or her, that came into existence only after the individual had acted, that was unintelligible, that was contradicted by another rule of the same system, that commanded the impossible, or that changed every minute. At some point obedience becomes futile: "A total failure in any one of these eight directions does not simply result in a bad system of law; it results in something that is not properly called a legal system at all" (pp. 38–39). These rules are consid-

TABLE 2–3 Fuller's Criteria for Valid Law

TO BE VALID LAW MUST	TO BE VALID LAW MUST NOT
Have generality in its application	Conflict with the administration of law
Be known and knowable to the people	Require the impossible or unreasonable
Be reasonably clear	Be contradictory to other laws
Be constant across time	Be retroactive

ered absolute standards for lawmakers, and the validity of the law rests not only in its content but also in how it was developed.

Philip Selznick—Normative Sociology of Law

Philip Selznick attempts to reconcile the natural law approach with empirical sociology. In natural law, the validity of the law is determined by evaluating it against some higher standard. According to Selznick, the notion of justice must be incorporated into our definition of valid laws. Without justice as a core concern of valid law, it becomes impossible to define or challenge illegal activities conducted by individuals under the guise of law (Selznick, 1968; 1961).

POSITIVISM

Charles Louis de Secondat, Baron de la Brede et de Montesquieu (1689–1755)—Spirit of Law and the Separation of Powers

According to Baron de Montesquieu (1748), a French political philosopher, historian, and jurist, law should be viewed as a reflection of the culture from which it arises. His book, *The Spirit of Laws*, details how the law reflects the customs, circumstances, and environment of any particular society. Montesquieu conducted a comparative analysis of three different types of government: republican, monarchal, and despotic. He posited no view as to the absolute nature of human behavior, rather that there exist multiple solutions to the many problems of governing and freedom. The guiding principles or norms of the society would lead to one solution or another. Therefore, laws are not static and universal but rather relative to the societal context. The idea that there are *good* or *bad* laws relates to the fact that there can be good and bad components in any society. Perhaps Montesquieu's greatest contribution was his influence on the development of government in the United States. He wrote about the need to separate the powers of government in a society in order to protect individual freedoms. Obviously this idea had a marked influence on the writers of the U.S. Constitution as they created the balance of U.S. governmental powers into legislative, executive, and judicial branches (Bodenheimer, 1974:49).

Analytical Jurisprudence

Some philosophers in the legal positivist tradition felt that the law was separate from morals and the cultural context, that it could be analyzed as if it were a closed system with a set of rules unto itself. Also called formalists, they advocated the total separation of legal analysis from moral and ethical questions concerning the nature and content of law.

John Austin (1790–1859)—Analytical Jurisprudence John Austin, a British legal positivist, advocated the idea that law is analytical because it lays out "a formal, logical, closed system of legal rules" (Schur, 1968:26). According to Austin, law is a command of the sovereign (Weinberg and Weinberg, 1980). A command is any indication for a person to act or not act in a particular way and is accompanied by a threat of harm if one does not comply. Commands are, in brief, "orders backed by threats" (Golding, 1975:26). Obviously the requirement of obeying an order has nothing to do with the goodness or badness of the desired act but relies solely on the source of the command. A sovereign, according to Austin, is anyone who is "habitually obeyed and who habitually obeys no one else" (Weinberg and Weinberg, 1980:10). In contemporary terms, the command of the sovereign is simply the laws of the state, and the issues surrounding the morality of laws do not enter into the question.

Hans Kelsen (1881–1973)—Pure Theory of Law Hans Kelsen (1970) also took an analytical jurisprudence approach to the study of law but with quite a different position: "Kelsen views the legal system as a hierarchy of norms, with legal acts and rules of any level traceable to norms at still higher levels, culminating in the 'basic norm'"(Schur, 1968:27). Law is valid if it can be traced back to the original norm on which the legal system is based. Therefore, "the laws of a legal system . . . form a hierarchical structure, and the validity of a lower legal norm is justified by appeal to a higher legal norm, either because the content of the former conforms to the latter or because the creation of the former is authorized by the latter" (Golding, 1975:40). Again, for Kelsen, the question of whether the law is moral or not may be an interesting but not a legal question. The legal positivist effectively separates questions on the legal nature of law from those on the moral nature of law.

Cultural Jurisprudence

While the earlier philosophers sought to describe the law in a closed system void of cultural influences, some later philosophers took a more cultural and historical view of the legal system. These individuals felt that the legal system was a reflection of the larger cultural and societal patterns of norms and values.

Friedrich Karl von Savigny (1779–1861)—Volksgeist Karl von Savigny was the founder of historical jurisprudence, arguing that laws arise from societal customs and cannot be arbitrarily imposed by either judges or legislatures

(Small, 1924/1967). This school of thought argued that the validity of the law was dependent on the larger social order and the cultural norms and values that support it. According to Friedrich Karl von Savigny, the law was not

> a deliberately created product of some artificially contrived legislator, but was a slow organic distillation of the spirit of the particular people (*volksgeist*) among which it operated . . . such a law must be understood as the product of a long and continuing historical process and its validity depended on the fact that its traditional character was rooted in the popular consciousness and was thus a true national law in accordance with the spirit of the people. (Lloyd, 1976:252)

Therefore, a law enacted by a legislative body may or may not be valid, depending on the beliefs and practices of the people whom it affects. Although Karl von Savigny's work is important in the sociology of law because it sensitized legal scholars to the fact that legal structure cannot be analyzed separately from its cultural and historical context, it was never made clear how one would come to define *volksgeist*, the spirit of the people. For example, if we define it just in terms of majority rule, laws concerning antislavery, civil rights, and affirmative action cannot be seen as valid. This blurring of the morality and validity issues is an important step in understanding the influence of law on the lives of individuals.

Sir Henry Sumner Maine (1822–1888)—Ancient Law Sir Henry Sumner Maine took a historical approach to the study of legal development, arguing that legal systems evolved and that in "progressive" societies the law would develop from a static or fixed system based on ascribed statuses.[2] In his classic book, *Ancient Law*, he states, "The movement of the progressive societies has been uniform in one respect. Through all its course it has been distinguished by the gradual dissolution of family dependency and the growth of individual obligation in its place" (Maine, 1861:170). He goes on to argue that "the movement of the progressive societies has hitherto been a movement from Status to Contract" (p. 170). Therefore, as Maine argues, the law in contemporary societies moves away from rights assigned to individuals based on their birth and moves toward duties and responsibilities that reflect a contract each individual holds with the society. The legal system in these contemporary societies is a reflection of the contract of agreement. One of the things not addressed in Maine's work is the fact that not all parties in a society have fair bargaining positions. If, in fact, the contract is the basis for legal development, those who hold and gain power, whether ascribed or achieved, will have an unfair advantage in this form of legal governance.

Utilitarianism

Utilitarianism refers to the analysis of the practical or working nature of law. It is based on theoretical principles of moral philosophy where actions are judged right or wrong according to their consequences. It has close ties to empiricism, the view that knowledge arises from experience, extending moral theory into a scientific mode of reasoning where causal consequences are defined and measured (Glover, 1990). The focus of utilitarianist theorists is on the influence law has on human behavior. In this regard, law is viewed as a social structure that promotes conformity among individuals in a society to prevent chaos. It is also viewed as a mechanism for social change since the legal structure reflects the changing mores and values (Bentham, 1789; Sidgwick, 1874; Mill, 1863/1971).

Jeremy Bentham (1748–1832)—Utilitarian Hedonism Jeremy Bentham combined a strong interest in what the legal system should do with his efforts to portray its actual workings. In his book *An Introduction to the Principles of Morals and Legislation*, published in 1789, Bentham established a set of principles of utilitarianism where the goal for both individuals and legislators in defining appropriate societal conduct is to achieve the greatest happiness for the greatest number.

Bentham's work is based on a premise of utilitarian hedonism, which is founded on the notion that people will behave in such a way as to maximize pleasure and minimize pain (Bentham, 1789). Therefore, law's purpose is to provide the greatest happiness for the greatest number. To accomplish this, laws must be established to curtail some forms of conduct. In other words, laws are made and enforced to produce the greatest good. The validity of a law is therefore determined by reference to the law's utility. Does it serve the greatest happiness for the greatest number?

One of Bentham's major contributions was the emphasis he placed on applying a scientific analysis to legislative outcomes. He was a strong advocate of a systematic assessment of the social consequences of legislation. Within this principle of "a legislative science," he proposed using hedonistic calculus as the measure by which punishments should be allocated to criminal behavior. That is, he proposed that criminal offenses should be classified by the harm done to society and should be accorded specific punishments, the severity of which would be no more than the precise amount needed to inhibit individuals from committing the offense. Bentham's theory is based on the belief that human beings are basically hedonistic; they will seek pleasure and avoid pain. Therefore, the criminal punishments should involve only slightly more pain than the pleasure one would gain by engaging in the behavior (Bentham, 1789). One of the major difficulties with the implementation of Bentham's ideas was the inability to accurately measure pain and pleasure. Bentham felt that his "hedonistic calculus" would enable decision makers to make moral decisions based on quantitative rather than impressionistic evidence. Yet this quantitative assessment often proves illusive (Harrison, 1983).

Bentham is known in the corrections field for his work in designing the "panopticon," the ultimate prison system. His design reflects his belief in punishment as a strong deterrent to criminal behavior. The panopticon model was used widely in the United States to model prison structures. It is characterized by tiers of cells, generally arranged in a circle around a central guard tower.

Rudolf von Jhering (1818–1892)—Social Utilitarianism Like Bentham, Rudolph von Jhering also placed a major emphasis on the consequences of law. He viewed law as a means of achieving societal goals. His theory, social utilitarianism, saw law as a social institution with the purpose of reinforcing the overall normative structure of society. Unlike Bentham, Jhering concentrated on social rather than individual purposes. The law is viewed as a mechanism or device for controlling human behavior so that it comes in line with societal goals.

Jhering classified societal purposes into three categories: individual, public, and social. These were later adopted by Roscoe Pound in his analysis of law as a social institution designed to satisfy "social wants." Much of Jhering's work was a forerunner of legal realists' principles, with their focus on the effects of judicial outcomes. According to Jhering, law was a significant instrument for promoting social change. He viewed the law not as simply a reflection of societal values and norms but also as an instrument that could influence those values (Weinberg and Weinberg, 1980).

Sociological Jurisprudence

There were many early contributions to the sociological understanding of law and society. These contributions, sometimes referred to as sociolegal perspectives, focused on the law as it exists in a changing society. Acknowledging that the law is not static but rather an interactive force with norms, values, and beliefs of the culture within which it exists, these theorists attempted to explain the validity of law within the framework of its cultural context.

Eugen Ehrlich (1862–1922)—Living Law Eugen Ehrlich made a distinction between what he referred to as the "positive law" and the "living law." He believed that behind all the formal laws, specifically statutory law (positive law), there existed a "living law," which was the law actually followed by people in the society. For a law to be effective, there must be agreement between the positive law and the living law (Ehrlich, 1936/1975). For example, when all the speed limits on the interstate highways in the United States were lowered to 55 miles per hour, very few people followed this "positive law." Ehrlich would have argued that the law was ineffective because of incongruence between the positive law (55 mph) and the living law (people felt more comfortable going 65 or 70 mph). Eventually, the law was changed, and the maximum speed limit was increased on stretches of interstate highways outside of cities and towns. We could argue that this was an attempt to diminish the incongruence between what the lawmakers felt people should do and what people felt was right.

Roscoe Pound (1870–1964)—Law in Action American philosopher, educator, and jurist, Roscoe Pound, extended Ehrlich's social analysis of law to the study of what he termed "law in action." Specifically, he wanted to see how well positive law conformed to the living law. He was a strong advocate of empirical research to answer questions concerning how the law could be utilized to meet human social needs (Pound, 1959). Pound believed that we should see the law as a tool for social change or social engineering and also that law needed to change as social conditions changed (McLean, 1992). We will discuss in more detail this contribution to the issue of law as an instrument for social change in Chapter 7.

Legal Realism

Legal realists focus on the judiciary branch of government by specifically addressing the ways in which judges influence the fabrication of law through their individual interpretations of law. Legal realists question the extensive use of deductive logic for resolving legal issues since all individuals in a society are influenced by their historical, cultural, and socioeconomic backgrounds. Judges, therefore, include their own personal notions of justice in their decisions. Law, according to Holmes (see below) and the legal realists, includes "a body of edicts representing the will of dominant interests in society, backed by force" (in Vago, 1994:41). In this view, the law would represent the dominant interests in society as they are reflected in the opinions and biases of judges. This viewpoint is expanded by the critical legal studies (CLS) movement, which is a radical critique of the current legal system. The CLS movement is described in more detail later in this chapter.

Oliver Wendell Holmes, Jr. (1841–1935)—Legal Realism President Theodore Roosevelt appointed Oliver Wendell Holmes, Jr., to the U.S. Supreme Court in 1902. Considered the "Great Dissenter" because of his numerous dissenting opinions, he was also respected for his eloquence. He published *The Common Law* in 1881 in which he presented his pragmatic approach to legal philosophy (Aichele, 1989). He wrote that judges act as agents, imposing and implementing law, rather than simply as interpreters of the law. Justice Holmes noted that judges always exercise choice when making their decisions. This gives them a great deal of influence in how laws are followed and, in some circumstances, how laws are made.

Holmes questioned the use of logic as a tool for objective and consistent decision making. In his essay, "The Path of the Law," Holmes (1897) wrote, "Behind the logical form lies a judgment as to the relative worth and importance of competing legislative grounds, often an inarticulate and unconscious judgment, it is true, and yet the very root and nerve of the whole proceeding" (p. 457). As Holmes stated in his dissenting opinion in *Lochner v. New York* [198 U.S. 45, 76 (1905)], "General propositions do not decide concrete cases."

This viewpoint raises the issue of how much subjectivity can be incorporated into legal decision making without violating the principles of legal reasoning. There is the necessity for an interpretive method of legal reasoning, which is "a way to evaluate the facts of a problem case to determine that some facts are or should be legally important while other facts are or should be irrelevant" (Burton, 1985:83).

INFLUENCES FROM SOCIOLOGY

Legal philosophers have concerned themselves primarily with questions concerning the definitions of law and justice and the morality and validity of law. Sociologists, as well as anthropologists, economists, and psychologists, however, have taken a multidisciplinary approach to law, addressing issues concerned with the roles that laws play in a societal context. According to Edwin Schur (1968), sociologists have an interest in the study of the legal system because it is "a distinctive and more or less coherent (though continuously changing) set of legal roles, norms, and organizations, together with characteristic patterns of interrelation between the legal order and other institutional realms of society" (p. 4). Figure 2–2 illustrates the sociological legal perspectives.

Talcott Parsons (1902–1979)—Structural Functions of Law

Talcott Parsons is a noted structural functionalist theorist in sociology. Structural-functional theory focuses on the advantages of the social structure for both individuals and society. Structural-functionalists analyze the social structure in terms of manifest (intended) and latent (unintended) functions. The focus is also on consensus and on how societal institutions must function in harmony for a society to be successful. The law is viewed as one social institution, which functions with other institutions, such as the economy and the family. The law's purpose is to maintain social order.

In his article "The Law and Social Control," Parsons ([1962] 1980) describes law as a generalized mechanism of social control. Law is an important component of the social structure and reinforces the values, norms, and rules that organize society. The primary function of law, according to Parsons, is to mitigate conflict and promote an integrative social process for social discourse. Through the law, the norms in a society are reinforced, often by the use of various legal sanctions.

Parsons identified four concerns of legal systems: legitimation, interpretation, sanctions, and jurisdiction. *Legitimation* refers to the basis on which the legal system has established the right to implement a system of rules. If a discrepancy exists between the legal system and society's normative structure, conflict will occur. A legitimated system is one that is responsive to individuals and groups in the society; for example, legislatures in the

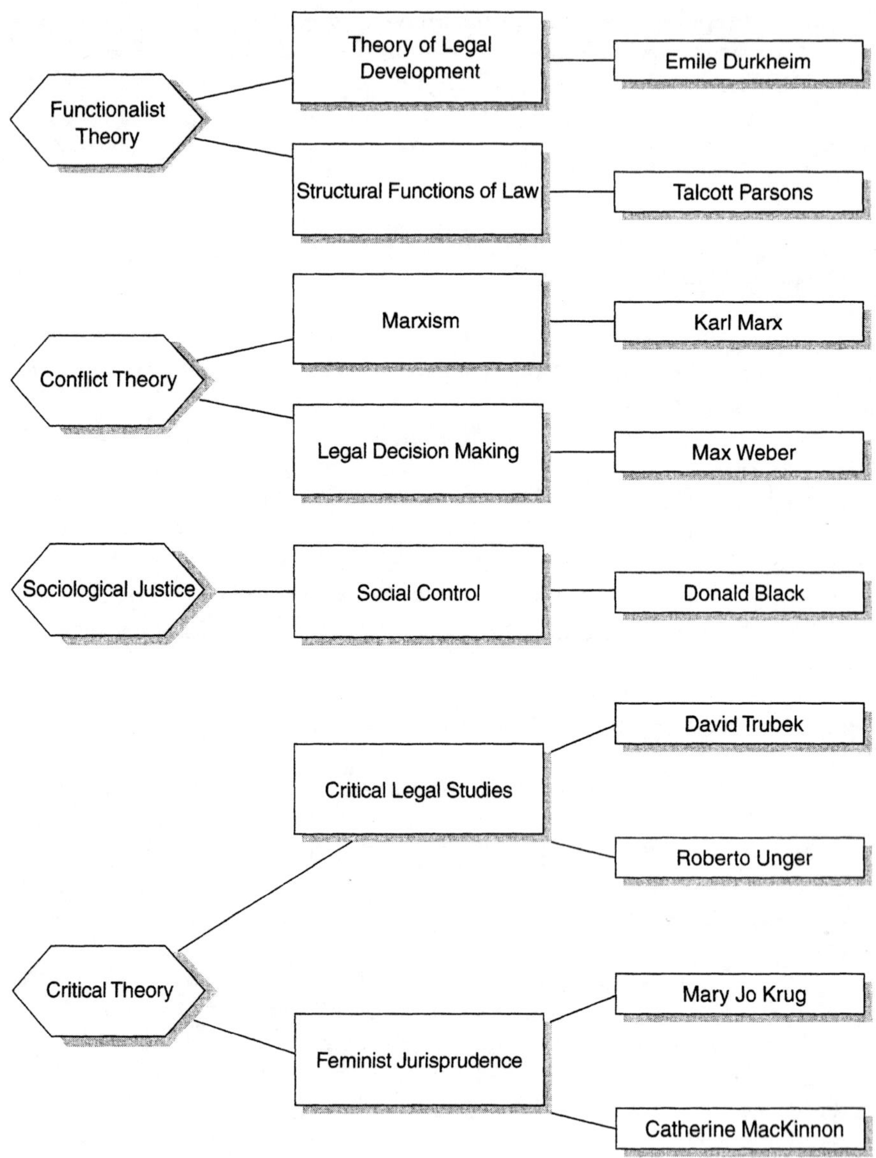

FIGURE 2–2 Sociological Legal Perspectives

United States are responsible to their electorates. The second problem is *interpretation*. Rules are commonly written in very general terms, whose application to specific situations may produce conflicting results. Also, the meaning of these rules may be different for two individuals in similar situations. The use of *sanctions* is the third area of concern for Parsons. Sanctions refer to the consequences to individuals when they conform or fail to conform to rules. Sanctions can be either positive, an inducement or reward for an action, or negative, a threat or form of coercion for nonperformance. Coercion is defined here as the use of force or the threat to use force to gain compliance. For law to function effectively, there must be a consistent system of consequences, or sanctions. The fourth area of concern for Parsons was *jurisdiction*. The jurisdiction issue asks the question, "Under what circumstances and to which individuals in a society do the rules apply?"

The structure of a legal system sets out to institutionalize responses to these concerns. The legal system will flourish in a society where there is not a great deal of conflict over general societal values. In a society where there is much agitation over basic values, the social disequilibrium creates conflict in the legal system.

Emile Durkheim (1858–1917)—Theory of Legal Development

The French sociologist Emile Durkheim, also a structural functionalist, is best known for applying the scientific method to the discipline of sociology in his 1897 study of suicide (Durkheim, [1897] 1951). Durkheim defined sociology as "the science of institutions, their genesis and their functioning" (p. 45), and within this tradition lies the foundation of sociological positivism in contemporary sociology.

In his work, *The Division of Labor in Society*, Durkheim ([1893] 1947) outlined the development of social order in different societies. Part of this social order includes the system by which rules are defined and enacted as law. Durkheim proposed a theory of legal development based on the social solidarity of society. Social solidarity refers to the cohesion of a society, that which holds the society together. Durkheim maintained that there were two basic types of solidarity: mechanical and organic. Mechanical solidarity prevails in relatively simple and homogenous societies, where unity is ensured by close interpersonal ties and similarity of habits, ideas, and attitudes. Organic solidarity is characteristic of modern societies, which are heterogeneous and differentiated by a complex division of labor. The grounds for solidarity is the interdependence of widely different persons and groups who perform a variety of functions (Vago, 1994:39). Table 2–4 depicts the characteristics of these two forms of solidarity.

Durkheim's theory illustrates the necessity of understanding the societal context when analyzing the legal culture. In small homogeneous societies based on mechanical solidarity, the law by necessity is repressive (see Table 2–1). Repressive laws are designed to punish individuals who do not conform to societal norms. In this way the law serves to reinforce the social cohesion, which is based on the similarity of the individual members. A highly heterogeneous society with a complex division of labor requires a great deal of interdependence among the individual members. To reinforce

TABLE 2–4 Durkheim's Theory of Legal Development

MECHANICAL SOLIDARITY	ORGANIC SOLIDARITY
Small, homogeneous society	Large, complex heterogeneous society
Highly dependent population	Highly independent population
Simple division of labor	Complex division of labor
Cohesion based on similarities	Cohesion based on differences
Law is *repressive*	Law is *restitutive*

ANOMIE

→

Transition from mechanical to organic solidarity, characterized by a state of anomie.

this interdependence, laws are restitutive. Restitutive laws focus on the individual and attempt to restore or reimburse the victim. The transition of a society from mechanical to organic solidarity is characterized by anomie, or a state of normlessness.

Karl Marx (1864–1920)—Marxism

Karl Marx often is called the earliest voice of conflict theory in sociology. Conflict theorists posit that society is in a state of constant conflict because interest groups always compete for scarce resources. One of the realities and ironies of the struggle is that the groups with the most resources are most likely to win the struggle. Marx viewed society as a system of economic forces in conflict, which generated social change through the tensions and struggles between classes. Social progress would occur through this process of continuing conflict. The development of Marxism was influenced by the rapidly emerging labor movements in England and France and the rapidly growing industrial enterprise governed by capitalist production. Marx believed that there was a basic relationship of exploitation between those who owned the means of production (bourgeoisie) and those who worked for the owners (proletariat). The exploitation of the workers by the owners would lead to such extreme alienation among the workers that class conflict would become inevitable. This focus on the economic relationship in a society is at the core of Marx's analysis of all social institutions, and his theory of law incorporates this economic perspective. Vago (1994) summarizes Marx's theory with three principle assumptions:

1. Law is a product of evolving economic forces.
2. Law is a tool used by a ruling class to maintain its power over the lower classes.
3. In the communist society of the future, law as an instrument of social control will "wither away" and finally disappear. (p. 37)

> The idea that law is a reflection of economic conditions is an integral part of the doctrine of "dialectical materialism." According to this doctrine, the political, social, religious, and cultural order of any given epoch is determined by the existing system of production and forms a "superstructure" on top of this economic basis. Law, for Marx, is part of this superstructure whose forms, content, and conceptual apparatus constitute responses to economic developments. This view maintains that law is nothing more than a function of the economy but without any independent existence. (Vago, 1994:37)

Marxist theories of law, as well as other conflict theories, view the legal system as an institutional mechanism that preserves the status quo and maintains the inequities between the owners and the workers, or the haves and the have-nots, which are intrinsic components of the capitalist relationship. Like legal realism, conflict theories describe laws as being neither neutral nor independent of influence but rather as reflecting the class-driven values of legislators and judges, leading to inequities in the social structure.

Max Weber (1864–1920)—Legal Decision Making

Max Weber's theoretical arguments concerning power and authority are basic tenets for a sociological understanding of the nature of law. Power is the ability to make people do things even if they don't want to do them. This power can be either legitimate, referred to as *authority*, or illegitimate, referred to by Weber as *coercion*. According to Weber (1992), there are three ways to gain authority: tradition, charisma, and legal-rational means. Traditional authority is generally based on devotion to the way things have been done in the past. Monarchies are classic examples of this form of authority, which a person gains through ascribed status, that is, a status with which one is born. Not long ago, as illustrated in the Myra Bradwell example in Chapter 1, men held authority in U.S. society; they received power and privileges simply because of their sex, an ascribed status. Charismatic authority is power that is vested in an individual because he or she has some unique, extraordinary characteristics. Many people followed the teachings of Martin Luther King, Jr., because he possessed a unique ability to motivate and organize others. Rational-legal authority refers to power that is vested in a position. This type of authority is based on a rational system of rules and regulations. Most bureaucracies are based on rational-legal authority, and individuals hold positions of authority over other individuals because of their particular job titles. It is not necessary to agree with the decision or to admire the person making the request; if the person holds a position of authority over you, it is expected that you will follow the rules. Voluntary compliance with authority is common among these three models, yet the possibility of coercion, the use of force or threat of force, is present in all of them. Noncompliance with these authority types puts an individual at risk of ostracism, loss of status, and in the case of a bureaucracy, loss of job and prestige.

In law, however, coercion is a primary tool used to gain compliance. Weber ([1914] 1954) argues that the law has three primary features that distinguish it from custom. First, the law pressures people into conformity through the use of threats and actions. For example, although you may be late for your next appointment, you may choose not to exceed the speed limit to get there on time because of the threat of getting a ticket and the actions that would be taken against you by both the court and the insurance company. Second, the use of these threats and actions always involves force or coercion. If you are speeding, you will feel compelled to pull over if the police come after you, just as you will feel *coerced* either to pay the ticket or to appear in court. The force or coercion used is generally backed by further threats and actions. Third, those who implement the threat are engaged in an official role to uphold the law. Although anyone could request that you pull over or slow down, only those with the official insignia of law enforcement have the backing of the state to force you to do so.

Weber also analyzed legal systems in terms of how legal decisions are made and the rationality of the procedures used to implement the system. Weber's typology of decision making, illustrated in Table 2–5, indicates whether or not rationality was present and whether or not the procedure was formalized. A rational system is one in which general rules are used to make decisions; an irrational system is one without a general system of rules. A formal system is one in which decisions are based on established rules of evidence and procedure, regardless of their fairness. A substantive system has no formal rules, and the circumstances of individual cases are taken into consideration alongside prevailing notions of justice.

The judicial decision-making process is defined according to the presence or absence of rationality and formality (see Table 2–6). A substantive

TABLE 2–5 Weber's Typology of Legal Decision Making

		RATIONALITY	
		Absent	*Present*
FORMALITY	*Absent*	Substantive irrational	Substantive rational
	Present	Formal irrational	Formal rational

TABLE 2–6 Legal Decision Making

SYSTEM TYPE	DESCRIPTION	EXAMPLE
Substantive irrational	Case-by-case decision making based on insight of charismatic judge	Quadi justice Solomon's justice
Substantive rational	Cases decided by applying rules from extralegal source, e.g., religion or ideology	Puritan use of biblical commandments
Formal irrational	Specialized legal procedures used, although decisions not derived from general rules but determined by supernatural forces	Oracle
Formal rational	Cases decided by applying logically consistent abstract rules that are independent of moral, religious, and other normative criteria; all cases of the same nature treated equally	U.S. system

irrational system is based on case-by-case decision making, often dependent on the insight of a charismatic judge. Quadi justice, a style of adjudication based on Quadi judges in Islamic towns, is an example of this system. In the marketplace a judge will arbitrate disputes between buyers and sellers. No formality exists; no explicit rules or legal principles guide the decision making; rather the judges arrive at insightful solutions on a case-by-case basis (see Chapter 3 for a discussion of the Islamic legal system). The legitimacy of the judgment arises from the charismatic gifts of the individual judges.

Substantive rational systems decide cases by applying rules from some extralegal source such as religion or a particular ideology (see Chapter 3 for a discussion of socialist law), for example, the Puritan use of Bible commandments. In the formal irrational system, specialized legal procedures are used, although the decisions are not derived from general rules but are determined by supernatural forces, for example the use of oracles. The oracles often rely on the interpretation of patterns of bones, flights of birds, or the content of dreams as signs, and generally certain ritual incantations are necessary.

In formal rational systems, cases are decided by applying logically consistent, abstract rules that are independent of moral, religious, and other normative criteria. All cases of the same nature should be treated equally. In theory, the current system used in the United States is a formal rational system. Weber describes an ideal type: if the system were perfectly rational, the sentences given out to individuals convicted of violating criminal laws would be highly correlated with the type and consequences of the crime. However, in the United States, actual sentencing has little correlation to criminal consequences, and thus the law in practice tends to be more substantive than rational. Some states have moved toward legislating strict sentencing guidelines for judges to limit judicial discretion and introduce more rationality into the system.

Donald Black—Social Control

Theorists such as Donald Black (1983, 1976) view law as a mechanism of social control. Black posits four styles of social control: penal, compensatory, therapeutic, and conciliatory, each being employed in specific circumstances. Penal and compensatory styles of social control are considered accusatory. In an accusatory system, one individual who has been harmed in some fashion is the complainant and the other individual, the one who is accused, must defend her or his behavior. Generally, there is a winner and a loser. In a penal system, if the accused person loses, he or she will be punished and in a compensatory system required to reimburse the victim through some form of restitution. These are not mutually exclusive outcomes, and an individual may be punished as well as expected to pay restitution. Therapeutic and conciliatory types of social control are considered remedial, in which the intent is to help the offenders stop their offending behavior. In the therapeutic type of social control, this help will be in the form of treatment. Conciliatory styles of social control generally involve intervention in individual disputes through mediation and conflict-resolution strategies. Divorce proceedings in the United States are based on the premise of conciliatory resolution of individual conflict.

Since the remedial forms of social control focus on treatment and resolution, they have the potential for enforcing social control in ways that may infringe on individual rights. For example, to prevent unwelcome sexual behavior, an individual may be involuntarily committed by government order, with few of the procedural guarantees afforded to criminal defendants. Table 2–7 differentiates the types of social control.

Black (1976) also argues that there is a relationship between issues of equality and the number of laws in a society. Indeed, the relationship between a society and its laws is inverse: the less equality in a society, the more laws enacted.

TABLE 2–7 Black's Types of Social Control

TYPE OF SOCIAL CONTROL	ACCUSATORY/REMEDIAL	EXAMPLE
Penal	Accusatory	Punishment
Compensatory	Accusatory	Restitution
Therapeutic	Remedial	Treatment
Conciliatory	Remedial	Dispute resolution

TWO ADDITIONAL PERSPECTIVES

Critical legal studies and feminist jurisprudence do not fit into any of the preceding categories. These two perspectives are fairly new and indicate how some contemporary theorists question the legal system rather than simply explain its existence.

Critical Legal Studies

Critical legal studies, or CLS, is a relatively new area of investigation in the sociology of law. Its beginnings are marked by a conference held at the University of Wisconsin at Madison in 1977 (Milovanovic, 1988). Within five years, a thousand individuals were attending yearly CLS meetings (Unger, 1986). This perspective was influenced by the social conditions, ideas, and people of the 1960s and 1970s in the United States, as well as by the legal realists.

While criticized for not really having a theoretical focus, CLS does have several beliefs that unite its adherents. First, traditional law, i.e., formalism, or the use of law in a neutral, objective manner, guided by precedent, is a big lie (Milovanovic, 1988:102). No distinction exists between law and politics, law and values, and law and goals. Second, as suggested by Marx and others, law is ideology and as such is simply the belief system of those in power. Third, CLS questions the Langdellian teaching method used in the majority of law schools in this country (see Chapter 6 for a fuller discussion of the professions). To CLS, the Langdellian method, and the other messages taught in law schools, simply prepare students to think like lawyers in order to fit into the legal hierarchy. The criticisms lie in the fact that lawyers are not trained to battle the status quo but rather are taught how to work within the system like "cheerful robots" (p. 102).

Critical legal studies, given its radical view of the legal system, engages in a process called "trashing," which is a methodological position used for examining existing case law and opinions (Milovanovic, 1988:103). It consists of a critical examination of underlying, unstated assumptions in case opinions. Given the trashing methodology, it is understandable that a major focus of CLS is antidiscrimination law. What are the laws doing? Who is helped and hurt by them? What is the reality of antidiscrimination, beyond the political ideology? What is the legal place of women, people of color, and the poor?

David Trubek has argued that law is indeterminate, making it unable to cover all possible situations and conditions that occur in a society (Trubek, 1989; Trubek and Esser, 1989). Like the legal realists, he argues that laws are not objective or value free but rather give legitimacy to the powerful in society by reinforcing the traditional value system. Through this process, the legal system becomes part of the system of power in society.

Most CLS scholars agree that the current legal system is repressive, but they disagree about how to create a more humane society and system. Although controversial, CLS is considered to be the cutting edge in the development of the sociology of law in the United States (Milovanovic, 1988).

Feminist Jurisprudence

Feminists have always considered the law a key factor in creating, reproducing, and obscuring gender inequality. According to this perspective, the law is male and patriarchal; the legal system identifies "male" as normative and has written and established a legal system from a male (as well as white and class-privileged) perspective. According to critics such as Dusky (1996), the legal system is sexist and backward and fails to recognize its problems.

Effective legal strategies to reduce gender inequality require a uniquely feminist understanding and critique of the law, a "feminist jurisprudence." This entails revealing the male world view that is substantively and procedurally embedded in law while simultaneously infusing law with a feminist perspective and sense of justice (MacKinnon, 1993). There is an ironic twist: feminists have relied on the law to relieve women's oppression and to improve women's social and economic position while they criticize the law as obscuring and promoting inequality.

Some key questions can be asked about this perspective (Otten, 1993): does the law protect women? Does the law protect the powerful (men) from the powerless (women)? Does the law work as an avenue of redress for women? Particularly problematic is the contemporary discussion of equality. Does equality mean treating women and men the same or differently? Or does it mean rewriting the rules to do both? If treating women and men exactly the same is equality, should pregnant women receive no special consideration? If treating women and men differently means equality, how do we get past the argument that women and men are the same (yet different)?

Historical practices such as those that affected Myra Bradwell (Chapter 1) are examples of how the legal system has treated women and men differently. Feminist legal theory, in line with CLS, is critical of the current system and the way it operates. Consequently, according to Otten (1993), MacKinnon (1993), and others, three more questions emerge in feminist debates about the law: First, have women benefited, and in what ways, from legal changes over the past two centuries? Has legal reform reduced gender inequality? Second, are the goals of freedom and protection mutually exclusive? And finally, does formal (legal) equality contradict substantive (actual) equality (Otten, 1993)?

CONCLUSION

While discussions of perspectives such as feminist jurisprudence and critical legal studies make obvious the effect of social conditions, people, and ideas, all theories are actually influenced by these social realities. Whether one is discussing Karl Marx or Lon Fuller, one must realize that theorists' ideas do not develop in a vacuum. Marx, as a German Jew chased out of Germany, felt and wrote about the oppressive power of economics. It is interesting that he was raised in a bourgeois family but, because of the privilege of attending college and studying economics, he was able to criticize the upper classes. Surrounded by social and political revolution, he witnessed and hypothesized about the current and future effects of capitalism and power. Other theorists also were influenced by their spatial and temporal environments.

NOTES

1. *Roe v. Wade*, Supreme Court of the United States [410 U.S. 113, 93 S.Ct. 705 (1973)]. Before 1973, abortion was a crime in all but four states. "Jane Roe" and "Mary Doe" [*Doe v. Bolton*, 410 U.S. 179, 93 S.Ct. 739 (1973)] requested abortions and were turned down. They successfully took the case to the Supreme Court, whose rulings abrogated abortion laws in thirty-one states as unconstitutional and made revisions necessary in the abortion laws of fifteen other states.
2. *Ascribed* statuses are those that are assigned at birth, such as sex and race. In many societies, wealth and poverty also are ascribed statuses, as power is handed down from generation to generation. In contemporary U.S. society, we generally consider wealth and power to be *achieved* statuses—those acquired by an individual throughout his or her life.

3 Cross-Cultural Context of Law

To illustrate how social conditions, social ideas, and people and groups in a region affect its legal structure, we examine legal systems around the world. It is important to understand that different cultures organize their legal systems in different ways and that these diverse organizations are referred to as *families* of law. Many scholars distinguish four primary families of law in the world: common law, Romano-Germanic (or civil) law, socialist law, and religious or philosophical law (Terrill, 1997:xiii; there are discussions concerning this categorization, see Reichel, 1994:94). Socialist law is best discussed within its historical context, so this family of law is demonstrated by looking at the former Soviet Union. We will consider the legal systems of France (Romano–Germanic) and Saudi Arabia (religious or philosophical) to illustrate the families of law they represent. Because this text mainly concerns the common law system, we will not go into additional detail about this family of law other than to describe its general characteristics. A variety of other legal systems has been created by combining characteristics of the four primary systems, and so we will look at Japan as an example. Finally, some systems have been organized and operate independently of the four families of law; an example is U.S. tribal law, and we will describe this system as well. First, we provide a brief synopsis of the general characteristics of the families of law and, second, we look at how these systems operate in various countries. It should be noted that the descriptions of the families of law are "ideal types"; no system conforms exactly to its archetype.

PROBLEMS WITH COMPARATIVE STUDIES AND ISSUES

Terrill (1997:xi–xii) suggests five approaches to the cross-cultural study of law and justice: the anthropological-historical, the institutional-structural, the political-legal, the social-philosophical, and the analytical-problems (for a more in-depth discussion of these approaches, see Terrill). Their existence suggests that one can look at law in a variety of ways. Indeed, the approach one chooses guides the questions one asks about legal systems. In our analysis we will focus on the following questions: How do social ideas influence law? How do social conditions influence law? And how do people and groups influence law? That emphasized, we must consider a few other issues.

Several problems are inherent in attempting a cross-cultural examination of law. Students of cross-cultural methodology are familiar with the reality that languages and ideas do not translate perfectly. While we seek to understand *the law* worldwide, we must understand that translation creates problems. Similarly, because of our own ethnocentrism, we often identify other systems through a lens that is less than pure. Bear this in mind, as we discuss the manner in which other countries and cultures around the world design, administer, and execute law, first by reviewing the various families of law in the world, and then looking at how the families of law are implemented in different countries.

ROMANO-GERMANIC (CIVIL) FAMILY OF LAW

Romano-Germanic (civil) legal systems are the most common in the world. They have evolved over a long period of time and are the basis for some other families of law, such as the socialist system. Civil law is a family of law that is codified, meaning that practitioners, as well as lay people, have access to the written codes established by a legal system. Four major historical influences have shaped the development of contemporary Romano-Germanic law.

In the sixth century, Byzantine Emperor Justinian drafted a compilation and codification of the law then in force in the Roman world. Justinian was primarily concerned with making the legal world more accessible to nonlegal scholars. Up to this point, only legal counselors could understand legal directions, and individuals were forced to rely on the interpretation of these counselors. Often the laws were unclear and contradictory. Justinian wanted to create a legal code that individuals could refer to when they needed legal answers. The result of Justinian's directive, finished in A.D. 534, was the *Corpus Juris Civilis*, a set of four books collectively referred to as *Justinian's Code*. Each book had a different purpose: the *Code* was a collection of ordinances approved by Roman emperors before Justinian; the *Novels* were the laws passed during Justinian's reign; the *Digest* was a collection of legal opinions by Roman jurists; and the *Institutes* was a handbook designed to introduce students to the study of law (Terrill, 1997:136).

At about the same time, canon law, the Catholic church's own set of rules which dealt with spiritual and church matters, was also being developed. Canon law included directives on family life, morals, and church governance, and was administered by church, or ecclesiastical, courts (Fairchild, 1993:30).

The Napoleonic Code was one of the many reforms put into place by the French Emperor Napoleon Bonaparte. It consisted of 2,281 codes and was drawn up by legal experts who combined the variety of laws in use throughout France at the time; it superseded any and all previous law in France. These laws came from numerous sources, including canon law, Roman law, commercial law, and some of the feudal practices of the medieval period. It was considered a simple, nontechnical piece of work (Fairchild, 1993:31) and resulted in five separate publications (Terrill, 1997:137): Civil Code of 1804, Code of Civil Procedure of 1807, Code of Commerce of 1808, Code of Criminal Procedure of 1808 (revised in 1959), and Code Penal of 1810 (revised completely in 1994).

The Germanic code was the polar opposite of the French code; it was long, academic, and complex. It took almost three decades, from the 1871 unification of Germany to its actual implementation in 1900, for legal scholars to develop the Germanic code. It was the end result of a massive scholarly effort to study previous law, develop a philosophy of law, and provide a rational basis for legal development (Fairchild, 1993:31).

The inquisitorial nature of the trial process in Romano-Germanic systems may be unfamiliar to students of common law systems. The term *inquisitorial* is misleading because of its association with the Grand Inquisition. In reality, an inquisitorial system is one that engages in an extensive pretrial investigation process, which is undertaken to ensure that innocent persons are not brought to trial. Furthermore, courtroom participants, i.e., judges and lawyers, interact with one another during this pretrial process, and all information acquired is divulged to the participants. Accused individuals are involved in the investigation from the beginning. This process can be contrasted to the adversarial system used in common law courtrooms, which can be characterized as a competition between two groups rather than an information-gathering system.

SOCIALIST FAMILY OF LAW

Karl Marx (see Chapter 2) predicted that law in the communist state of the future "will wither away and die." This statement was grounded in his belief that societies and individuals would be radically different in their thinking by the time communism became a reality. Instead of an individualistic attitude, he believed that people in a communist state would concern themselves with the needs of the community and the collective good. While Marx has been criticized as utopian and simplistic, his writings and thoughts have had a profound impact on the organization of another family of law, the socialist system. Of the four families of law we discuss here, this is the newest. Some scholars believe it would more appropriately be called a "legal tradition" rather than a legal system (Reichel, 1994:106).

The socialist family of law is a codified system; six characteristics distinguish it from other legal families (Fairchild, 1993:36–39):

1. The public law/private law distinction
2. The importance of economic crimes
3. The educational or "social engineering" function of law
4. The distinctive role of the procurator
5. The distinction between political and nonpolitical justice
6. The mitigated independence of the judiciary

Public versus Private Law

Socialist systems are philosophically organized toward the ultimate goal of achieving communism. As such, they downplay private ownership of goods and production. Factories, farms, and other business enterprises are owned by the central government. The sale of goods and the output of production is government regulated. Laws are written to support the achievement of the communist end, the collective good.

Economic Crimes

While workers in capitalist systems are motivated by competition for scarce goods, they have a relative degree of freedom in terms of their industry at work. Expectations are that individuals will arrive at work on time, produce a sufficient and reasonable amount of work, and do the best job they can. The same expectations hold in a socialist system. However, work behavior, such as punctuality and productivity, is a subject for legislative regulation, and failure to comply is punished as an *economic crime*.

Educational Function of the Law

While most systems attempt to educate their population about the law, socialist systems utilize the law itself as an educational tool for spreading the concepts and importance of socialism. This educational indoctrination supports the development of the consciousness of the collective good.

Role of the Procurator

A procurator, in general, can be compared to a prosecutor in a common law system. However, in a socialist system, procurators are often more powerful than judges. Because procurators represent the state, they have the final say in prosecution. They also are involved in government reform and administrative decision making. Procurators are said to have nine roles: "criminal investigator, grand jury, criminal prosecutor, judicial ombudsman, executive branch ombudsman, general ombudsman, prison ombudsman, military ombudsman, and propagandist of soviet law" (cited in Fairchild, 1993:38).

Political versus Nonpolitical Justice

The notion of nonpolitical justice is informed by the belief that all people should be treated fairly and equitably. Political justice, on the other hand, is not so informed. Behavior that is considered heinous because of its lack of support for the state is subject to state sanctions in the form of political justice. Political justice occurs when the state machine steps into and supersedes the process of justice.

Mitigated Independence of the Judiciary

In socialist systems, judges are instruments of the state and decide cases with only the collective good and the state's best interests in mind. This is not to imply that judges are the tools of political leaders but rather that it is acceptable and expected that the interests of the state inform a judge's decisions.

In addition to these six principles, Reichel (1994) argues that Marxist-Leninist ideology provided the impetus for the socialist family of law and that, further, the belief that law is something which is truly "artificial" characterizes this system (p. 108).

RELIGIOUS OR PHILOSOPHICAL FAMILY OF LAW—ISLAMIC LAW

The secular nature of the legal system is a defining characteristic of the previously discussed families of law, but legal systems based on religious beliefs do not have this characteristic. The Islamic *Sharia*[1] is an example of a system in which the principles of the religion of Islam are the guiding precepts. *Sharia* literally translates as *pathway* but is used to mean *law* in Islamic justice systems. Sharia includes the commands that specify what is right and wrong, illegal and legal, and proper and improper in a Muslim's life. The ongoing task of Sharia law is to impose a "dual responsibility" on believers: "to do what is good and to abstain from what is blameworthy" and to keep in line the behavior of nonconformists (Souryal, Alobied, and Potts, 1996:435; Reichel, 1994:111–112).

Sharia regulates all human conduct by demanding, authorizing, and prohibiting certain behaviors. It includes all religious and secular behavior, with no exception (Souryal et al., 1996:433). The origins and scope of Islamic law are fundamentally different from those of any other (Moore, 1996:390). Six characteristics of Islamic law have been distinguished:

1. It is not given by a Ruler but rather by God and can be identified in part through the *Koran.*
2. It has been amplified by leading Muslim jurists Abu Hanifa, Shafi, and Malik among others.
3. Islamic law remains valid whether recognized by the State or not.
4. The origin of Islamic law is Divine Revelation.
5. Islamic law is so comprehensive and all embracing that it covers every aspect of the legal system—personal law, constitutional law, international law, and criminal law.
6. It is not in the nature of "should be"; it specifies "what is." (cited in Fairchild, 1993:40)

In countries where Islamic law is not state law (see point 3 above), a voluntary compliance with Islamic teachings and beliefs is required of Muslims. In that sense, Islamic law is law, even if not the law of the state. For a state to abolish Islamic law, it must often actively pursue its destruction. As with religions worldwide, when devout followers adhere to religious teachings, it constitutes law whether recognized as such or not.

The primary source of Sharia is the *Koran (Qur'an),* the Islamic holy book. The *Koran* is not a book of laws as such, since fewer than 200 of the 6,000 verses qualify as actual legal rules. Another important source is the *Sunna,* or *Sunnah,* which contains decisions made by the prophet Mohammad.

Four schools of Islamic jurisprudence have been derived from different Islamic leaders in different countries through time: Hanafi, Hanbali, Maliki, and Shafi'i. The main differences among these schools are matters of emphasis, judicial reasoning, and the elaboration of the Koran. Countries that adhere to Islamic law tend to follow one or another of these schools.

Gender is an important issue in Islamic law. Many laws in the Sharia treat women and men quite differently. For example, women often cannot be called as witnesses for certain crimes, and when they are called to testify, their testimony is given only half the weight of male witnesses. Property law and family law (marriage, divorce, and custody issues) are also weighted in favor of men.

COMMON LAW FAMILY OF LAW

The common law system is the family of law most familiar to those reading this text. According to Fairchild (1993:32), this system is more complex and difficult to deal with than civil law. It is found predominantly in Anglo-Saxon countries, including the United States and most commonwealth countries, having been developed in Great Britain. The beginning of common law is generally designated as 1066, when William the Conqueror defeated British troops at the Battle of Hastings and began his reign as king of England. To bring the country together under his rule, William established, among other things, a new legal order. He set up a court system, referred to as the King's Court (Curia Regis), in which judges traveled around the country to hear cases. This centralized court system was the first of its kind in Great Britain. Common law systems are so called because the law became common, or applicable, to all people in the land.

Because the judges in the King's Court did not have a body of written laws as reference, they relied on custom and past judicial decisions. This practice, now called *precedent,* comes from the Latin *stare decisis* ("to stand by decided cases"). Another characteristic of common law systems is the development of *judge-made,* or case, law. The King's Court developed a common set of procedures for handling cases, and the importance of judicial procedures is still evident today in common law systems. Over the course of time, judges came to see themselves as bound more to the law than to the king, resulting in an independent judiciary (Fairchild, 1993).

Common law systems also are characterized by the adversarial trial process used in courtrooms (as mentioned in Chapter 2). Adversarial courts establish a win-lose process, which is true in both criminal and civil cases.

In the eighteenth century, Sir William Blackstone (1993) compiled all of the laws common in England at the time. His document, known as "Blackstone's Commentaries," was a collection of his Oxford lectures published between 1765 and 1769, and was a major step in the written consolidation of British common law. As noted by Blackstone, the common law established rules for dealing with all matters that might arise in court, whether civil or criminal.

Contemporary discussions of this family of law include the question of whether it actually still exists. It is true that with the rise of legislative democracies in the contemporary world, the rule-making power once exercised by judges has been taken over by legislative bodies. However, many of the laws written by legislative bodies are phrased in terminology that is particularly vague (see the discussion in Chapter 4 on specificity), so the vagaries of public statutes are often left to judicial interpretation. Furthermore, much tort and property law still draws heavily on precedent and the common law tradition. Because this text deals primarily with a discussion of common law, we will not include an example in the following discussion.

EXAMPLES OF THE FAMILIES OF LAW

France

France, largely urban and industrial, has a Romano-Germanic legal system. It is a unitary state, meaning that it does not have to balance the concerns of individual states with those of a federal government. France is renowned for its contributions in music, art, philosophy, literature, and science, as well as to political and social theory. Indeed, the Napoleonic Code was one of the primary influences in the development of civil families of law around the world.

The history of France, particularly since the French Revolution of 1789, has been one of constant change and instability. Social conditions and radical ideas of reform led to the overthrow of the French monarchy during the revolution and were intended to create a better society. Unfortunately, the revolution left many political questions unanswered, and seemingly contradictory ideals continue to plague French society. The attachment to individual liberty and political equality is counterposed with an abiding faith in authority and belief in the rule of the majority (Terrill, 1997:98–99). These contradictions predate the revolution and continue to influence how the French people perceive their country (p. 102).

The current constitution of the Fifth Republic was essentially the creation of Charles de Gaulle in September 1959. It is divided into twenty-four titles and includes ninety-two articles. Each title addresses an aspect of constitutional authority (Terrill, 1997:100). There are two primary officeholders in contemporary France: the president, who actually decides government policy, and the premier (or prime minister), who is appointed by the president and is the link between the president and the Parliament. The two primary government bodies are the Council of Ministers, which is selected by the premier with the president's approval, and the Parliament. The Parliament is a bicameral legislative body, consisting of the Senate (or upper chamber) and the National Assembly (or lower chamber). The Senate is made up of 283 people who are elected for nine-year terms by the Electoral College; the National Assembly has 491 deputies, elected directly by the voters for five-year terms. The National Assembly is the more powerful of the two legislative bodies, since it is the first body to examine the national budget, it has the power to dismiss the government, and the Council of Ministers is responsible to it. Numerous political parties vie for power in France, and it has been postulated that they contribute to the instability of the government.

One island of stability in France over the last two hundred years has been the civil service bureaucracy, a highly regarded centralized administrative system. It was created by Cardinals Richelieu and Mazarin to wrest power from the nobility, and Napoleon increased its effectiveness. The job of the civil service is to directly implement national policy through ninety-five departments spread throughout the country (Terrill, 1997:105). *Magistrates,* a term used to refer to the tripartite offices of judge, procurator, and officials of the central administration of justice, are members (p. 124).

To better understand the interplay among people and the ideas that influence legal systems, we need to recognize that Napoleon's reworking of the civil service coincided with the implementation of his code. For several hundred years before the establishment of the Napoleonic Code and the civil service, no centralized system of law existed in France. There was no uniform standard for legal decisions, and this situation created some of the instability in the society. From the 1500s through the 1700s, the people of France needed and wanted a codified system of law that would create a set of statutes applicable nationwide and that would eliminate inequities in the law. Distinctly different laws applied to each social class. Napoleon's rise to power in the late 1700s was due, in large part, to successfully satisfying this centuries-old desire of the French people (Terrill, 1997:134, 136).

There are two general categories of law in France: public law, which includes criminal, constitutional, and administrative law, and private law, which pertains to two parties (Terrill, 1997:134). The Napoleonic Code dealt with each of these issues. For example, the Civil Code of 1804 and the Code of Civil Procedure of 1807 both dealt with private law, while the Code Penal, the Code of Criminal Procedure, and the Code of Commerce all defined public law.

The Code of Criminal Procedure (revised in 1959) explains methods of investigation and adjudication. The Penal Code (revised in 1992; in effect in 1994) identifies various types of offenses and their appropriate sanctions (Borricand, 1997). Three kinds of criminal offenses exist in France: crimes, which are felonies; misdemeanors, which are serious misdemeanors; and violations, which are minor misdemeanors (Borricand, 1997). These classifications also make distinctions among the courts: crimes are heard in the assize courts; misdemeanors are heard in the correctional courts; and violations are heard in the police courts, which handle over 50 percent of all criminal cases. The public law codes specify that major civil cases be heard in the Courts of Major Jurisdiction, and minor civil cases are heard in the Courts of Minor Jurisdiction (p. 168).

France has a national police system, which is headquartered in Paris. Police officers are representatives of the state, and law enforcement is thus administered, supervised, and coordinated by the central government. Ensuring that the laws are observed and enforced is the primary role of police personnel (Borricand, 1997). This system was first organized in the 1600s by Jean Baptiste Colbert, finance minister to Louis XIV, to solidify the authority of the monarchy. Even after the French Revolution, the national police system remained intact. The French police have extensive rights. They may intervene in the lives of citizens for a variety of reasons because of the philosophical support of authority and belief in the rule of the majority (Terrill, 1997:108).

There are two principal police systems in France, civilian and military (Fairchild, 1993:67). The National Police (PN), which employs about 133,000 people, established the following goals in 1995: (1) to ensure a sense of public security, (2) to control illegal immigration, (3) to combat organized crime, (4) to protect citizens from terrorism, and (5) to maintain public order. The PN operates under the Ministry of the Interior, and the establishment of this set of goals reflects the country's current internal concerns. The PN is responsible for typical policing activities in Paris and other urban centers; it is also responsible for the majority of criminal investigations. The National Gendarmerie (GN) is part of the Ministry of Defense and supplies military police for the French army, navy, and air force, as well as for overseas territories; it is also responsible for policing activities in towns of fewer than 10,000 people (Terrill, 1997:110–112). Of the two forces, the GN is older and has the greater prestige.

There are two main kinds of courts in France, administrative courts and ordinary courts. Each court system has its own hierarchy. The administrative courts, first established by Napoleon to help control the empire and keep him aware of citizens' complaints (Fairchild, 1993:108), are responsible for supervising government actions and for attempting to balance the state's interests with those of citizens (Terrill, 1997:124). Thirty-one administrative courts hear cases brought by citizens against agents of the government for violation of citizens' rights (however, the courts do not hear cases concerning the abuse of power by the police or the judiciary). At the top of the administrative court hierarchy is the Council of State. This court is known as the "guarantor of the rights of French citizens" (Fairchild, 1993:170). Access to the administrative courts is cheap and easy; citizens file a petition without an attorney, and the state takes the process from there. The current backlog, however, is extensive.

The ordinary courts, the other half of the court structure in France, handle civil and criminal litigation. The principle of unity (as discussed at the beginning of this section) is also applicable to the legal system; the same court can hear both criminal and civil cases (Reichel, 1994:88). Some of the ordinary courts have already been mentioned in this discussion (assize, police, correctional, major jurisdiction, and minor jurisdiction). At the pinnacle of the ordinary courts hierarchy is the Court of Cassation. This court is the highest appeals court in France and hears both criminal and civil cases. Its primary concern is with points of law, and therefore it often does not hear an entire case on appeal. It is this court's responsibility to make sure that the law is interpreted uniformly throughout France (Terrill, 1997:126). The court of appeal also may hear criminal and civil cases but, as the first appellate body, may review not only points of law but also factual descriptions in a case (p. 126).

There is no court similar to the U.S. Supreme Court in France. The notion of judicial constitutional review does not exist according to Fairchild (1993:108) for two primary reasons. First, the revolutionary tradition in France is such that there was and continues to be great distrust of a corrupt judiciary. Second, in a codified system of law and justice, the notion that judges would, on a case-by-case basis, examine the constitutionality of issues is deemed absurd by the French. The legal codes are supreme—not the individual decisions of judges.

The inquisitorial nature of France's legal system becomes clearer upon examination of the criminal court process. Three primary parties may be involved in the investigation of a crime. The first is the procurator, a civil servant whose job is not to secure a conviction in a case (unlike the prosecutor in a common law system) but to ensure that justice is done and that society's interests are served. Procurators are considered the "guardians" of society's interests (Fairchild, 1993:129) and thus do not represent the state, even though they are civil servants. Procurators do have the power, in some instances, to decide if cases should or should not be initiated. In cases involving minor crimes (particularly violations), these individuals direct the police investigation. As mentioned earlier, the National Police is the primary group involved. Finally, judges, called examining magistrates when dealing with felony cases, play a major role in the investigation of criminal cases. If a case is considered sufficiently serious, an examining magistrate conducts an extensive pretrial investigation.

Reliance on pretrial investigations is one of the characteristics that sets civil law apart from other systems. The investigation is closed and secret to protect the accused, although he or she is actively involved in the process. The examining magistrate, along with the police and the procurator, call witnesses, question the accused, and gather facts and testimony before the trial. Generally, defendants do not enter a plea to the court; if a plea is offered, it is taken as another piece of evidence in the investigation (Reichel, 1994:245). The point of this investigation is to avoid bringing innocent persons to trial. The result of the investigation is a dossier, or file, which records all of the information gathered. Once sufficient information is collected, the examining magistrate either dismisses the case or sets the case for trial. Individuals who do plead guilty do not escape trial. Each case must be proven in court, to preclude the possibility of a guilty plea offered to protect someone else, for example.

Individuals can be held in police custody for twenty-four hours without being charged; police do not need to show probable cause. With the permission of the procurator, an individual can be held for forty-eight hours. The accused has the right to an attorney but only after an initial examination by a magistrate (Terrill, 1997:114). If bail is granted, it is deposited with the clerk of the court. Bail serves two functions in the French system: it acts as security to guarantee the appearance of the accused in court, and the funds posted are used to cover costs and/or any fines that may be assessed (p. 141).

Once a case is brought to trial, professional magistrates preside. Magistrature judges in France are trained specifically for membership in the judiciary. They must compete for entry after two years of training at the National School of Magistrature (Borricand, 1997). They are civil servants and often begin their careers in the judiciary as early as their late twenties. Usually, judgments are rendered by a panel of three judges rather than one judge alone. Stare decisis as a theory of law does not exist in the French system. Cases are decided on the general principles found in the codes, and decisions are written to illustrate complete accordance with the law (Fairchild, 1993:128).

In the Assize Court, a nine-member jury may be seated. The jury is placed behind the three judges in the courtroom. Because of today's overburdened dockets, procurators have begun to reduce charges in some cases to misdemeanors. As a result, examining magistrates handle only about 10 percent of all cases under investigation (pp. 149–150). This discretionary role of procurators has become the source of much controversy.

Japan

Like France, Japan is a unitary country, urbanized and highly industrialized. However, unlike many Western urban, industrialized nations, Japan's culture stresses the importance of group goals and group solidarity. Competitiveness is accepted, but only within a group context. Loyalty to one's superiors is stressed over individual rights, and the attainment of individual and group harmony takes precedence over self-aggrandizement (Terrill, 1997:257) The ideology of individualism is scorned, while individual effort on behalf of the group is considered laudable (p. 240). These values are reflected in the Japanese attitude toward deviance and criminality. In Japanese society, deviants and criminals are pitied rather than condemned. Offenders themselves feel shame more than guilt (p. 268). This viewpoint may help explain Japan's low crime rate.

After centuries of Shogunate rule, the imperial Japanese family returned to the throne in 1868. This is commonly referred to as the Meiji Restoration, which marks the beginning of contact with the West. In 1889, Japan adopted its first constitution, modeled after constitutions in the West. The document, considered transitional (Terrill, 1997), divided the government into three branches, with an established cabinet, a bicameral legislative body, and a government bureaucracy. However, no system of checks and balances was established among the three branches, such as may be found in Western governments. The emperor, as supreme executive, still acted as absolute sovereign.

This arrangement lasted for approximately fifty-five years, until the end of World War II. From 1945 to 1952, the United States controlled the reconstruction of Japan. During this period, referred to as the Occupation, a second constitution, the Showa or Peaceful Constitution, was drafted in 1947. The new constitution, modeled on the British system, reduced the status of the emperor to that of figurehead. Ultimate power rested with the bicameral legislature. The document retained the Cabinet and created a prime minister's position, as well as a new judicial system that included a Supreme Court. Also, the rights and duties of Japanese citizens were delineated (Terrill, 1997:241).

The legislative body in Japan is called the Diet. The lower chamber, the House of Representatives, has 512 members, elected to four-year terms. Representatives elect the prime minister, who must be a representative, and control the national budget. The upper chamber is the House of Councillors, with 252 members, elected to six-year terms. Both houses rely on a committee system, which considers bills prepared by government bureaucrats before sending them on to the houses at large, to be adopted into law or rejected.

The Cabinet is a group of approximately twenty members selected by the prime minister. The majority of those serving in the Cabinet must be members of the Diet. Some Cabinet ministers control specific ministries; others head subministries within the government. The prime minister is the leader of the government and his or her party. Japan has a multiparty system, although the Liberal Democratic party has controlled the government since World War II (Fairchild, 1993:55).

The government is organized around a three-level model: the national, county (called prefectures), and local levels. At the national level is the central administration, which includes government ministries, the bureaucracy of a large, modern state. There are forty-seven prefectures in Japan. Each has its own elected assembly and a governor who acts as chief executive officer. The local level is made up of cities, towns, and villages, all of which have their own elected assemblies and a mayor. Most of the work at the prefecture and local level involves the implementation of national policy, decided by the Diet and prime minister.

The police in Japan are responsible to the prime minister. According to Terrill (1997), law enforcement in Japan has gone through five phases. The third phase began in 1872, shortly after the Meiji Restoration. At that time, a representative of the emperor was sent to Europe to study law enforcement, and he recommended following the police systems in France and Germany. This led to the establishment of a highly centralized, federal police force controlled at the national level but operative at the prefecture level (p. 245).

The fourth phase of law enforcement began during the Occupation. The Showa Constitution explicitly listed the rights of citizens, changing the way in which law enforcement personnel did their jobs. Also, the police system was decentralized. In towns and cities throughout the country, 1,600 independent police forces were established. The fifth and final phase in policing came in 1954, two years after the Occupation ended. The Police Law of 1954, passed by the Diet, abandoned the decentralized system and established the civilian National Public Safety Commission (NPSC). The NPSC falls under the jurisdiction of the prime minister and is responsible for the administration of policing in Japan. It also sets the budget, is involved in police operations, does research and planning, and engages in a variety of other tasks (Terrill, 1997:245–246).

The NPSC also supervises the National Police Agency (NPA), which is responsible for the control and coordination of officers at the prefecture level. Approximately 1,200 officers and 5,500 civilian personnel work for the NPA, and seven regional bureaus have been established. The prefectural police (PP) operate in each of the forty-seven prefectures (larger prefectures have more than one office). There are approximately 220,000 PP officers who engage in law enforcement and order maintenance (Terrill, 1997:247–248; Moriyama, 1997).

Before the restoration, judicial matters were handled by government administrators. The first judicial code was introduced in 1872 and established a court hierarchy and the offices of judge and procurator. Although the system met with societal resistance, between the time of the Meiji Restoration and the end of World War II, the Japanese judiciary became an established body (Terrill, 1997:256). However, as noted by Fairchild (1993:56), "The use of the law or legal system to settle disputes suggests that social values have broken down." Even today, Japanese tradition is dedicated to avoiding disputes in favor of compromise, conciliation, and mediation before taking a case to trial.

Japan has a four-tiered hierarchy with five courts. The Supreme Court, with one chief justice and fourteen associate justices, has the primary responsibility for constitutional interpretation. The court has not, however, become a leading institution in Japanese government. Its few major decisions regarding unconstitutional laws passed by the Diet have been largely ignored (Fairchild, 1993:112). Its most important task appears to be the administrative responsibilities related to the oversight of the legal profession. The

Supreme Court has responsibility for the Legal Training and Research Institute, which trains new attorneys and judges, as well as court clerks and family court investigators (Terrill, 1997:258).

The eight high courts, each with three judges, serve as the intermediate courts of appeal for both civil and criminal cases. The fifty district courts, which usually have one judge on the bench, handle both civil and criminal cases of note. Cases in these courts may go to trial. The 575 summary courts handle criminal and civil cases for trivial matters. No trials are held in these courts, and only one judge hears the case. The district and summary courts make up one tier in the court system. The final tier is the family court system, which handles domestic and juvenile cases (Fairchild, 1993:178).

The legal profession is divided into three groups: judges, procurators, and attorneys. There are relatively few legal professionals in Japan, largely because Japanese society is not particularly litigious. Furthermore, only 2 percent of law students pass the national bar exam in Japan, and lawyers do not have the kind of monopoly on legal matters that they do elsewhere. Many corporations, for example, employ individuals who are not attorneys to manage their legal matters. In addition to passing the bar, an individual who wishes to become a judge, procurator, or attorney must undergo an additional two years of training at the Legal Training and Research Institute. Once this is completed, he or she may then choose which path to follow (Terrill, 1997:260–261).

Judges, generally trusted and esteemed (Moriyama, 1997), are appointed by specific authority. For example, Supreme Court judges are appointed by the Cabinet (Terrill, 1997:261). Although stare decisis does not exist in Japan, many judges have adopted the principle when deciding cases before them (p. 262). Since trials are adversarial in nature, but there is no principle of stare decisis, Japan's judicial system is sometimes referred to as hybrid. Technically, precedent does not exist, yet because of years of Western influence, this characteristic of the common law system is sometimes evident.

Procurators in Japan enjoy a great deal of discretionary power. They are members of the civil service bureaucracy and are charged with prosecuting criminal cases and determining the disposition of cases. They have the authority to investigate, arrest, and detain individuals. The discretionary power of procurators also allows them to decide what cases not to charge, although they are expected to be impartial (Terrill, 1997:262–263; Moriyama, 1997).

Attorneys are required to be members of the Federation of Bar Associations, as well as members of one of the fifty-two prefecture bar associations. All accused individuals have the right to hire a private attorney or have one appointed by the court. Of the 14,500 attorneys in Japan, most represent individuals involved in litigation. As mentioned earlier, most corporate legal matters are dealt with by non-attorneys. Juries were introduced into Japan in 1923 with the establishment of the Jury Law. However, the use of juries was officially suspended in 1943.

Three separate codes define the criminal law: the Penal Code, the Code of Criminal Procedure, and the Penal Law. The Penal Code defines crimes and the types of punishments associated with them. This code is very general, hence the ad hoc adaptation of stare decisis. The Code of Criminal Procedure sets legal standards to be followed in determining guilt or innocence. The Penal Law defines the nature of commitment to correctional facilities.

Once arrested, an individual must be informed of the reason for arrest and at that point may retain counsel. Within seventy-two hours, a judge must issue a warrant of detention in order for the individual to remain in custody. A bail system is used in Japan, and bail may be requested by the accused, the accused's counsel or the accused's family. Once a case goes to trial, the likelihood of a conviction is high; in 1988, only .01 percent of accused persons were found not guilty (Moriyama, 1997).

Former Union of Soviet Socialist Republics

The socialist family of law began in 1917 with the Russian Revolution and, for all intents and purposes, ended in December 1991 with the collapse of the USSR. Before the revolution, Russian society was ruled by a succession of czars and has been characterized as absolutist, totalitarian, and ruthless. There were degrees of tyranny under the various czars, and Russian society suffered frequent periods of instability and turmoil. The influence of ideas associated with the Renaissance, the Reformation, and the Enlightenment was essentially absent from Russian history (Terrill, 1997:293). The laws of pre-revolutionary Russia were codified in the eleventh century and were strongly influenced by the Germanic tradition. Even though Russia and the German states were often at odds with each other (Fairchild, 1993:53), the overall effect and influence of Europe on Russia has historically been minimal. The system of absolutism and concurrent instability did not change with the advent of the socialist family of law. What made this family, or tradition, of law unique and distinct was the "substance of the law and the purpose of its legal mechanism" (Terrill, 1997:325). The socialist ideology informed the development of the legal system and the legal hierarchy. The primary distinction in the USSR was between socialist and nonsocialist law (p. 343).

The USSR was a federal nation with fifteen separate republics within its borders. Under the Soviet regime, centralized planning was encouraged and individual creativity discouraged. The result of this ideology was that the Soviet Union became industrialized but not advanced. The constitution proclaimed free speech, free press, and free assembly. However, the government came to suspect everyone, both foreign and domestic, of counterrevolutionary intentions.

The Communist party of the Soviet Union (CPSU) was a centralized, all-powerful administration. The judiciary, the police, and the legislature all were tied to the party. The CPSU had several purposes over the course of its existence. Before the revolution, its purpose was to foment unrest and achieve power through force. After the revolution, the CPSU maintained its power by determining and implementing policy for the future socialist state. The only legal political party in the USSR, its basic organizational units were the primary party organizations (PPO). More than 380,000 PPOs existed throughout the country. Above them were rural, city, district, provincial, and republic organizations. At the top of this hierarchy was the Party Congress (Terrill, 1997:304–305).

The Party Congress had three organs: the Central Committee, which coordinated the work of the party in various government agencies throughout the USSR; the Politburo, which was a subgroup of the Party Congress; and the Secretariat, which included the top leaders of the CPSU. The Politburo formulated party policy, while the Secretariat had responsibility for executing and supervising its implementation. Government policy was carried out by three police systems, which were often considered to be above the law.

In December 1917, the first state security force was established: the Extraordinary Commission for Combating Counter-Revolution and Sabotage (Cheka). Cheka disbanded in 1922, after the success of the revolution, and was replaced by the State Political Administration (GPU), administered by the People's Commissariat of Internal Affairs (NKVD) (Terrill, 1997:308).

In January 1924, the USSR ratified its first constitution. This replaced the GPU with the Unified State Political Administration (OGPU), which reported directly to the Central Committee (Terrill, 1997:308), and Joseph Stalin became the "undisputed ruler of Russia" (p. 309). To maintain his position, Stalin used the OGPU to execute or imprison millions of people suspected of antisocialist behavior or who opposed Stalin's absolute authority.

The Militia, the second police force, was created in November 1917 and was the principal mechanism of law and order. The Militia engaged in the traditional policing functions of law enforcement and order maintenance, but its powers extended well beyond that. It was accountable to the central government and Communist party, but it operated within local Soviet districts (Terrill, 1997:314). Uniformed and nonuniformed Militia officers in local units were responsible for investigating criminal behavior. They also dealt with the investigation of economic crimes, as well as passport violations (p. 315).

After World War II, the NKVD became the Ministry of Internal Affairs (MVD) and was given control of the Militia. The NKGB became the Ministry of State Security (MGB) and took on that responsibility (Terrill, 1997:309). Upon Stalin's death, the MVD and the MGB merged. In 1954, the Committee for State Security (KGB) was created and made accountable to the Council of Ministers. Under party control, the purpose of the KGB was to maintain and extend the power of the Communist party throughout the USSR and the world. Domestically, the KGB's active surveillance created a "subtle pall of terrorism [that] hung over every Soviet citizen" (p. 310).

The third police force, the Ancillary Forces, was organized to "protect socialist property from theft and waste, and to defend the country and promote social order" (Terrill, 1997:316). The Ancillary Forces, also known as People's Guards, had a significant impact on law enforcement. In socialist ideology, they were seen as a way to work toward the end of state power and civilian empowerment (Fairchild, 1993:71).

In 1922, a three-tiered court hierarchy was created: people's courts, provincial courts, and the Supreme Court. The people's courts were original trial courts, and judges were elected by the people. Provincial courts heard both criminal and civil cases, and the judges were elected by representative bodies in the government. The federal Supreme Court supervised lower courts, acted as the court of original jurisdiction for important criminal and civil cases, and settled disputes between republics. Constitutional review was not a primary responsibility of the judiciary at this level. Each province also had its own supreme court, which operated as a court of final appeal. In 1922 and 1923, a series of new legal codes was created that dealt with civil law, criminal law, and procedural law (Terrill, 1997:326). According to the 1922 Criminal Code, any act deemed "socially dangerous" was a crime (p. 343).

Since the official view of a socialist state is that law will eventually wither away and die, the importance of lawyers and the judiciary was considered transitory. Directly after the revolution, the bar was formally abolished (Fairchild, 1993:153). In 1936, Stalin reversed this policy, realizing that the law and lawyers could serve his purposes (Terrill, 1997:330). At this point, the Soviet judiciary fell under the influence of the CPSU. Lawyers became judges, procurators, or defense attorneys. Almost all defense attorneys worked for the state, whereas all judges and procurators were considered civil servants. Stalin's Constitution of 1936 proclaimed judges to be independent and subject only to the law as it was written. It also enumerated rights to defense counsel and other issues (Reichel, 1994:232).

The office of the Soviet Procurator was established in 1922. It was a highly centralized office, and the procurator general was appointed by the Supreme Soviet (Terrill, 1997:334). The procurator's office served in all phases of the administration of justice in the USSR. As is the case in Romano-Germanic systems, the procurator's office undertook an extensive pretrial investigation. Defense counsel had the option only of requesting that the procurator call witnesses on behalf of the defense. During trial, "social accusers" and "social defenders" could appear to support either the state's or the accused's case (Reichel, 1994:227). Individuals who pled guilty were still required to go through the trial process. Judges rarely sat alone, and there were no juries.

This discussion has necessarily been historical. Since the dissolution of the USSR in 1991, other socialist systems have collapsed. While some systems, in China, for example, still exist, the future of this family of law is questionable. In the West, our perception of the judicial system in the former Soviet Union is colored by media reports of political show trials. Although those accused of political crimes were not afforded the rights common to other families of law, it should be stated that in general criminal cases the Soviet legal system adhered to the process described above (Fairchild, 1993:130).

Saudi Arabia

To understand the Saudi system of law and justice, one must understand the importance of the Islamic religion in that country. Justice, in Islam, can have several meanings. It can refer to the quality of being morally responsible, to the mutual respect between individuals, to the idea of communalism among all people, and to the notion of a commandment from God (Souryal et al., 1996:432). The last two meanings are probably the most commonly evoked in Islamic jurisprudence. Muslims are expected to act as if they are always in the presence of God. Furthermore, community takes precedence over the individual because the community is perceived as God's community. Islamic societies are based "on a spiritual commitment to social decency" (p. 433) and God is considered the only lawgiver. Thus, behavior is classified into five categories: obligatory (*fard*), meritorious or recommended (*mandub*), indifferent (*mubah*), reprehensible (*makruh*), and forbidden (*haram*). These behaviors are discussed in the Sharia.

Under Islamic law, the Sharia is the only permissible source of legislation, and "for all practical purposes, Huddad serves as the Constitution, the Penal Code, and the Code of Criminal Procedure, all in one" (Souryal et al., 1996:433) in Saudi Arabia. The main body of the Sharia is the Huddad Allah, or the limitation on behavior that is prescribed by God; a *had* is a God-prescribed punishment (*huddad* is a plural form of *had*). *Had* penalties are absolute because they are prescribed by God; they cannot be altered, negotiated, forgiven, or pardoned.

Because God is the highest ruler, the king or civil government may not initiate legislation that is not within the natural order of God. The king, in this circumstance, may only issue regulations in the form of royal decrees consistent with the Sharia. In Saudi Arabia today, decrees are formulated by a committee within the Council of Ministers. If approved, these recommendations are sent to the king, who issues royal decrees that, when published, become law (Moore, 1996:391, 392). There is no law other than Sharia, and authoritative acts are valid only to the degree they are in accordance with Sharia.

Early in the twentieth century, King Abdul Aziz ibn-Abdul Rahman al Faisal Al Saud established the Saudi monarchy. Saudi Arabia is divided into five counties, each with a governor. Much of its population is nomadic (Fairchild, 1993:72), although there are urban areas. The fundamentalist Hanbali school, adopted by Al Saud as the form of Islamic jurisprudence, specified the organization of the courts and the procedures to be used by the legal system (Moore, 1996:392). Authors have noted that no "modern" constitution exists in Saudi Arabia (Fairchild, 1993:115), and as stated by Al Farsy (cited in Fairchild, p. 115), "It is the fundamental assumption in the polity of Saudi Arabia that the Holy Qur'an, correctly implemented, is more suitable for Saudi Muslims than any secular Constitution."

The king is at the pinnacle of the justice system; he is the final court of appeal and the source of pardons. The Ministry of Justice (created in 1970) is the second level of the judicial system. There are two court systems under the Ministry of Justice: the Sharia courts and the administrative tribunals (Moore, 1996:394). The administrative tribunals comprise a number of committees that handle secular concerns of the kingdom. The two most important are the Labor Committee and the Commercial Dispute Settlement Committee (p. 392).

The Sharia court system hears civil and criminal cases but has no established court jurisdictions. Likewise, it does not distinguish between private and public law (Reichel, 1994:114). All courts have general jurisdiction and are set up under the Ministry of Justice. There are four tiers of courts in this system. The lower, or ordinary, courts hear minor civil or criminal matters and are presided over by one judge. The general courts hear more serious cases and are also presided over by one judge. The first-level appeals courts, of which there are two in the country, are presided over by three judges. In cases where the punishments of death, stoning, and amputation have been conferred, five judges listen to the appeal. This is the final court of appeal for all cases except those involving the punishments just mentioned. In these cases, the Supreme Judicial Council is the final court of appeal. In general, criminal procedures are left to each jurisdiction and its court systems. A codified set of procedural rules does not exist (Fairchild, 1993:132).

In the Saudi court system, the belief is that a judge (*quadi*) is a judge for every matter (Souryal et al., 1996:434). Whether dealing with criminal, family, private property, or personal injury law, Saudi *quadi* are expected to closely adhere to Islamic Sharia. In theory, a defendant is entitled to an open trial. However, trials often are closed "in the interest of morals" (Moore, 1996:398).

Crimes in the Islamic justice system are of three types: *huddad* crimes, *quesas* crimes, and *ta'azir* crimes. *Huddad* crimes are grave crimes committed against God. Prosecution of these crimes is mandatory, and punishment is meted out exactly as prescribed by God's commandment. Because of the severity of these crimes, the evidentiary rules are far stricter than in any Western criminal justice system (Souryal et al., 1996). There must be numerous witnesses to the crime, and/or the accused must offer a confession. Confessions may be withdrawn at any time, in which case a trial must be held. There are seven *huddad* crimes: adultery, defamation, drinking alcohol, theft, highway robbery, apostasy from Islam, and corruption in earth. The punishment for all of these crimes is either death or mutilation. *Quesas* crimes are considered retaliation crimes and include murder, manslaughter, assault and battery, and other crimes against a person. Penalties for these crimes are not specifically ordained in the Koran and are therefore not fixed. The goal of punishment is equal retaliation and may include the death penalty. *Ta'azir* crimes represent an "open ended category which can cover all other conducts" (p. 443). Witnesses in any trial must be adult male Muslims (although in some jurisdictions two women can count as one man) of upstanding character (Reichel, 1944:114).

Jurisdiction in civil cases lies only in the hometown of the defendant, regardless of the location of the contract or property in the dispute (Moore, 1996:393). Plaintiffs must file civil actions at the governor's office. The governor's office will first attempt to achieve a compromise between the parties involved, but if no compromise can be reached the case will go to court.

During the trial, a clear statement of the charge must be read, but it does not have to be written down or stated in any particular format. The trial process is informal by most Western standards (Moore, 1996). The judge listens to the charge and then asks both sides to tell their story. Each side may bring witnesses to support their claims (Reichel, 1944). The accused in Islamic justice is considered innocent until proven guilty (Souryal et al., 1996:447). If the accused admits guilt, the judge renders his decision on the spot; if the accused claims innocence, a trial follows. There are no juries in the Saudi court process. Defendants do not have legal representation in criminal trials. Although they may request assistance of counsel in preparing their cases, defendants must present their own defense, and counsel is not allowed to be present. In civil cases, defendants may be represented by an attorney (Moore, 1996:397).

The police in Saudi Arabia are controlled by the Interior Ministry. The head of the Saudi police is the director of public safety, generally a relative of the king, as are most government officials. The director appoints most county and local police officers. The *mutawa,* or religious police, is an organization that is technically separate from the police department but that works closely with it. This morals force is responsible for monitoring people's behavior for any deviation from Islamic expectations.

CONCLUSION

Each country discussed in this chapter illustrates a different family of law. The differences between the ideal type and the working descriptions lie in the social conditions, people, and ideas that have been influential in the formation of the legal system. Whether generated by Bonaparte in France, the Occupation in Japan, or the idea of socialism in the former USSR, the development of the legal system reflects the social order.

NOTES

1. We have chosen to use the standard newspaper spelling of the word for this edition.

4 | Types of Law

All individuals in a society are governed by a variety of norms, or rules, which define appropriate and inappropriate behavior. The law is a mechanism to prevent people from violating certain societal rules. Many rules fall outside the scope of the legal culture; religious and moral codes, rules imposed by parents, and etiquette standards for politeness are norms, not laws. All the rules that govern our lives reflect some aspect of the ethical and moral beliefs of our cultures. If we think of rule violations as wrongs, there are basically three types of wrongful behavior: criminal, tort, and moral. Criminal behavior is a public wrong against society, and the criminal courts determine the nature of the wrong and the appropriate sanction. Torts are private wrongs against an individual or individuals, and civil courts have jurisdiction in these cases. Moral wrongs are violations of moral or religious codes and are not dealt with by the courts; however, they may involve some formal or informal sanctions brought about by extralegal sources. These wrongs are not mutually exclusive; rape or murder can be considered a crime, a tort, and a moral wrong. Being rude and abusive is not criminal and generally does not involve a tort; however, it could be viewed as a moral wrong, and the sanctions may include the loss of friends and social status. These relationships are illustrated in Figure 4–1.

This chapter will consider these types of wrongs, and also three specific

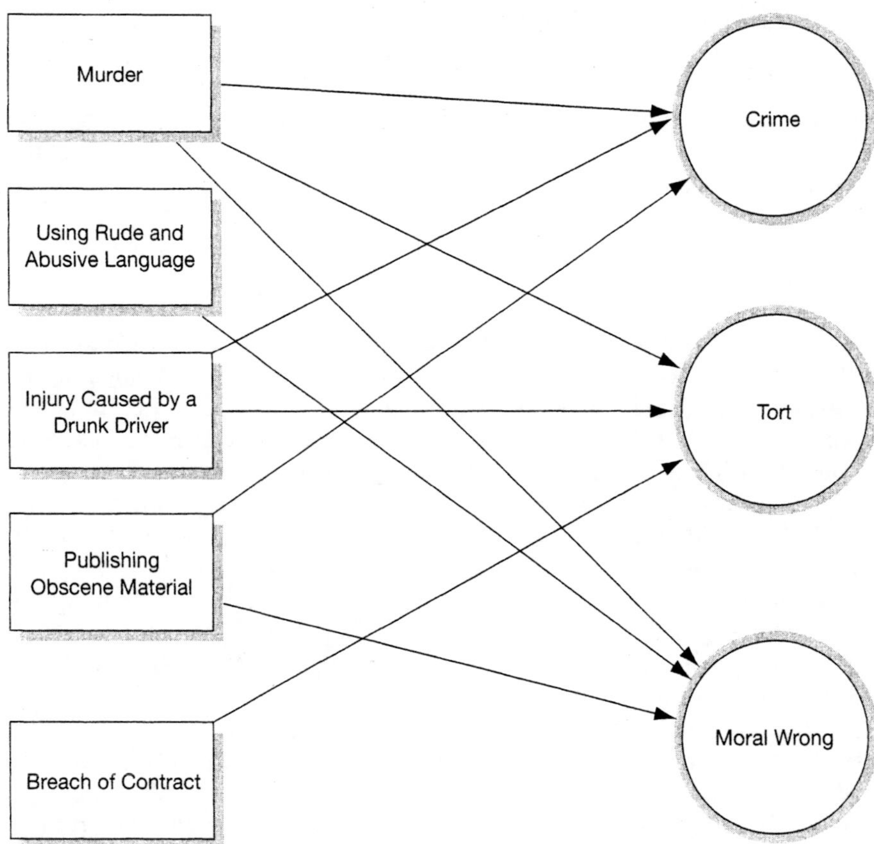

FIGURE 4–1 Types of Wrongs

bodies of law that deal with them. Besides the Constitution, U.S. citizens may be subject to different legal codes. The two we will discuss, in addition to Constitutional law, are the Uniform Code of Military Justice (UCMJ) and Tribal Law. These forms of law evolved to address two different and unique situations, one involving military personnel and the other members of Native American nations.

In the United States, the two most commonly known forms of law are criminal law and civil law. Although many behaviors can actually be considered violations of both criminal and civil law, there are some important distinctions between how these types of laws are defined and how they are enforced. Civil law is concerned with wrongs against a particular individual; criminal law is defined as a wrong against the state. In criminal law the state prosecutes the case (e.g., *State v. Metzger*, a brief of which is included in this chapter). An individual or company brings charges in a civil case (e.g., in a divorce case it is usually *Jones v. Jones*). When a criminal wrong has occurred, the redress is initiated by the state because the behavior imperils the welfare of the entire society. Therefore, although individual victims are harmed when crimes are committed, the victim does not bring charges against a criminal aggressor; rather, the state brings the charges and prosecutes the case and the victim serves as a witness for the state.

CIVIL LAW

All noncriminal laws that govern interaction and behavior between individuals or organizations are civil laws. Although the media cover more criminal cases, there is a much higher probability that all of us will end up in a civil court. There are almost four times as many civil cases as criminal cases in the United States. Laws that involve divorce settlements, contracts, property rights, and individual losses are all considered civil laws. In addition, torts are specific types of individual wrongs for which the law allows an individual to seek redress, such as when a person is injured or slandered. Many tort violations are also violations of criminal law, as in assault cases. However, it is in civil court that a victim of assault can seek personal redress through the collection of financial damages. In a criminal trial, the state will seek to punish the offender for a wrong to society.

Criminal and civil courts have different trial procedures and evidentiary requirements. Because only the state is authorized to take away an individual's life or liberty (i.e., through probation, parole, incarceration, or death), the evidence must be especially convincing. Therefore, a criminal trial prosecutor must convince a jury *beyond a reasonable doubt* that the individual who is accused of the crime is, in fact, the person who committed the crime and that he or she committed it with criminal intent. If the jurors have a reasonable doubt about whether the prosecution has adequately presented the case, the individual must be acquitted. Defining reasonable doubt is difficult, and there is much discussion about its meaning. In the *Dictionary of Criminal Justice*, Rush (1994:114) defines reasonable doubt as the inability of a juror to feel "an abiding conviction or moral certainty of the truth of the criminal charge." In a civil trial, the party bringing the charges must demonstrate through a *preponderance of the evidence* that the harm claimed by the accuser is, in fact, due to a wrong committed by the accused. The evidence presented by the wronged party must outweigh, by being more impressive or convincing, the evidence presented by the accused. Figure 4–2 helps to clarify the distinctions between these two levels of evidence.

Recently, the U.S. Supreme Court has increased the protections afforded in some civil commitment proceedings by increasing the standard of proof to "clear and convincing" rather than a "preponderance of the evidence." The Court believes that since commitment hearings may deprive a

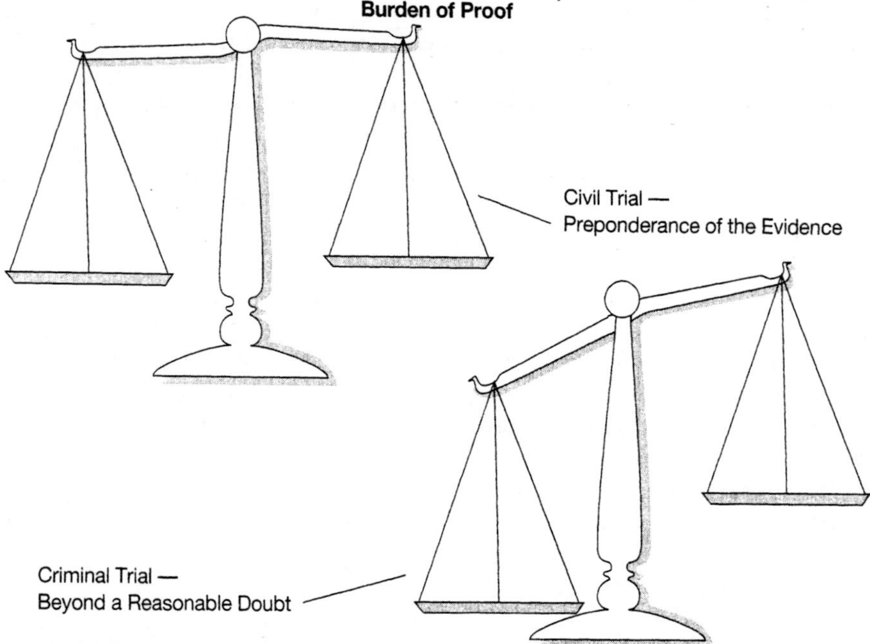

FIGURE 4–2 Burden of Proof

person of liberty, it is important to increase the safeguards against abuse of the system. The Court held that any significant deprivation of liberty by the state must be attended by heightened scrutiny.

CRIMINAL LAW

Although many human behaviors can be considered wrong or deviant, only behavior that violates a criminal statute is considered a crime in the United States. When wrongful behavior is written into a criminal law, it becomes criminal behavior, thus differentiating it from other forms of deviance. Therefore, no matter how immoral or reprehensible a behavior seems, it is not a crime unless it is specifically prohibited by law.

Criminal law is geared toward prosecuting *mala in se* behaviors. The Latin phrase translates "wrong in themselves," that is, behaviors that all reasonable people in a society would acknowledge to be wrong and that require punishment. Today, we view such acts as murder, rape, arson, and robbery, to name a few, as mala in se behaviors. These are crimes in virtually all societies, and there is general agreement among the population that these are wrongful behaviors and that society should do what it can to prevent them from occurring. The most serious crimes in the United States are classified as Index Offenses, or Part I Offenses, according to the Uniform Crime Reports. These include four violent crimes (murder, forcible rape, robbery, and aggravated assault) and four property crimes (burglary, larceny-theft, motor vehicle theft, and arson). All of these are considered mala in se acts.

In comparison, *mala prohibita* refers to behaviors that are wrong because they are prohibited by written law. Often there is no general agreement that the acts are *wrong in themselves*, but the state has encoded them into law for the overall purpose of maintaining social order. Speed law violations, abortion restrictions, and prostitution would be considered examples of mala prohibita acts, as would most of the crimes included as Part II Offenses in the Uniform Crime Report. Table 4–1 lists the official categories of crimes according to the Uniform Crime Report. Under the earlier forms of common law in the United States, it was possible to prosecute individuals for committing mala in se, or wrongful, acts even if they were not direct violations of statutory, or written, law.

Characteristics of Criminal Law

Edwin Sutherland (1939) specifies four characteristics, politicality, specificity, uniformity, and penal sanction, that distinguish criminal law from other types of rules that guide everyday life. Only laws prohibiting behav-

TABLE 4–1 Official Categories of Crime

PART I, OR INDEX, OFFENSES	PART II OFFENSES
Murder and nonnegligent manslaughter	Forgery and counterfeiting
Forcible rape	Fraud
Robbery	Embezzlement
Aggravated assault	Stolen property—buying, receiving, possessing
Burglary	Other assaults
Larceny-theft	Vandalism
Arson	Weapons—carrying, possessing
Vehicle theft	Prostitution
	Sex offense (other than rape and prostitution)
	Drug abuse violation
	Gambling
	Bookmaking
	Offenses against family and children
	Driving under the influence
	Liquor laws
	All other offenses (except traffic)
	Curfew and loitering violations
	Public drunkenness

TABLE 4–2 Characteristics of Behavior Defined as Criminal

Politicality	Violated rules must have been enacted by the state
Specificity	Rules must be very specific and spell out in clear terms what one must do to break the law
Uniformity	Rules are to be applied equally to all members of society without respect to age, social status, race, gender, education, etc.
Penal sanctions	Violation of the rules must have a specific punishment or a threat of punishment

iors that violate state-made rules (politicality), are very exact about what must occur (specificity), are applied equally to all members of society (uniformity), and have a specific punishment or threat of punishment (penal sanction) are considered criminal (see Table 4–2).

Politicality The historical origins of the legal system in the United States can be traced to the principles of common law, which evolved from the royal courts of Anglo-Norman England. Historically, it was not necessary to actually violate a written law but simply to do a *wrongful act* that caused harm to society. Over time, however, this less formal situation changed. Two cases which illustrate the transition that occurred in judicial decision making are *Ohio v. Lafferty* and *McBoyle v. United States*. In the former case, Lafferty was convicted in 1817 for selling unwholesome provisions. The defense moved to arrest judgment since there was no law in the state of Ohio that specifically prohibited an individual from selling unwholesome provisions. However, the court upheld the conviction, stating that even though there was no direct breach of statutory law, clearly the act was an "offense against the public" and the premise of common law was to protect the public good. Therefore, in 1817, the courts upheld a conviction based solely on common law when statutory law was completely silent on the subject. The motion for arrest was overruled, and the defendant was fined $50 for each violation, with costs. However, the precedent established in this case was not to remain intact for long.

Between the early 1800s and the early 1900s, the judicial system in the United States moved toward a stricter interpretation of statutory law. By 1931, in *McBoyle v. United States* [283 U.S. 25 (1931)], the Supreme Court had moved toward the requirement of specificity in legal interpretation. McBoyle was convicted of transporting a stolen airplane from Ottawa, Illinois, to Guymon, Oklahoma. He was initially convicted and sentenced to serve three years and pay a fine of $2,000. The question that was raised before the Supreme Court was whether or not the National Motor Vehicle Theft Act applied to aircraft. The definition of a motor vehicle according to the act was automobiles, trucks, wagons, motorcycles, or "any other self-propelled vehicle not designed for running on rails." Airplanes were not mentioned in the description even though they were known in 1919 when the act was passed. The Supreme Court ruled that the law did not apply to airplanes in this case and that the courts did not have the right to speculate about whether the legislature would have included airplanes had they thought of it. The judgment in this case was reversed.

As demonstrated, until the late 1800s, convictions based solely on common law were customary and acts that were construed to be mala in se, even with no legal statute, could be prosecuted. Since the early 1900s, however, the courts have taken a stricter interpretation of written law. Today, for a behavior to be considered a crime it must be written in statutory law or interpreted and defined by case law, established through precedent.

Specificity Corresponding to this transition from common law violations to statutory law was the requirement that criminal law must be specific. As opposed to civil law, in which an individual or company can be brought to court for committing a wrongful act that causes harm to another, in criminal court an individual can be charged only with violations of statutory law. These laws must be precise, clearly spelling out what an individual must do to break the law.

Along with the trend toward a strict interpretation of criminal statutes, many legislatures developed catchall provisions to define as criminal any behavior that fell outside of the norms of society and was not precisely included in other criminal statutes. These statutes were generally very ambiguous and could include almost any behavior that had the potential to harm another. Thus, they raised a number of constitutional issues regarding the need for specificity in criminal law. The main difficulty was that the average citizen would not necessarily know beforehand whether or not a certain behavior was criminal. To prevent this ambivalence, the "void for vagueness doctrine" and the "overbreadth doctrine" were designed to compel legislatures to be specific:

> A criminal statute is constitutionally void for vagueness when it is so vague that men of common intelligence must necessarily guess at its meaning and differ as to its application. 269 U.S. 385, 391. A statute is void when it is vague either as to what persons fall within the scope of the statute, what conduct is forbidden, or what punishment may be imposed. (Gifis, 1975:221)

Overbreadth is similar in nature. It describes a situation in which a statute may proscribe not only behavior that is legitimately criminal but also behavior that is constitutionally protected. A statute that is overbroad may have a chilling effect on individuals; that is, they choose to limit their legitimate constitutional rights because they are fearful of the possible application of these laws and their subsequent punishments. A statute that was found void for vagueness is included in the brief of *State v. Metzger*.

State v. Metzger
Neb. 319 N.W. 2d 459 (1982)

Douglas E. Metzger was convicted in Nebraska of violating a municipal code that prohibited indecent behavior. Metzger, on April 30, 1981, was standing nude inside his garden-level apartment in front of his window when a neighbor noticed him from the parking lot. The neighbor phoned the police, and when the police arrived they saw Metzger standing naked in front of the window, eating a bowl of cereal. Metzger's nude body was completely visible down to his mid-thigh.

Lincoln Municipal Code, section 9.52.100 stated, "It shall be unlawful for any person within the City of Lincoln . . . to commit any indecent, immodest or filthy act in the presence of any person, or in such a situation that persons passing might ordinarily see the same."

Does standing in front of one's window, eating a bowl of cereal in the nude constitute an "indecent, immodest or filthy act?" Obviously the answer to this question will differ, depending on whom you ask. What specific behaviors would be considered criminal and what non-criminal? If two people were kissing in public and a third party saw them, would they be committing a criminal act? What if these two people were of the same sex? The principle of specificity in criminal law connotes that an individual must be able to determine in advance what is lawful and what is unlawful. The court ruled that this ordinance was so vague that it was unconstitutional since it was possible for the statute to encompass both lawful and unlawful behavior.

Conclusion: "We therefore believe that . . . 9.52.100 of the Lincoln Municipal Code must be declared invalid. Because the ordinance is therefore declared invalid, the conviction cannot stand" (p. 463).

REVERSED AND DISMISSED

Uniformity Criminal law is designed to be applied equally to all members of society, regardless of age, class, gender, or any other variable unrelated to actual criminal behavior. Obviously, this is a principle of an ideal and rational system of criminal law. Although legislatures dictate laws that are to be applied equally, other agencies such as law enforcement and the judicial system do much more than simply apply them. There is a great deal of discretion in whether or not an individual will be arrested and/or prosecuted. Also, juries can be influenced by a number of factors outside of the actual innocence or guilt of the accused party.

A classic study by Donald Black (1970) found that several variables influenced whether or not a police officer would make an arrest, including whether the crime was a felony or a misdemeanor, the wish of the complainant, whether the complainant and the alleged offender knew each other, how deferent the complainant was toward the police officer, and whether the crime was a street crime or a white-collar crime. Since Black's study, many researchers have addressed the issue of police discretion and have found that biases, specifically as they relate to class, race, and gender, may be lessening (Krohn, Curry, and Nelson-Kilger, 1983; Smith, Visher, and Davidson, 1984). However, typical police practices may produce unequal arrest policies. For example, the police may patrol more heavily in low-income areas or where there is a higher proportion of minority individuals, resulting in higher arrest rates for low-income and minority individuals.

Prosecutors demonstrate wide discretion in deciding whether or not to prosecute a case; they also decide which specific charges will be brought against the alleged offender. Decisions to prosecute may revolve around the nature of the evidence, the type of offense, previous convictions of the offender, and ultimately the resources of the system.

In the uniform application of the law, many factors must be taken into account. However, when deciding to arrest or prosecute someone, the ideal behind criminal law is its uniform application. Even with discretion, the process inherent in making a wise or intelligent decision must not take into consideration age, race, religion, gender, or social class. These would be considered extralegal variables and would fall outside the scope of the law.

Penal Sanction The final characteristic of criminal law is that it has a corresponding penal sanction. For all criminal law violations, there is punishment or a threat of punishment. Because criminal laws are designed to protect the good of society, the state is authorized to impose sanctions on individuals who violate the criminal codes. It is only through the criminal judicial process that an individual can lose the right to life, through the death penalty, and liberty, through incarceration. In addition, criminal courts can impose fines, monitoring (electronic monitoring or probation), and other sanctions like education programs or participation in a treatment program, as determined by the case. The primary purpose of the corrections system is to dispense the sanctions imposed by the criminal courts.

Characteristics of Criminal Behavior

Criminal acts are very specific types of wrongful behavior. For a behavior to be considered criminal, it must include all seven of the following characteristics:

1. There must be certain external consequences or harm to society.
2. The act must be legally forbidden or proscribed in law.
3. Some form of conduct must occur, either intentional reckless action or inaction.
4. Criminal intent, or *mens rea*, must be present.
5. Mens rea and conduct must occur together.
6. There must be a causal relationship between the societal harm and the misconduct.
7. There must be a legally prescribed punishment.

First, as mentioned earlier, a criminal act is an act against society. Therefore, behavior is considered criminal only if it harms society, not simply an individual victim. This is why the state prosecutes: it is the state's effort to maintain social harmony by preventing behavior that is considered destructive to the social fabric. Individuals who have been harmed by an act that does not threaten societal interests have recourse through the civil system. Second, the behavior must be legally forbidden. This does not mean that certain behaviors are not wrong or immoral because they are not identified by statutory law but simply that they are not criminal. Third, some form of conduct (*actus reus,* the criminal act) must occur—either intentional reckless action or inaction. For the most part, simply thinking about committing a crime does not constitute criminal behavior. The one exception to this rule is the crime of conspiracy, in which the actual plotting of a crime, such as a presidential assassination, is considered criminal. It is important to note, however, that a person charged with conspiracy can only be convicted of plotting the crime and cannot be charged with the actual crime.

Fourth, mens rea, or criminal intent, must be present. The notion of criminal intent is critical to the understanding and functioning of the U.S. criminal court system. For someone to commit a crime, she or he must be aware of the wrongdoing and intend to commit harm. It is because of this intent premise that most states exclude from the criminal process certain individuals who are unable to intentionally commit harm. For example, in the United States there is a separate system for juveniles who engage in harmful behavior. The juvenile court system is based on the premise that children do not have a sufficiently formed conscience to be able to adequately distinguish right from wrong. Therefore, when juveniles commit a criminal act, they are not tried in our adult criminal system but rather are brought into the juvenile court system, where they are adjudicated delinquent. Also, individuals who are mentally retarded or insane generally are not considered capable of committing criminal acts. This is not to say that they cannot be held accountable in other venues. For example, juveniles can be institutionalized for being a danger to themselves or to others.

Individuals must also have knowledge of the act to be held accountable for it. In some cases, however, individuals can be held criminally liable for actions that they may have been individually unaware of but for which they are responsible. The *doctrine of respondeat superior* is an example in which a company or an individual is held responsible for protecting the public in situations in which the members of the public are not in a position to protect themselves. The brief of *U.S. v. Dotterweich* illustrates the use of this doctrine in the manufacture and distribution of drugs. In this case, Dotterweich, the corporate president of a pharmaceutical company, was held criminally liable for mislabeling and shipping drugs. Although he may not have had direct knowledge of the act of mislabeling, it is his responsibility as corporate pres-

U.S. v. Dotterweich
320 U.S. 277 (1943)

Dotterweich, as president and general manager of Buffalo Pharmacal Company, Inc., was charged along with the company with violating the Federal Food, Drug, and Cosmetic Act enacted by Congress on June 25, 1938. The company had purchased drugs from their manufacturers, repacked them under their own label, and shipped them in interstate commerce. The drugs were mislabeled. The statute prohibits "the introduction or delivery for introduction into interstate commerce of any . . . drug . . . that is adulterated or misbranded." "Any person" violating this provision was guilty of a misdemeanor. Three counts went to the jury. The jury disagreed about whether the corporation could be held accountable but found Dotterweich guilty on all three counts. The conviction was reversed on appeal. The Supreme Court ruled that Dotterweich was to be held accountable since the conventional requirement for wrongdoing, that is, awareness of the act, was not necessary when protecting the public good.

"Such legislation dispenses with the conventional requirement for criminal conduct—awareness of some wrongdoing. In the interest of the larger good it puts the burden of acting at hazard upon a person otherwise innocent but standing in responsible relation to a public danger" (281).

REVERSED

ident to make certain that the drugs being shipped from his company are appropriately labeled, as established in the Federal Food, Drug, and Cosmetic Act of 1938.

Fifth, the mens rea and conduct must occur together. The intent can either be specific toward a particular act (specific intent), or as in the case of the *misdemeanor-manslaughter, felony-murder doctrine*, intent encompasses not only the act but also its consequences (general intent). In this doctrine, if someone has the intent to commit a misdemeanor and someone dies as a result of that action, the defendant can be charged with manslaughter; if someone commits a felony and someone dies as a result, the defendant can be charged with murder.

Sixth, there must be a causal relationship between the societal harm and the criminal misconduct; seventh, there must be a legally prescribed punishment (*nullum crimen sine poena*, no crime without punishment) for the behavior to be considered criminal.

Criminal acts are ideally identified as behaviors that fit into these seven characteristics. However, in some situations individuals (or their lawyers) argue they have not really met the mens rea qualification. This argument is generally proposed by the introduction of the legal concept of insanity.

Insanity and the Insanity Defense

The utilization of the insanity defense in well-publicized cases and trials has made this legal strategy a topic of much debate and speculation. It is a very difficult defense to argue and is actually used only in 1 to 2 percent of all felony cases that go to trial (as cited in Katsch, 1995). It is most often used with murder or other serious felony charges and often when the evidence against the defendant is overwhelming.

The earliest insanity defense was argued in 1843 in England in the case of *Rex v. M'Naghten.* Daniel M'Naghten lived in London and believed that Sir Robert Peel, then British home secretary, was conspiring to kill him. M'Naghten killed Peel's private secretary, Edward Drummond, when he mistook him for Peel. M'Naghten's defense lawyer argued that he was incapable of being responsible for his actions when he killed Drummond because he was suffering from mental delusions at the time. The British jury agreed, and the "right and wrong" test emerged as a result of that trial. Now referred to as the M'Naghten rule, the legal standard is that an individual must be able to distinguish right from wrong before being held responsible for criminal behavior. Specifically, a person is not responsible if he or she were "laboring under such a defect of reason, from diseases of the mind, as not to know the nature and quality of the act he was doing, or, if he did know it, that he did not know that what he was doing was wrong" (Gardner, 1989:97).

Since 1843, various other mental insanity defenses have been proposed. However, the M'Naghten rule was used by virtually all the American courts until late in the 1970s and is still used by at least half of the state courts. Table 4–3 describes other tests being used currently in U.S. courts to determine criminal responsibility.

The "substantial capacity test" is defined by the Model Penal Code (published by the American Legal Institute, or ALI), which is a generalized, modern codification of the principles considered basic to criminal law (Rush, 1994:220). This test, which is used by the federal courts and by about half of the state courts, states,

> Section 4.01 Mental Disease or Defect Excluding Responsibility
>
> (1) "A person is not responsible for criminal conduct if at the time of such conduct as a result of mental disease or defect he lacks substantial capacity either to appreciate the criminality (wrongfulness) of his conduct or to conform his conduct to the requirement of law."
> (2) As used in this Article, the terms "mental disease or defect" do not include an abnormality manifested only by repeated criminal or otherwise antisocial conduct (Robinson, 1988:1032).

The term *mental disease or defect* does not include an abnormality manifested only by repeated criminal or otherwise antisocial conduct (Gardner,

TABLE 4–3 Criminal Insanity Tests

TESTS OR PROCEDURES USED TO DETERMINE CRIMINAL RESPONSIBILITY

Test or Procedure	Year When First Used	Type of Test	Extent of Use at Present Time
M'Naghten "right or wrong" test	1843	Test is based on ability of defendant to know the difference between right and wrong.	Used by almost all American courts until the 1970s; now used by only half the state courts.
Model Penal Code "substantial capacity" test	1955	Did defendant have the "substantial capacity" to distinguish between right and wrong or to conform conduct to the requirements of law?	Used by many states, but California and the federal government returned to the M'Naghten test after using this test. See *U.S. v. Gould*, 801 F.2d 997 (1986), and *People v. Skinner*, 38 CrL 2002 (Calif. Sup. Ct., 1985). The Hinkley shooting and the Dan White shooting had much to do with these changes.
Diminished capacity defense	1957	*Only* partial forgiveness is possible if an abnormal mental or emotional condition is shown to have existed at the time of the crime (murder would be reduced to manslaughter).	Few states use this defense since the "Twinkie defense" was used in the slaying of San Francisco Mayor Moscone and Harvey Milk. States are not constitutionally compelled to recognize doctrine of diminished capacity. *Muench v. Israel*, 33 CrL 2506, 715 F.2d 1124 (7th Cir. 1983).
"Guilty but mentally ill" alternative verdict and plea	1975	Defendant may be found "guilty but mentally ill" if all the following are found beyond a reasonable doubt: (1) defendant is guilty of offense, (2) defendant was mentally ill at time offense was committed, (3) defendant was not legally insane at time offense was committed.	Used in eight or more states with either the M'Naghten test or the "substantial capacity" test. States using "guilty but mentally ill" pleas are Michigan (1975); Indiana (1980); Illinois (1981); and New Mexico, Alaska, Georgia, Kentucky, and Delaware (1982).

Note: Tests that are no longer used in the United States include the "irresistible impulse" test and the "Durham product" test.

Source: Thomas J. Gardner. *Criminal Law: Principles and Cases,* 4th ed (St. Paul, MN: West Publishing Company, 1989), p. 102. © 1989 by West Publishing Company. Used by permission of Wadsworth Publishing Company.

1989:98). A person must act purposely, knowingly, recklessly, or negligently to meet the minimum requirements of culpability according to the Model Penal Code, Section 4.01 (Robinson, 1988:1032). In the mid-1970s, some states began to allow "guilty but mentally ill" verdicts, which generally call for treatment of the mental illness, followed by incarceration for the crime. Michigan, in 1975, was one of the first states to enact such a law following a series of murders that occurred after defendants had been acquitted and released by utilizing insanity defenses. Although there have been a number of attacks on the constitutionality of the "guilty but mentally ill" statutes, none has been successful.[1]

In addition, emotional and mental health factors are often taken into consideration during plea bargaining.

U.S. MILITARY, CONSTITUTIONAL, AND TRIBAL LAW

Although there are many similarities among these three legal codes, military and tribal laws cover specific persons in specific situations. Military and tribal codes may affect not only military personnel and tribal members, but also may affect persons on military or tribal property who are not members of these groups. The codes may limit or expand certain Constitutional rights, and involve methods of administration that are unique to each.

U.S. MILITARY LAW

Throughout human history, the men and women who organized to fight each other have been accorded special consideration for their efforts. In some cultures, a distinct warrior class may evolve, such as the Helots of ancient Greece. In most modern societies, fighters are recruited or conscripted from the population, or employed from outside the society as mercenaries. Regardless of the source of the fighters, or the character of the organization to which they belong, a distinct set of rules applies to them, whether codified or traditional. Because they are expected to use arms against the enemies of the society, including deadly force, they are exempt in specified cases from the ban on taking human life, a proscribed act in all societies, although not in all situations. Since the expectation is that their enemies also will use deadly force, it is necessary to instill strict discipline in order to protect the fighters and the fighting unit. Failure to obey orders can mean disaster in combat.

In cultures accustomed to tyranny and harsh, everyday discipline, such as was known in Czarist Russia during the nineteenth century, military discipline could not have been much worse for the armed services. But in Great Britain, with its long history of democratic sentiment, even under a monarchy, a move from civilian to military life could be perilous, even outside of combat. On the field or aboard ship, the commanding officer's word was law. Historically, failure to obey orders brought swift, brutal punishment, up to and including death. During the time of the British Empire, usually considered the eighteenth, nineteenth, and early twentieth centuries, blind loyalty and obedience were required and expected of British soldiers and sailors, and any deviation was ruthlessly sanctioned. There was no appeal to civilian authority in most cases, since the military was expected to do anything necessary to safeguard British culture. Only in extreme cases, such as mutiny, was British military discipline ever called into question.

As with many British traditions, discipline in the U. S. armed forces followed their pattern throughout much of its history. During the American Civil War, flogging, branding, and execution by hanging or shooting were common punishments for desertion in the U.S. Army. As U.S. criminal law became less brutal during the last hundred years, so did military law. The introduction of the Uniform Code of Military Justice (UCMJ) in 1951 consolidated and simplified the structure of law that affected men and women in the U.S. armed forces (United States Judge Advocate General, 2000). The UCMJ specifically prohibits cruel and unusual punishment, such as flogging and branding (855. Art. 55) and self-incrimination (831. Art. 31), yet although members of U.S. armed forces take an oath to uphold and defend the Constitution, while they participate as military personnel they are not defended by it.

The UCMJ provides information, definitions and instructions that cover every facet of law as it pertains to the military. It consists of twelve chapters on subjects from Apprehension and Restraint (Sub Chapter II) to Courts of Military Appeal (Sub Chapter XII). Persons subject to the UCMJ are listed in the first sub chapter. These include active duty personnel, National Guard members when their unit is in Federal service, civilians employed by the armed forces outside the United States and its territories, retired members of the armed forces who receive pay, retired reservists who are hospitalized in armed forces facilities, prisoners of war in armed forces custody, those serving with or accompanying armed forces units in time of war, and any person within an area outside the United States or its territories leased or acquired for use by the armed forces (802. Art. 2).

General Court-Martial

Trials under the UCMJ are conducted by courts-martial, which are divided into three types: general, special, and summary. General courts-martial may hear any case for any offense covered by the UCMJ, including capital cases, meaning the sentence of death is possible. The general court-martial consists of a military judge and not less than five other members, although the defendant can request trial by the judge alone, if the accused is aware of the judge's identity and makes the request after advice of counsel [816. Art. 16. (1)(B)]. The judge must be a commissioned officer and a member of the bar of a Federal court or the highest court of a State, and must be certified for duty by the Judge Advocate General (JAG) of the armed force in which he or she serves. The other members of the court may be any commissioned officer, i.e., Navy or Coast Guard ensign or above, or Army, Marine, or National Guard second lieutenant or above. A warrant officer, that is, an officer above noncommissioned officer but below commissioned officer, may serve unless a commissioned officer is a defendant in the case. Although there are exceptions, officers lower in rank than the defendant are not allowed to serve. Enlisted personnel, that is, all ranks below commissioned officer and warrant officer, may request that other enlisted personnel serve on the court. When an enlisted defendant requests that other enlisted personnel serve on the court, enlisted members must comprise at least a third of the court panel, and must not be in the same unit as the defendant. Exceptions to these general rules are allowed only when obtaining the needed personnel is completely impossible due to logistical constraints, such as might occur during time of war or national emergency. If such exception is made, trial counsel, i.e., the officer or officers who act for the prosecution, must fully document the reasons for the exception in the trial record.

Special Court-Martial

Special courts-martial are similar to general courts-martial. They are comprised of a military judge of the same qualifications as those of a general court-martial judge, and a panel of officers or enlisted men, three instead of five. The accused may waive the panel in favor of trial by the judge alone. The jurisdiction of the special court-martial, however, is limited in that it cannot hear capital offense cases, except as ordered by the President, nor can it hand down sentences of dishonorable discharge, dismissal, confinement for more than six months, hard labor without confinement for more than three months, forfeiture of pay in excess of two-thirds monthly salary, or forfeiture of pay for more than six months (820. Art. 20).

Summary Court-Martial

A summary court-martial, as the name implies, is not a formal trial, and is referred to as "commanding officer's non-judicial punishment" (815. Art. 15). It is convened by the commanding officer of a military detachment, who acts as sole judge, and its authority is limited. This type of court may not try officers, cadets or midshipmen, i.e., students enrolled in one of the national military institutions such as West Point or the Coast Guard Academy, and the accused may refuse trial by a summary court-martial. If the accused refuses a summary court-martial, a special or general court-martial may be convened, at the discretion of the commanding officer and his or her superiors. A summary court-martial may not adjudge any punishment of death, dishonorable or bad-conduct discharge, confinement for more than one month, hard labor without confinement for more than 45 days, restrictions to specified limits for more than two months, or forfeiture of more than two-thirds of one month's pay (Sub Chapter III).

Except in a summary court-martial, the accused has the right to counsel. The court usually appoints defense counsel, although the defendant may request a specific person as counsel or may retain civilian counsel at his or her own expense. Counsel for the accused must be of equal qualification and competence, as defined by the Judge Advocate General's office, to the trial counsel who acts for the prosecution (827. Art. 7.). Conviction requires a two-thirds majority vote of the judge and the panel, except in cases where the death sentence is mandatory, and then a unanimous verdict is necessary (852. Art. 52.). The trial judge must charge the panel prior to their vote on a verdict. In charging the panel, the judge informs the other members of the court that the accused is presumed innocent until guilt is established by evidence, that reasonable doubt of guilt must be resolved in favor of the accused, and that reasonable doubt as to the degree of guilt must be resolved in favor of a lower degree of guilt for which there is no reasonable doubt (851. Art. 51.).

Chapter X of the UCMJ lists all offenses punishable by the military code. For some offenses, type and duration of sentence is stated along with the offense, while some offenses are punished "as a court martial may direct." In addition to murder, rape, theft and other crimes that would be punishable under civilian law, there are several offenses listed that are peculiar to the military. Among these are "contempt" for U. S. institutions or persons in authority (888. Art. 88), "disrespect" for a superior officer (889 Art. 89.), and actions that cause "prejudice of good order and discipline" or "conduct of a nature to bring discredit upon the armed forces" which "shall be punished at the discretion of [a court-martial]." Catchall provisions, which are strictly prohibited as too vague in U.S. criminal law, are incorporated into the military code through this General Article that covers "all disorders and neglects . . . not specifically mentioned in this chapter. . . ." (933. Art. 134).

CONSTITUTIONAL LAW

Constitutional law, derived from the U.S. Constitution, incorporates the federal oversight of all legal processes in the United States. The authority to base final decisions on constitutional law rests with the Supreme Court.

U.S. Constitution

The American social and legal systems have proved themselves to be adaptive, resilient, and innovative, largely because of the fluidity of the sociolegal underpinnings of the Constitution. The study of constitutional law is a complex field in its own right, constantly in transition as sociological constructs and legal rulings stimulate an ongoing, interactive cycle of mutual cause and effect. Throughout this book we continue to reiterate this relationship between law and society, which remains valid regardless of which society and corresponding legal system are being considered. The U.S. Constitution is a unique and vibrant document. It was born of conflict to ensure "domestic tranquility."

The Constitution is made up of a preamble and seven articles, denoted as I, II, III, and so on. The Bill of Rights was ratified in 1791 and embodies the first ten "articles of amendment." Subsequent amendments were added pursuant to Article V, to address the needs of a constantly evolving social and legal reality. Table 4–4 is an annotated overview of the Constitution and Bill of Rights, with the topics most germane to the sociology of law and the criminal justice system in bold type. The additional seventeen articles of amendment can be found in the Appendix.

Historical, Social, and Political Foundations

The Constitution of the United States is a document that provides the quintessential example of the social context of the law. Fifty-five of the leading citizens of a newly emerged nation sought to blend particularistic state goals into the creation of a strong federal identity to withstand foreign efforts that could usurp newly won autonomy. The Constitutional Convention of 1787 was essentially a summit conference, representing the interests of thirteen nation-states, each with specific sociological realities, ideologies, and conditions. This differentiation led each to embrace and prescribe divergent value and legal systems, with laws reflecting the religious, economic, political, and social priorities of local and regional significance. Their collective abrogation of the divine right of kings, as eloquently stated in the Declaration of Independence on July 4, 1776, formed the basis of the former colonies' common national identity. A 1976 Commission on the Bicentennial of the U.S. Constitution concluded, "The Declaration of Independence was the promise; the Constitution was the fulfillment" (Burger, 1976).

The Constitutional Convention (May 25–September 17, 1787)

It is hard to envision that an instrument of law as short as the Constitution could provide for every contingency necessary to achieve consensus among so many competing social, economic, and political agendas. This de facto

TABLE 4–4 Annotated Constitutional Overview

Preamble	**Statement of constitutional purpose**
Article I	**Legislative branch powers**
Article II	**Executive branch powers**
Article III	**Judicial branch powers**
Article IV	State governments
Article V	Mechanism for amending the Constitution
Article VI	The supreme law of the land
Article VII	Mechanism for ratification

Bill of Rights Amendment

First	**Religious freedom; rights of free speech, press, peaceable assembly, and to petition the government to redress grievances.** Practical application has proved difficult; subject of constant redefinition as technological advancements provide new social forums. Equally difficult has been the **religious "establishment and free exercise" clause**, particularly with regard to education. Freedom of speech (or by extension, expression) and press are frequent subjects of tort, as is the definition of **"protected" language** vs. yelling "Fire!" in a crowd. Right to assembly has evolved to a **"freedom of association,"** as well as a social and legal justification for **civil disobedience.**
Second	**Right to a regulated militia, right to bear arms.** The issues of social control vs. societal protection and individual liberty continue to be at issue. The 3.5 million members of the National Rifle Association (NRA) interpret this as proscribing any attempt to limit access to weapons, while gun control lobbies posit that the right to bear arms extends only to members of government military units, like the National Guard.
Third	**No imposed quartering of soldiers,** part of the foundation for constructing a **right to privacy** in 1965 in *Griswold v. Ct.*
Fourth	**Search and seizure provisions; warrants only if probable cause.** Basis of **exclusionary rule—fruit of the poisonous tree doctrine;** main vehicle to privacy right.
Fifth	**Rights associated with criminal prosecution: grand jury indictment, no double jeopardy, no compelled self-incrimination; no deprivation of life, liberty, or property without due process of law.** Foundation for many procedural reforms in the criminal justice system; basis of the **Miranda warning.**
Sixth	**More rights associated with criminal prosecution: speedy/public trial by jury; notice of charges; to confront adversarial witnesses and compel testimony of favorable ones; and to have assistance of counsel in presenting a defense. Right to counsel** was originally construed to mean "self-pay," until cases in the 1960s solidified the right for **indigent** defendants, or those ***in forma pauperis.***
Seventh	Suits at common law (civil litigation as opposed to criminal) right to jury trial where disputed amount exceeds $20. A very clear example of changing social and economic conditions, necessitating adaptation through judicial review. For example, a federal diversity case had an established minimum dollar amount of $50,000 in 1996, reflecting the degree of economic inflation over 200 years.
Eighth	**Prohibitions against excessive bail and fines and cruel and unusual punishment.** Prime basis of **Manhattan Bail Project** by the **Vera Institute.** Most

TABLE 4–4 (Continued)

	important, nexus of **death penalty debate,** as well as conditions of imprisonment. The former issue has spanned the liberal–moderate conservative continuum of judicial interpretation, as well as the degree of actual use. Prime area of inquiry for social scientists has turned on the extent to which ethnic and socioeconomic factors affect sentencing outcomes. Cruel confinement issues similarly span a continuum, from documentably horrendous ones that prompted judges to mandate release of hardened felons to frivolous suits by inmates on every conceivable issue, including the color of Jello served. Ultimately resulted in abrogation of avenues for legitimate appeals.
Ninth	**Rights not enumerated in the Constitution are retained by the people.**
Tenth	**Reserve clause—rights not enumerated in the Constitution as specifically belonging to the federal government are reserved to the states or to the people.** Rallying point of states' rights proponents, who maintain that the intrusiveness of big federal government outweighs any concomitant benefit. The debate has seen ebb and flow since preconstitutional days. The Constitution itself was a product of this very debate between the Federalists and Anti-Federalists, or Jeffersonians (remember Montesquieu's separation of power), a social reality that produced the Bill of Rights as a compromise.

adaptability to constant societal transition was actually the result of significant disharmony among the Constitutional Convention delegates. There was great discord between those who wanted a strong central government (Federalists) and those who demanded state-level autonomy (anti-Federalists). Rhode Island refused even to send delegates to the convention, and only thirty-nine of the original fifty-five delegates from the other twelve states stayed to the end (Miroff, Seidelman, and Swanstrom, 1995:28).

Ultimately, the success and longevity of the Constitution as the law of the land must be attributed to the very diversity and discord of purpose that erupted constantly at the convention. To resolve the raging disharmony that arose from the disparate social ideals of the delegates, the best economic, political, and legal leaders of the time were forced to carefully contemplate, prioritize, and negotiate to achieve a consensus born of heterogeneity. Their only shared vision of society under a federal nation was repudiation of the monarchy from which they had just wrested freedom.[2]

The Separation of Powers

As the effort to achieve compromise and develop an affirmative social construct wavered, delegates who had taken their legal training in Europe offered a radical perspective of law to the mix of ideas and agendas. They predicated their view of government on the sociolegal theorizations of Baron de Montesquieu ([1748] 1886), advancing the notion of a requisite "separation of powers" to avoid disproportionate power in the hands of a few.

(Montesquieu, a French legal positivist, is discussed in Chapter 2.) James Madison, as an anti-Federalist, embraced this concept, offering his corresponding Virginia Plan at the convention as the preferred model for government organization (Miroff et al., 1995:30). By providing for a system of checks and balances in legislative (Article I), executive (Article II), and judicial (Article III) roles, the United States became the ultimate living model for Montesquieu's theory. In contrast, France remained in political upheaval after its own revolution in 1789, resulting in "five republics, two empires, and one monarchical restoration . . . with fifteen constitutions since 1789" (Fairchild, 1993:48). Meanwhile, the United States prospered and became the undeniable world leader in freedom and opportunity.

The Bill of Rights

The rights and freedoms embodied in the Constitution, which was ratified on June 21, 1788, were significantly expanded by the additional compromise needed to secure ratification by *states' rights* constituencies. In June 1789, Madison proposed twelve articles of amendment specific to the liberty of citizens. On September 15, 1791, Virginia was the final state to ratify ten of the twelve amendments, and these became known as the Bill of Rights.

As illustrated in Figure 4–3, contemporary constitutional issues focus on such matters as freedom of speech, the right to privacy, the right to a fair and speedy trial, the right to due process in trial proceedings, and freedom of religion. All of these issues, while reflecting the historical guidelines established by the writers of the Constitution, are continually being shaped and defined by the current sociocultural environment.

U.S. TRIBAL LAW

Before white Europeans came to the Americas, a vast complex of Indian communities with distinct cultures, norms, and societal structures already were established. Currently there are over 500 separate societies of indigenous peoples in the United States, each with its own unique sociocultural way of life. It would be a gross overgeneralization to paint all these cultures with one broad stroke. One commonality, however, was the attempt by white Europeans to assimilate indigenous peoples. Because these societies were well established prior to colonization of the Americas by Europeans, a system of tribal law does exist which is unique and distinct from other forms of law in the United States. Tribal law refers to the philosophy of law within and among indigenous nations, tribes, and bands. It is distinct from the laws and legal interactions between Native Americans and the U.S. federal and state governments, which can be called U.S. Indian law.[3] Tribal law, there-

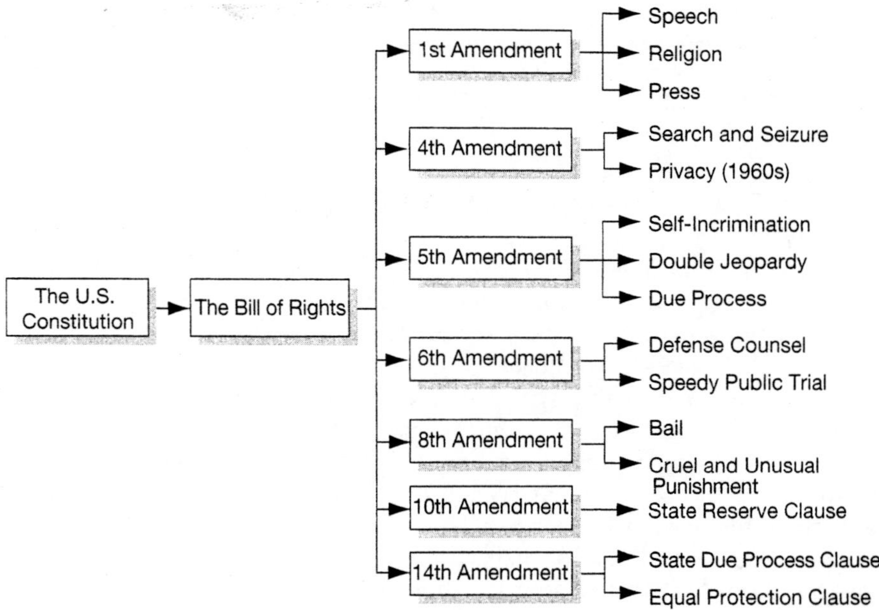

FIGURE 4–3 Summary of Significant Constitutional Rights

fore, is the law of sovereign peoples, responding to their unique social conditions, ideas, and culture; U.S. Indian law is the cross-cultural legal interaction between indigenous peoples and the overarching U.S. culture and its government agencies.

The terminology used to describe tribal law can be a problem. The term *Indian*, as in U.S. Indian law, has been viewed as a historical misnomer that reinforces negative stereotypes and groups many different cultures into one all-encompassing term. However, we are forced to deal with public policy and procedures and the organizations that guide them, such as the Bureau of Indian Affairs (BIA) and the Indian Gaming Commission. Also, the terms *nation* and *tribe* are often used interchangeably, although it is more accurate to refer to the nation as the larger sociopolitical unit, usually with a common language root, that is made up of tribal entities. For example, the Lakota (Sioux) are generally considered a nation comprising many tribes, including the Brule, Oglalla, Sisseton, and Yankton. Similarly, the Apache nation includes the White Mountain, Chiricahua, and Mescalero. In addition, *Indian country* is a term used to define land that has been specifically set aside for Indians' use. This designation is important because it is the legal designation for land where only federal and tribal law have jurisdiction. According to 18 U.S.C. 1151, Indian country includes

1. all lands within an Indian reservation,
2. all "trust" and "restricted" allotments of land regardless of location within or without an Indian reservation, and
3. "all dependent Indian communities" in the United States. (Hemmens, 1997)

A dependent Indian community was first defined in *United States v. Sandoval* [231 U.S. 28 (1913)] as an Indian tribe that is the responsibility of the U.S. government (Hemmens, 1997).

Prior to contact with Europeans, traditional tribal law was based on the body of norms and rules that governed the community. From an ethnographic perspective, the hunter-gatherer subsistence pattern of social organization (see Table 2–1), would be a generic descriptive of Native-American society. Tribal political and legal structures were based on the extended family and kinship ties, extending variously into the clan, band, village, tribe, and perhaps, nation. As cited in *Ex parte Tiger* [47 S.S. 304 (1898)], "They are strangers to the common law. They derive their jurisprudence from an entirely different source" (Harring, 1994:vi). The laws of the Indian tribes, as all laws, were a reflection of their culture, people, and ideas. The common law tradition that came to define early U.S. law was often at odds with the tribal traditions.

In contemporary interaction with U.S. society, many Native-American nations have developed legal structures that closely resemble that of the United States, combining electoral, economic, and legal resources. In doing so, tribes have formed coalitions to reinforce the authority of the tribal nation in order to maintain their sovereignty in public policy areas. Most notably, natural resource issues such as water and mineral rights, fishing, hunting, and wildlife management, as well as control of traditionally sacred lands, have been repeatedly litigated by Native-American nations.

The bases of current law that solely affect Native Americans, their lands and their cultures include the traditional mores and folkways of the Native-American culture, much of which has been superseded or replaced by statutory U.S. law. Since the early years of European colonialism, white hegemony forced Native Americans to adapt their structures of governance to conform to those of the encroaching society (Harring, 1994:26). The Cherokee, Creek, Choctaw, Seminole and Chickasaw nations were called the Civilized Tribes by whites because they adopted governmental forms similar to those of the United States. These adopted laws worked alongside informal band and village law, often at cross purposes.

In traditional Native-American cultures, relationships are governed by ties of family and tribe, often dependent on oral history. Limits on behavior are understood and internalized; actions are guided by shared social norms, and sanctioned by societal approval or punishment within the intimate confines of the extended family or village. As a general rule, a council of tribal elders resolves serious disturbances of tribal order, such as theft and murder.

The council meets not to adjudicate the merits of a case, but to mediate and bring about reconciliation among the principals and with the community as a whole. This is in sharp contrast with U.S. criminal law, which is highly defined, abstract and imposed by a hierarchical bureaucracy, a concept foreign to indigenous cultures. White law's rigidity and lack of reconciliatory intent made it unpalatable in the Native-American context (Nelson and Sheley, 1985).

European colonialism had nearly wiped out indigenous peoples by the early 1800s. In a desperate bid for self-preservation, Native Americans adopted this alien codification of laws and regulations. The Native-American population east of the Mississippi River decreased by 90 percent between the advent of colonization and the beginning of the nineteenth century. The Cherokee of the Southeast United States were one tribe who adopted a governmental form based on the United States' system, including a similar constitution. Their hope was to negotiate on equal terms with the U.S. government, but the innate racism and imperialism of U.S. officials made this impossible (Harring, 1994:169). However tortuously reasoned, legislative, executive, and judicial acts that affected indigenous peoples ultimately had the effect of transferring Native-American lands to white control. Entire indigenous nations were forced to relocate because they stood in the way of western expansion by white people convinced of their manifest destiny (Harring, 1994:23).

Even when U.S. judicial decisions were written in favor of Native Americans, the outcomes seldom were enforced, as in the case of *Worcester v. Georgia* (31 U. S. ((6 Pet.)) 515) (1832). The Reverend Samuel Worcester broke Georgia law regarding the Cherokee by living on their land without a state license, and was sentenced to prison at hard labor. Georgia enacted the law to prevent northern missionaries from fomenting dissent among the Native Americans in Georgia. Justice John Marshall held that the tribal territory constituted a domestic dependent nation with primary authority over its own affairs. The state of Georgia had no control over the tribe on its own land and could not require a state license of anyone who chose to live there. Worcester's conviction was overturned. But the state defied the court, President Jackson refused to enforce its decision, and Worcester was forced to take an oath of allegiance to the State of Georgia in order to be released from prison. Although the term *tribal sovereignty* was used often during discussion and litigation regarding Native Americans, its meaning varied in the different contexts of U.S. policy. The concept was used in this case by Justice Marshall to undermine state control of Native-American lands in favor of federal control. The inherent racism of the time is reflected in Justice Marshall's comments when he referred to Native Americans as "an inferior race of people . . . under the perpetual protection and pupilage of the government . . ." in *Johnson v. McIntosh* (21 U.S. ((8 Wheat.)) 543) (1823). Native Americans were viewed by nineteenth

Worcester v. Georgia
31 U.S. (6 Pet.) 515 (1832)

In the 1820s, the state of Georgia enacted special laws designed to control the Cherokee Nation within its borders, which constituted a direct challenge to federal authority regarding both treaty and Indian commerce clauses of the U.S. Constitution. The intent of these laws was to destroy the social, political and economic infrastructure of the Cherokee people. Tribal council meetings and tribal courts were forbidden; no non-Indian could enter Cherokee land without a state license; whites who lived there already were obliged to take an oath of allegiance to the state of Georgia.

Eleven missionaries who lived among the Cherokee were arrested under this last law, tried in Georgia, and sentenced to 4 years at hard labor. Nine were pardoned and released after taking the oath of allegiance. The Reverend Samuel Worcester and Elizur Butler refused to take the oath and went to prison. The state refused to acknowledge the jurisdiction of the Supreme Court, and took no part in the appeal proceedings. Justice Marshall stated that the Cherokee Nation constituted a distinct community, responsible for its own affairs, and that the state of Georgia had no jurisdiction on Cherokee land. He made it clear, however, that the Cherokee were not an *independent* nation, but were under the protection of the federal government, which had exclusive authority in dealing with Native Americans. In addition, Worcester held the position of postmaster, and the Constitution states that no federal appointee can be required to hold a state permit. The convictions of Worcester and Butler were

REVERSED AND ANNULLED.

But Georgia defied the court and refused to release the men. President Jackson refused to enforce the decision in order to avoid an armed conflict with the state. After a year and a half in prison, Worcester and Butler took the oath of allegiance and were released.

The failure of the Supreme Court and the Jackson administration to uphold territorial sovereignty and federal authority over the Cherokee nation weakened the Native Americans' already tenuous hold on their lands. Many Cherokee people subsequently took the Trail of Tears to the Indian Territory in the West.

century white Americans as children who needed to be protected from themselves and others.

As Native Americans were forced onto reservations during the eighteenth and nineteenth centuries, they experienced enormous cultural stress. In order to cope with the assimilation and acculturation demands of whites, some Native Americans attempted to accommodate the requests of the white government. These accommodations caused friction among Native-

American people, creating factions. Native Americans mistrusted those who worked with the whites and who embraced the belief in assimilation. They were called treaty Indians, because of their willingness to cooperate with the whites. In most cases, only those members of the tribe who cooperated with the whites were favored by the white bureaucrats, who controlled the reservations. An extreme example of such factionalism is the case of Crow Dog (Harring, 1994).

Ex Parte Crow Dog [109 U.S. 556 (1883)]

Since 1871, the Bureau of Indian Affairs (BIA) has controlled U.S. reservations. Agents of the BIA live on or near the reservations and oversee all activities on them. This oversight has been paternalistic at best, feudal at worst. One tactic of control initiated early on by the BIA was the practice of hiring a police force from Native Americans who live on the reservation. The BIA often hired traditionalists in the hope of diverting them into the mainstream. Crow Dog was a traditionalist, and had been a chief of tribal police on the Great Sioux reservation in Dakota Territory for a short time. Spotted Tail was the Chief of the Brule Sioux who lived at the Rosebud Indian Agency in South Dakota. He was a fine politician who kept the band out of two major Indian wars and managed to walk the line between the progressive and traditionalist factions, in spite of the hostility shown by many traditionalists, including Crow Dog. Crow Dog shot and killed Spotted Tail on August 5, 1881. He never denied killing Spotted Tail, and the matter was settled under traditional tribal law. The families of the two men met, and it was agreed that Crow Dog would pay Spotted Tail's family $600 cash, eight horses, and one blanket. As far as the Native Americans were concerned, that was the end of it (Harring, 1994).

The BIA agent, however, had Crow Dog arrested and tried in a U.S. court. The agent knew that the matter had been settled under tribal law, supposedly the law of the land in the sovereign nation, but he acted anyway. The BIA had already made several attempts to extend U.S. criminal law enforcement onto the reservations, and this was one more test of the U.S. government's ability and willingness to eliminate the last vestiges of Native-American rights of self-determination. Crow Dog was arraigned in territorial court in Deadwood in the spring of 1882. The prosecution presented the defendant as a factionalist troublemaker and assassin. Crow Dog refused to speak English on the witness stand, although he had been educated at the Carlisle Indian School. The all-white jury convicted Crow Dog of murder, despite defense testimony that Spotted Tail was armed and had reached for his pistol. The BIA then paid for Crow Dog's appeals all the way to the Supreme Court in hopes that the justices' ruling would extend U.S. criminal law into the reservations.

The Supreme Court in this case upheld limited sovereignty for reservations and vacated the lower courts' convictions of Crow Dog, but the language of the dicta intimated that the sovereignty was transitory and eventually would give way to complete assimilation of Native-American peoples (*Ex parte Crow Dog,* 109 U. S. 556) (1883). Over the next few years, both Supreme Court case law and acts of Congress further eroded Native-American rights on their reservations. In 1885, Congress passed the Major Crimes Act by tacking it onto an appropriations bill. This act gave the United States jurisdiction over a short list of heinous crimes committed on reservations, regardless of the race of the perpetrator or of the victim. *United States v. Kagama* (118 U. S. 375) (1886) introduced the concept that Congress's power over Native Americans could not be limited by treaty or by tribal sovereignty. The Dawes Act of February 8, 1887, forced the allotment of Indian lands to individual tribe members. The effect was to destroy their communal way of life, divide bands, villages, and extended families into isolated farmsteads, and further the process of assimilation into the mainstream of a white, U.S. lifestyle.

Even before the Major Crimes Act and *Kagama,* the BIA had worked hard to force assimilation on Native Americans. It established the Indian police in 1879 and courts of Indian offenses in 1883. Neither institution had any legal standing, under tribal law or the U.S. Constitution, but were installed by the BIA as administrative tools of social control. Demoralized and impoverished by their prison-like existence on reservations, some Sioux traditionalists turned to the Ghost Dance, a nationalist and religious movement. This attempt to reestablish traditional, uncivilized folkways was intolerable to the BIA and to local settlers, who feared that the Ghost Dance was a prelude to violence. The only threat in the Ghost Dance was its power to undermine the assimilation strategy of the BIA, so they outlawed it and sent Indian police to enforce the ban. The Indian police held authority only from the BIA, and many resigned rather than fight the traditionalists (Harring, 1994).

The courts of Indian offenses were specifically designed to "aid the Government in its efforts to abolish rites and customs so injurious and so contrary to civilization . . ." (BIA, *Annual Report, 1883,* xxi), such as traditional dances and other cultural traditions. Judges in these courts were Native Americans appointed by the BIA agent. These Native-American judges operated the courts at the pleasure of the agent and further fragmented the traditional Native-American legal structure. Any act by a Native American on the reservation could be construed as an offense and fall under these courts' jurisdiction. Malicious lying, seduction, evil speaking, and family quarrels were among the cases heard by the courts. Offenders were routinely sentenced to the agency guardhouse, a BIA-run jail, for from 10 to 90 days. The legality of these administrative courts was upheld in *United States v. Clapox* (34 Fed. Rep. 575) (1888). Judge Matthew Deady of the Oregon federal district court defended the tribal courts, not as Constitutional institutions, but as governmental instruments to "improve and elevate the condition of these dependent tribes to whom it sustains the relation of guardian." Thus, the reservation became a school where Native Americans were taught to defer to whites, since they could be jailed for any action that did not meet the agent's criteria for *civilized* (Harring, 1994).

Despite the Supreme Court, the Congress, and the BIA, Native-American culture and law survives in the United States, but only as a shadow of its former self. Native Americans on reservations face serious poverty and unemployment, and attempts to introduce industry into tribal lands have been largely unsuccessful due to their geographic isolation and lack of resources. Even the advent of casino gambling on reservations and Indian-owned land, as successful as it has been in some cases, has not solved many Native-American problems—and contributes to others (Dahl, 1995).

CONCLUSION

In this chapter we have discussed the important differences among the types of law, civil, criminal, and constitutional. We have pointed out the importance of different burdens of proof in civil and criminal cases; discussed the history and use of insanity as a defense; and explained the role of people, ideas, and social conditions in the development of the Constitution. In addition, we looked at two unique codes of law, the UCMJ and Tribal Law, that affect only specific groups in our society, and discussed their origins, the characteristics that make them unique, and the effects on the people and institutions to which they apply. In the next chapter we will examine systems of law by looking at the U.S. court structure and the movement of cases through the system.

NOTES

1. See *People v. McLeod,* 288 N.W. 2d 909 (Mich., 1980); *Weismiller v. Lane,* 815 F. 2d 1106 (7th Cir., 1987).
2. It should also be noted that their idea of who comprised the "we" in "We the people" was exclusive and elitist, being limited to the white, male, property-owning citizens eligible to vote. Not until the Twenty-sixth Amendment in 1971 and the intervening ratification of the Fourteenth (1868), Fifteenth (1870), Nineteenth (1920), and Twenty-fourth (1964) Amendments, as well as the Civil Rights Act of 1964 and the Civil Rights Voting Act of 1965, were status-based exclusions to voting largely eliminated.
3. This is the distinction made by Sidney Harring (1994) in *Crow Dog's Case.* A similar distinction was made by Vine Deloria, Jr. (1985), in *American Indian Policy in the Twentieth Century.*

5 | Systems of Law

The U.S. Constitution, as amended by the Bill of Rights, was ratified in 1791. Although the entire body of law in the United States derives from such sources as common law traditions and complex administrative codes, the Constitution ultimately takes precedence over any other law in the country. The founders of the United States provided for a collateral body of law to be determined by the individual states that was to reflect the moral, socioeconomic, and legal priorities of each particular jurisdiction. The Tenth Amendment, or *reserve clause*, reserves powers not specifically delegated to the federal government as the province of the state legislatures. This, in essence, is the notion of *dual federalism* that defines the system of law in the United States or, rather, fifty-one systems of law, the federal government and one for each state. Every state has its own constitution, which must conform to the federal Constitution. This balance of authority between the federal and state governments has evolved over time.

There was a significant move for renewed states' rights in the 1990s. For example, the Supreme Court heard oral arguments on the constitutionality of the Brady Bill in December 1996. The Brady Bill is named for James Brady, who was shot and injured during an assault on President Ronald Reagan by John Hinckley, Jr., in 1981, when he was President Reagan's press secretary. The 103rd Congress adopted The Brady Handgun Violence

Prevention Act, which required a background check before handgun sales, along with a ban on assault weapons, and restrictions on the transfer of handguns to juveniles. The 104th Congress [H. Con. Res. 65], in a statement of support, indicated that this act had been responsible for preventing the sale of over 40,000 handguns to individuals legally barred from purchasing them. The basic question before the Supreme Court concerned the extent to which such federal legislation can be imposed on the states when no federal dollars are allocated to implement the mandate.

The *balance of powers* schema employed at the federal level, with executive, legislative, and judicial branches forming a triparte system of checks and balances, is replicated at the state level. Given the numerous statutes, administrative rules and regulations, and case law, at both state and federal levels, as well as district, county, and city laws at the local level, determining which jurisdiction has authority is often a challenge.

In Chapter 6, we will deal more specifically with the lawmaking function of state and federal legislatures. We will observe that the laws legislatures enact do not always apply to all situations. A bill may be structured in such a way as to gain a consensus that will enable it to be passed in the bicameral legislative structure, avoid a veto, or withstand judicial review. Often legislation is left deliberately vague and omits certain details to avoid antagonizing significant portions of the population.

Before the consideration of legislative enactments of law, we will examine in this chapter the contemporary court and legal system in the United States. The role of the judicial branch of government was initially considered benign and not particularly significant. It had neither the "power of the sword, nor of the purse." But as will become evident in the brief on *Marbury v. Madison* (1803), astute political maneuvering by Chief Justice Marshall established a precedent for judicial review and exponentially expanded the role and scope of judiciary authority. We will now analyze this role in greater detail, and then we will present two conceptual models designed to explain the legal process.

THE COURTS

The primary function of the courts in the United States is to determine solutions to conflicts through the application of the law. This premise applies to all courts, both criminal and civil, and in all levels of jurisdiction, i.e., limited, general, and appellate. The courts are charged to objectively hear the case presented by the parties to a dispute and to find and apply the appropriate law to resolve the conflict. Appeals notwithstanding, the court's ruling legitimizes the outcome, giving other disputants in similar situations a basis for predicting whether or not their position is truly rational under the law. This predictability in the law is, of course, constantly in flux, as discussed in previous chapters. As social ideas and conditions change, so, too, will the law, through legislative enactments and/or judicial case law.

At the most basic level, conflicts occur when at least two parties seek a distinct outcome to a given situation, but there can be many parties to a dispute (e.g., a 1995 class action suit against Dow Chemical had thousands of parties who sought reparations for alleged product liability). Goldman and Sarat (1989) identify three kinds of disputes. (1) Private dispute is a conflict between two private parties. Examples are the disputes associated with marital dissolution; that is, it must be determined who is awarded the house and car, the responsibility for jointly incurred bills, and child custody and parenting issues. (2) Public initiated dispute is a conflict between the government and one or more individuals. Criminal prosecution is a prime example, but the dispute could be over a late tax penalty. (3) Public defendant dispute is that in which an individual, agency, or other body associated with the government is a party in the conflict. Section 1983 actions are a growing example of this type of conflict. City governments, who often self-insure against liability for negligence by city employees (usually law enforcement), must litigate or settle claims for damages brought by citizens (for a specific example, see the brief of *Tennessee v. Garner*).

Case Mobilization

Courts differ from legislative bodies because they do not initiate subject matter or issues. The manner in which a legal system acquires cases is referred to as case mobilization. An assumption about the U.S. court system is that individuals will vigorously pursue whatever is in their own best interest. Cases can be initiated by individuals or by the state. When the legal system relies primarily on individuals to initiate legal action, it is called a *reactive mobilization process* (Weinberg and Weinberg, 1980). Unless private individuals assert that they have been wronged in some way (a breach of contract, for example), the legal system will make no contribution to solving the problem. Government officials do not file suit on behalf of individuals if their stereo doesn't work, the landlord has refused to fix the steps, or the mail-order company never shipped the gift. The reactive model rests on the assumptions that people are (1) well informed of their legal rights, (2) rational, and (3) will pursue their own best interest (Black, 1970).

When the state is the major source of case initiation, it is called a *proactive mobilization process* (Weinberg and Weinberg, 1980). The proactive model rests on the assumption that the legal well-being of citizens is best determined by the government. It is argued that this is a social welfare model of law in which the legal system imposes its beliefs on the individual (Black, 1970).

The United States has developed a mostly reactive system, even in criminal law. While the state has the formal role of initiating criminal proceedings, the fact is most criminal charges arise out of complaints made by individual citizens. The system is reacting to what is being brought into it. Furthermore, when the complaining party decides not to testify against an alleged offender, the criminal process becomes less effective because of a lack of witnesses for the state.

Mention should be made of special-interest litigation groups such as the American Civil Liberties Union (ACLU) and the National Association for the Advancement of Colored People (NAACP). As groups with visibility and resources, they have systematically and successfully challenged laws and policies in this country and are exemplary models of reactive mobilization. They protect the rights of citizens, keep themselves well informed, and seek to pursue outcomes that best meet the rationales of their organizations.

Requirements and Principles of the Courts

Because the courts are passive and can consider only cases brought before them, cases must meet several criteria (Abadinsky, 1995:200):

Standing is the requirement that a plaintiff who challenges a law or tries to settle a conflict show evidence of direct harm. This eliminates frivolous suits that slow an already clogged legal system. A genuine dispute, i.e., a case with standing, must exist between two parties who will gain or lose something as a result of the court's decision. The most common claims are financial loss and harm, physical loss, or the loss of liberty. In recent years, standing has been liberalized to include less obvious threats, such as danger to the environment. If there is no standing, the legal issue is moot, or not significant. People or groups with an interest in a case but who do not meet the test for standing may still express their views on the matter through briefs of *amicus curiae*. These are friends of the court briefs, which summarize a viewpoint on a particular issue.

De minimus non curat lex translates as "the law will not concern itself with trifles." If a friend owes a (soon to be ex-) friend $1, the court does not want to hear about it (Vago, 1997:258). This is a trivial matter, and more important issues should be the focus of the court's work. An exception to this doctrine is a case of ideological importance that is being litigated for nominal damages. A token award identifies the victor in the conflict and sets a precedent for future decision making on a closely related issue.

Justiciability (Vago, 1997:257) means that a case is appropriate for a specific court to hear and render a decision. The court must also be able to provide a remedy for the situation. For example, divorce cases can be heard only in specific civil courts and cannot be brought before a federal criminal court.

Government immunity is also an aspect of the court process. Originally, in the United States, neither the federal nor the state governments could be sued without their permission, based on the doctrine of sovereign immunity, which derived from the English view that "the king can do no wrong." Immunity can also extend to officials in the performance of their duty. As the government expanded, government immunity lost some of its force. For

Tennessee v. Garner
471 U.S. 1 (1985)

At about 22:45 (10:45 P.M.) on October 3, 1974, the Memphis, Tennessee, police dispatch received a "prowler inside call." Officers Elton Hymon and Leslie Wright were subsequently dispatched to the crime scene in progress. While Wright radioed the dispatch and talked to the neighbor reporting the disturbance, Hymon started to investigate the adjacent house. He observed a figure scrambling across the back yard, stopping short when he encountered a six-foot chain link fence. Using his service "Maglite," Hymon was able to distinguish the suspect's face and hands. He saw no sign of a weapon and later stated that he was "reasonably sure" and "figured the suspect was unarmed." He judged the frightened suspect to be about seventeen or eighteen years old and about 5′5″ or 5′7″ tall. In reality, the object of Hymon's scrutiny was a fifteen-year old eighth grader, one Edward Garner, who was a mere 5′ 4″ tall and weighed somewhere around 100 or 110 pounds." Hymon demanded that Garner halt, prompting the teenager to attempt to climb the high fence. According to Hymon's deposition, "I knew he was going to get away, because . . . there was no way I could have caught him." Hymon further stated that he "was carrying a lot of equipment and wearing heavy boots, and that Garner, being younger and more energetic, could have outrun him." Thus convinced that if Garner made it over the fence he would elude capture, Hymon shot him in the back of the head. At the hospital where his death was certified, $10 and a purse from the B & E were found on his slight body.

In using deadly force to prevent the escape, Hymon was acting under the authority of a Tennessee statute and pursuant to police policy. The statute provides that "if, after notice of the intention to arrest the defendant, either flee or forcibly resist, the officer may use *all means necessary* to effect the arrest" (emphasis added). Appalled over the untimely demise of his son and the total lack of rationality attendant to the killing, Garner's father filed suit under the provisions of 42 U.S.C., Section 1983, which allows claims for damages to be filed against negligent employees or entities of the state, despite the doctrine of sovereign immunity. The complaint alleged that the unprovoked shooting and the statute sanctioning it, violated the Fourth, Fifth, Sixth, Eighth, and Fourteenth Amendments of the Constitution. The Federal District Court for the Western District of Tennessee concluded that Hymon had employed the "only reasonable and practicable means of preventing Garner's escape."

The Court of Appeals for the Sixth Circuit affirmed that Hymon had acted in good-faith reliance on the Tennessee statute and was therefore within the scope of his qualified immunity. It remanded for reconsideration the question of any liability of the city, in light of *Monell v. New York City Dept. of Social Services,* 436 U.S. 658 (1978). (Monell greatly increased the scope of Section 1983 claims against city entities and was decided after the district court's ruling in *Garner.*) In a somewhat misguided spurt of judicial independence, the district court refused to reconsider its prior holding, despite the new case law. The court of appeals reversed and remanded, reasoning that the "killing of a fleeing suspect is a 'seizure' under the Fourth Amendment, and is therefore constitutional only if it is 'reasonable'" [710 F. 2d 240 (1983)]. The Supreme Court noted probable jurisdiction and granted certiorari.

Justice White delivered the opinion of the Court, affirming the Sixth Circuit's perspective of the Fourth Amendment liberty issue, noting the need for "balancing the extent of the intrusion against the need for it." "To determine the constitutionality of a seizure 'we must balance the nature and quality of the intrusion on the individual's Fourth Amendment interest against the importance of the governmental interests alleged to justify the intrusion'" (cite omitted). The Court noted that the fundamental "question was whether the totality of the circumstances justified a particular search or seizure." Stating that peaceful submission of suspects was the optimal outcome, Justice White wrote that "an officer may not always [seize a suspect] by killing him." "We are not convinced that the use of deadly force is a sufficiently productive means of accomplishing them [police objectives] to justify the killing of nonviolent suspects." "It is not better that all felony suspects die than that they escape. Where the suspect poses no immediate threat to the officer and no threat to others, the harm resulting from failing to apprehend him does not justify the use of deadly force to do so." "Officer Hymon could not reasonably have believed that Garner—young, slight, and unarmed—posed any threat."

Finding the Tennessee statute to be unconstitutional, the Court limited the legitimate use of deadly force by the police to situations where it is necessary to prevent escape *and* the officer has probable cause to believe that the suspect poses a significant threat of death or serious physical injury to the officer or to others.

JUDGMENT AFFIRMED

example, governments can now be sued when their actions are proprietary rather than governmental, that is, when they are acting more like a business. Some pieces of legislation, such as the Federal Tort Claims Act, have expanded the rights of injured persons to seek damages from the government, even though immunity is still relatively entrenched.[1] Such claims are still rather hard to pursue on the presumption that government employees must be allowed latitude to perform their jobs and make decisions without constantly anticipating legal consequences. The critical component is whether the individual acted maliciously or in good faith.

Besides these requirements, several other principles constrain courts in the United States (Eisenberg, 1988 in Abadinsky, 1995:141–142).

1. *Objectivity* requires judges to be impartial and not to have previous connections to the parties involved in a dispute. If they do, judicial ethics requires them to recuse, or remove, themselves from the case. The courts derive their legitimacy from their perceived adherence to objectivity.
2. *Support* involves the principle that courts must be supported by the general standards of a society and its legal system.
3. *Replicability* is the principle that aids in the dissemination of *sound legal advice*. With reasonable dependability, replicability is the belief that legal decisions are to be written in a standard format—so that advice can be based on past legal outcomes. Replicability allows lawyers to properly advise their clients, and it allows the courts to function in a fair and consistent manner.
4. *Responsiveness* suggests that courts are obligated to be responsive, not to the citizenry at large but to the legal profession. That is, responsive to, but not obligated to follow, the argument being made and the briefs being written.

5. *Jurisdiction* is another very important issue to consider. A court must have jurisdiction to hear a case and thus be able to rule. *Jurisdiction* is a term that is often used and has context-specific meanings. Courts must have jurisdiction over the parties involved in a dispute. This may be assigned in one of three ways (Altschuler and Sgroi, 1996): through a compulsory process in which individuals are served with a summons and are then required to appear before that court, giving it jurisdiction; because the persons in the dispute live in the state or have a business in the state; or by consent, in which an individual appears in court voluntarily.

A court also must have jurisdiction over the subject matter it hears. Questions about federal law are heard in federal courts; questions about state laws are heard in state courts. Courts of general jurisdiction can hear any type of case (civil or criminal, felony or misdemeanor). Limited jurisdiction means that a court can hear only certain kinds of cases, for example, magistrate or traffic courts. Appellate jurisdiction refers to a court's authority to review cases from a lower court on appeal by one of the litigants. The term *venue* denotes the actual geographic jurisdiction of the court and refers to a particular district, city, county, or state (Abadinsky, 1995:145).

Courts and the Last Word

Courts rarely have the last word in a given situation. As a matter of fact, it is very common for cases, or issues associated with cases, to reappear in court. Indeed, it often appears that court cases are on a cyclical track. A court may retain jurisdiction and parties will reappear in court to offer clarification or introduce additional details, for example, in a divorce. Even though a divorce may be settled, some parties return to the courtroom to argue about child support or to continue to discuss the property settlement. In addition, even when a court has rendered a verdict or decision, the appeals process allows parties to continue the case in a different jurisdiction.

Courts rarely have the last word for a number of reasons. Some court decisions are difficult to implement. The language may be vague, necessitating further court action. Some court decisions are defied. It is relatively rare and considered highly unprofessional when a lower court refuses to follow the rulings of a higher court, but it does happen. Defiance may take the form of simply ignoring a court's order. Some parties practice avoidance, that is, using procedural or technical considerations to avoid implementing a higher court's decisions. Finally, limited application is another normal response to many judicial decisions; a judge simply argues that the precedent is not applicable to the case at hand.

HIERARCHY OF THE COURT SYSTEM

The court system in the United States has a dual hierarchy (similar to the notion of dual federalism, discussed at the beginning of the chapter). All cases ultimately are tried in one of two jurisdictions, either state courts or federal courts. Each state's court system is unique, making it difficult to accurately describe the court system in the United States as if it were a unified system. Rather, it is decentralized; that is, no central court guides all other courts. Figure 5–1 is a generic structural model of the U.S. appellate court system. All states have limited and general trial courts, and all but twelve states have an intermediate appellate court (although these are referred to by different names). A court of last appellate resort, usually called the state supreme court, also exists in all states. The notable exception is New

FIGURE 5–1 Structure of the U.S. Appellate Court System

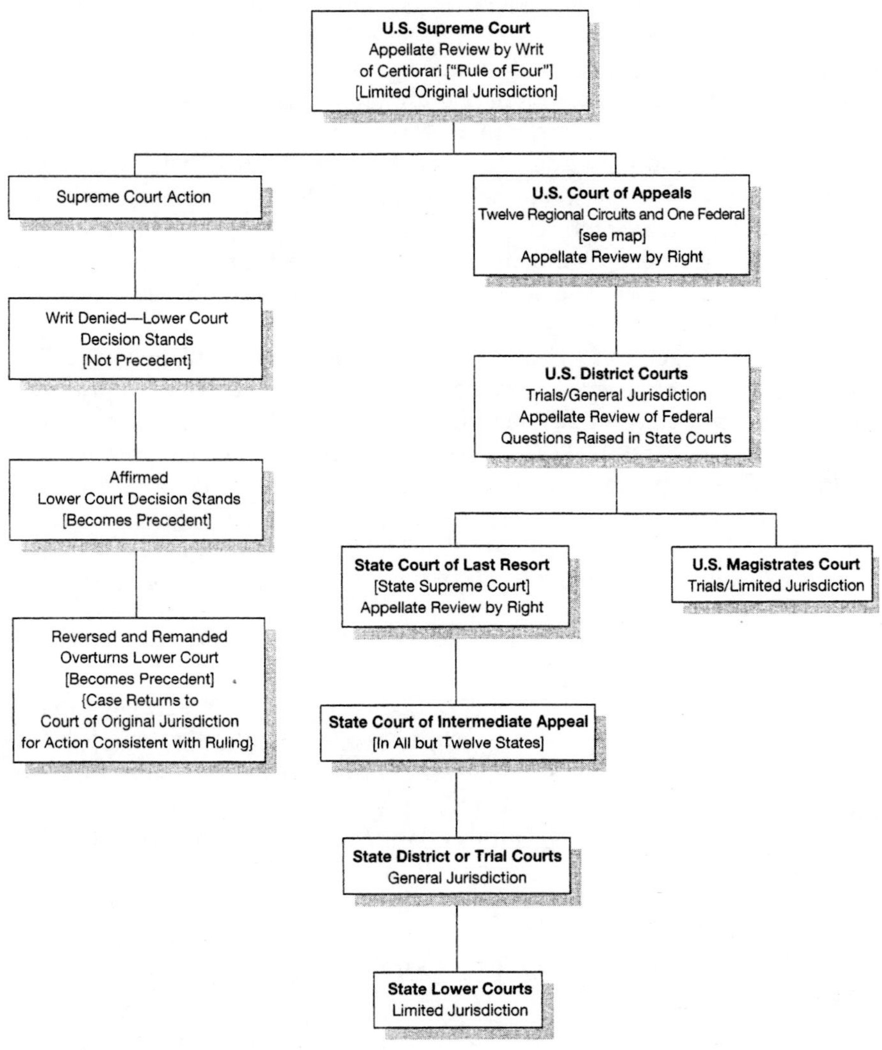

York State, where the Supreme Court is the general trial court, not an appellate court.

In general, disputes change as they move from trial courts into appellate courts. Routinely they become discussions about law or procedure and not about *fact*. If significant facts are at issue, the case is remanded to a general court for an evidentiary hearing. A trial de novo occurs only upon reversal of the decision, and the case is then returned to the original court. The original court tries the case over, absent whatever flaws caused it to be overturned or appealed. Most legal business in the United States is settled in state courts.

The federal court system is organized in a fashion similar to that of the state courts, with some variations based on the complexity and size of the federal government. At the federal level, courts have general or original jurisdiction over specific subject matter: cases in which the United States is a party; cases concerning specialty matters such as patents, copyrights, customs, and bankruptcy; cases involving foreign officials; cases involving parties from different states if more than $50,000 is involved; and cases involving the U.S. Constitution and federal laws. The states and federal courts share jurisdiction in the last two categories; the federal courts exercise exclusive jurisdiction in all other cases. The ninety-four basic trial courts at the federal level are called U.S. district courts, and each has a geographically determined jurisdiction. The district courts handle most of the legal business at the federal level.

The federal government also has an intermediate appellate body called the U.S. Court of Appeals. It is divided into thirteen circuits (see Figure 5–2), eleven nationwide geographic circuits; the U.S. District Court of Appeals in Washington, D.C.; and the Federal Court of Appeals for the federal circuit. A minimum of three judges must sit on these appellate benches, but often there are more, particularly on important issues; then the justices sit *en banc* (by the full court). The highest appellate court in the United States, which can receive cases from both state and federal courts, is the U.S. Supreme Court.

THE UNITED STATES SUPREME COURT

Predicated on the idea of separation of powers, to provide a system of government checks and balances the framers of the Constitution established a Supreme Court in Article III, giving the Court both original and appellate jurisdiction (its primary role) over "cases and controversies" in "Law and Equity, arising under this Constitution, the Laws of the United States, and Treaties."

Original Jurisdiction

Original jurisdiction (which the Court rarely exercises) extends to all cases that affect

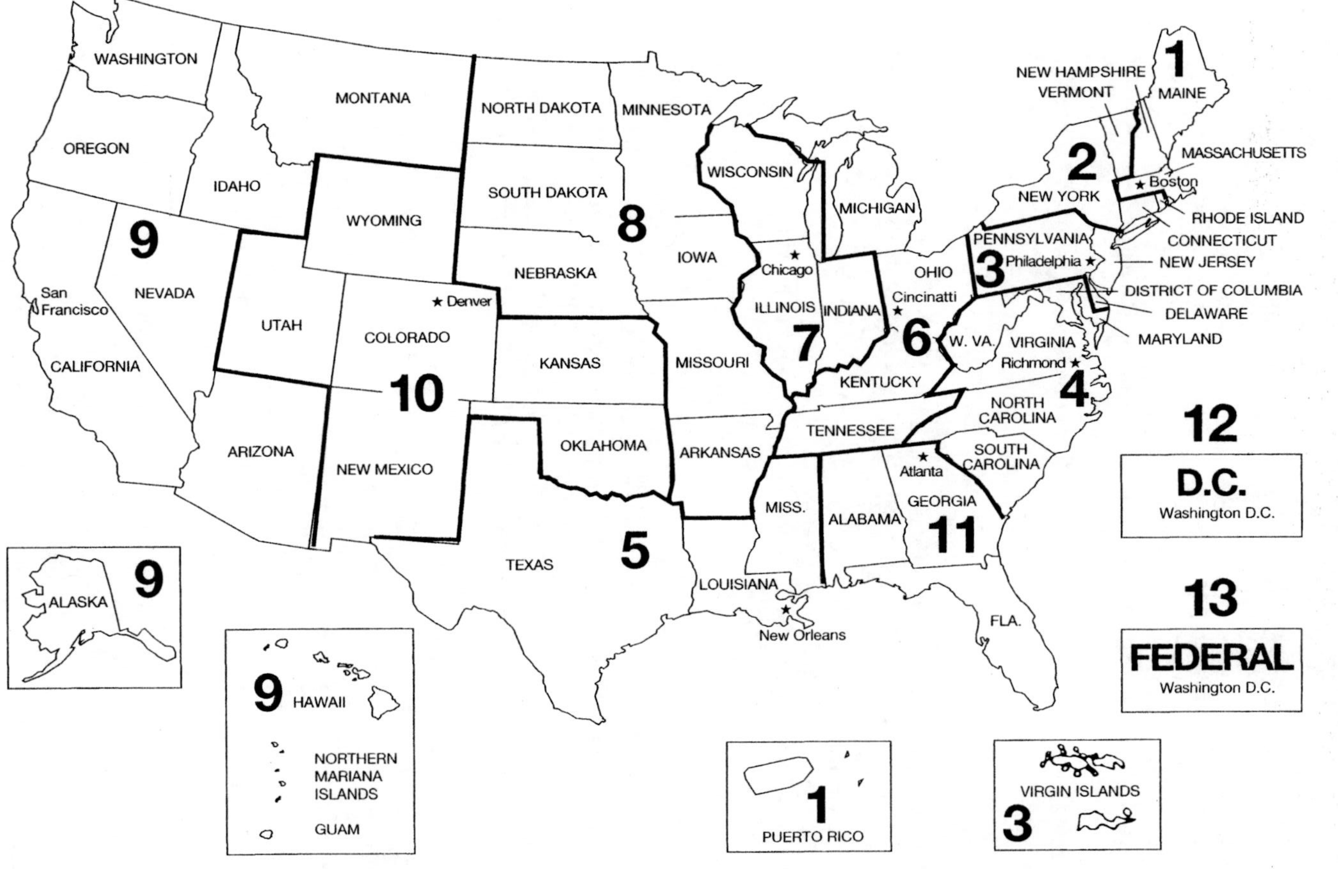

FIGURE 5–2 Number and Composition of Federal Judicial Circuits

1. Ambassadors
2. Public ministers and consuls
3. Admiralty cases
4. Maritime cases
5. Any case to which the United States [government] is a party

The remainder of originating powers all involve cases in which "a State shall be a party"

6. Between two or more states
7. Between a state and citizens of another state
8. Between citizens of different states
9. Between citizens of the same state who are claiming lands under grants of other states
10. Between a state and its own citizens
11. Between a state and a foreign state
12. Between a state and foreign citizens
13. Between a state and foreign subjects

Appellate Jurisdiction

The Supreme Court is a primary source of law in the United States. The Court has seen (and fought for) an explosive expansion in the scope of its influence on the law and, by extension, our society. The mechanisms for the increase in the High Court's role in "judge-made law" are twofold: the Judiciary Act of 1789 and the pivotal case of *Marbury v. Madison* in 1803 (see the brief).

The Judiciary Act of 1789 The Judiciary Act of 1789 established the structural integrity of the Supreme Court, the thirteen federal district courts, three ad hoc circuit courts, the position of attorney general, and the U.S. Marshals Service as an enforcement mechanism. The fledgling federal government in 1789 attempted to interpret the founders' original intent in Article III and to define more specifically which branch of government had ultimate power in a federal system that was already growing increasingly large and complex. Debate was inevitable in the interpretation process and illustrated the intended function of checks and balances provided for by the founders.

Marbury v. Madison *Marbury v. Madison* (1803) set the premise of judicial review and established the right of the U.S. Supreme Court to overrule statutes of Congress which violated the Constitution. The case found that Section 13 of the Judiciary Act of 1789, passed by Congress, was unconstitutional. Chief Justice John Marshall managed to placate the disgruntled parties to the debate, clarify the role and scope of the Supreme Court, and establish and assert the Court's power of judicial review as a new area that he called "implied powers." This case is basic to the history and ultimate development

Marbury v. Madison
1 Cranch 137 (1803)

Selected excerpts from Chief Justice Marshall's opinion

It has been insisted, at the bar, that as the original grant of jurisdiction, to the Supreme and inferior courts, is general . . . the power remains with the legislature, to assign original jurisdiction. . . . If it had been intended to leave it in the discretion of the legislature to apportion the judicial power . . . according to the will of that body, it would certainly have been useless to have proceeded further. (174)

If congress remains at liberty to give this court appellate jurisdiction, where the constitution has declared their jurisdiction shall be original; and original jurisdiction where the constitution has declared it shall be appellate; the distribution of jurisdiction, made in the constitution, is form without substance. (174)

To enable this court, then, to issue a mandamus, it must be shown to be an exercise of appellate jurisdiction, or to be necessary to enable them to exercise appellate jurisdiction. (175)

If an act of the legislature, repugnant to the constitution, is void, does it, notwithstanding its invalidity, bind the courts, and oblige them to give it effect? Or in other words, though it be not the law, does it constitute a rule as operative as if it was a law? (177)

It is emphatically the province and duty of the judicial department to say what the law is. Those who apply the rule to particular cases, must of necessity expound and interpret that rule. If two laws conflict with each other, the courts must decide on the operation of each. (177)

So if a law be in opposition to the constitution . . . the court must determine which of these conflicting rules governs the case. This is of the very essence of judicial duty. (178)

Those, then, who controvert the principle that the constitution is to be considered, in court, as the paramount law, . . . would subvert the very foundation of all written constitutions. . . . It would be given to the legislature a practical and real omnipotence, with the same breath which professes to restrict their powers within narrow limits. . . . That it thus reduces to nothing what we have deemed the greatest improvement on political institutions, a written constitution. (178)

The constitution is either a superior paramount law, unchangeable by ordinary means, or it is on a level with ordinary legislative acts, and, like other acts, is alterable when the legislature shall please to alter it. If the former part of the alternative be true, then a legislative act contrary to the constitution is not law: if the latter part be true, then written constitutions are absurd attempts, on the part of the people to limit a power in its own nature illimitable. (177)

In declaring what shall be the *supreme* law of the land, the *constitution* itself is first mentioned; and not the laws of the United States generally, but those only which shall be made in *pursuance* of the constitution, have that rank. Thus, the particular phraseology of the constitution of the United States confirms and strengthens the principle, supposed to be essential to all written constitutions, that a law repugnant to the constitution is void; and that *courts*, as well as other departments, are bound by that instrument. (179; emphasis added)

THE RULE MUST BE DISCHARGED

of the federal government, but it is complicated with subtle, yet tremendously important, points that are largely indistinguishable from the more mundane issues. Given the strategy and legal justification Marshall employed, such subtlety was probably intentional, diffusing any possible negative responses to the highly charged discussion. Looking back, it is easy to identify the pertinent issues from the trivial, but the logic used and arguments made are nevertheless long and circuitous by contemporary standards.

President John Adams, acting in a lame duck capacity, appointed forty-two new justices of the peace to the District of Columbia, the only exclusively federal jurisdiction, one week before he was to leave office. One of his appointees was the Marbury of *Marbury v. Madison*. When Thomas Jefferson assumed the presidency on March 4, 1801, the formal political appointments and commissions had not been delivered to the Secretary of State. President Jefferson was an anti-Federalist (and the driving force behind the Bill of Rights), who was highly displeased with Adams's (a Federalist) *packing* maneuver; that is, Jefferson wanted to appoint people who were in conformity with his own political ideology. Marbury petitioned the Supreme Court for a *writ of mandamus* (a civil court order to compel an official to perform an official duty) that would force Jefferson's new secretary of state, James Madison, to deliver the disputed commission.

Marbury applied for the writ pursuant to Section 13 of the Judiciary Act of 1789, the legislation authorized in the body of the Constitution in Article III, Section 2, which states, "The judicial Power of the United States shall be vested in one supreme Court, and in such inferior Courts as the Congress may from time to time ordain and establish." Marshall interpreted Section 13 of the Judiciary Act of 1789 to be in conflict with Article III, Section 2, of the Constitution, which had narrowly defined specific areas of original jurisdiction for the Supreme Court. This reading, simple on its face, actually asserted the supremacy of the Constitution over any act of Congress. Marshall reasoned that a constitution that could be altered at the whim of Congress would be functionally absurd. The genius of Marshall's logic lay in its presentation; he appeared to limit the power of the Court while, in actuality, he established the Court's authority to review congressional acts for conformity with the Constitution. One of the Court's areas of original jurisdiction, as specified by the Constitution, was over controversies concerning constitutional and federal issues. By establishing that congressional acts must conform to the Constitution and affirming that the Supreme Court was the final arbiter of constitutionality issues, the power of judicial review of legislation was firmly in place. According to Marshall's logic, the doctrine of judicial review was an implied power derived deductively from the Constitution's stated powers for the Supreme Court. Marshall used the newly deduced power of the Court to say that Congress had no authority to grant original jurisdiction to the Court; therefore the Court had no power to issue the writ of mandamus on Marbury's behalf. Jefferson was pleased that he had blocked Marbury's appointment, Congress was happy that the Court had limited judicial authority, and the Supreme Court was pleased to have expanded judicial authority.

The decision made by the Court in Marbury overturned federal legislation, a unique historical event. This situation did not occur again until fifty-four years later in *Dred Scott v. Sanford*. In *Dred Scott*, the Court upheld that a black slave could not become a U.S. citizen given the wording of the Constitution. Part of the reasoning behind this finding was the opinion written by then Chief Justice Taney who argued that Scott was not free just because of the passage of the Missouri Compromise of 1820–1821. (The Missouri Compromise was federal legislation which attempted to resolve disputes between free and slave states and, according to Taney, was itself unconstitutional.)

Originally, as has been pointed out, the Supreme Court was not a body imbued with the power it has today. The contemporary Supreme Court, however, is equal in importance to the other branches of government—because of the decision in *Marbury v. Madison* (1803). The Court can declare a statutory enactment void because it is unconstitutional. The decisions of the court affect the lives of everyone in the United States.

Except in very limited areas of constitutionally specified original jurisdiction, cases will come before the Supreme Court only if the following conditions are met:

1. Two or more U.S. circuit courts have reached different conclusions on the same constitutionally related issue.
2. The individual appellant has exhausted all other appeals.
3. A request for Supreme Court review or writ of certiorari is filed.
4. The "rule of four" is met; that is, four justices have agreed to hear the case.

There are approximately 8,000 requests for review annually. Four of the High Court justices must agree that the case, or group of cases on the same issue, is of sufficient merit to warrant the Court's full consideration. The most typical response is *certiorari* denied.

At the state court level, if a federal constitutional question is alleged, the defendant may opt to have the case heard in a federal district court. However, this rarely occurs since most defendants would prefer to have the original trial conducted at the state level and establish a record for possible future review.

The justices of the Supreme Court influence law in the United States for decades into the future. It is with this recognition that the importance of the appointment of Supreme Court justices becomes clear. Cases are dependent on an individual justice's opinions, ideas, and attitudes (backed by precedent), which are in turn influenced by the times in which she or he grew up and the ideas then current. Thus, when people talk about the Berger Court or the Rehnquist Court, they refer to the trend of decision making that occurred during an individual's time as chief justice.

Table 5–1 identifies all the Supreme Court chief justices since 1789,

TABLE 5–1 United States Supreme Court Justices Since 1789

John Jay	1789–1795
John Rutledge	1795–1795
Oliver Ellsworth	1796–1799
John Marshall	1801–1835
Roger B. Taney	1836–1864
Salmon P. Chase	1864–1873
Morrison R. Waite	1874–1888
Melville W. Fuller	1888–1910
Edward D. White	1910–1921
William H. Taft	1921–1930
Charles Evans Hughes	1930–1941
Harlan Fiske Stone	1941–1946
Frederick M. Vinson	1946–1953
Earl Warren	1953–1969
Warren E. Burger	1969–1986
William H. Rehnquist	1986–

TABLE 5–2 Supreme Court History

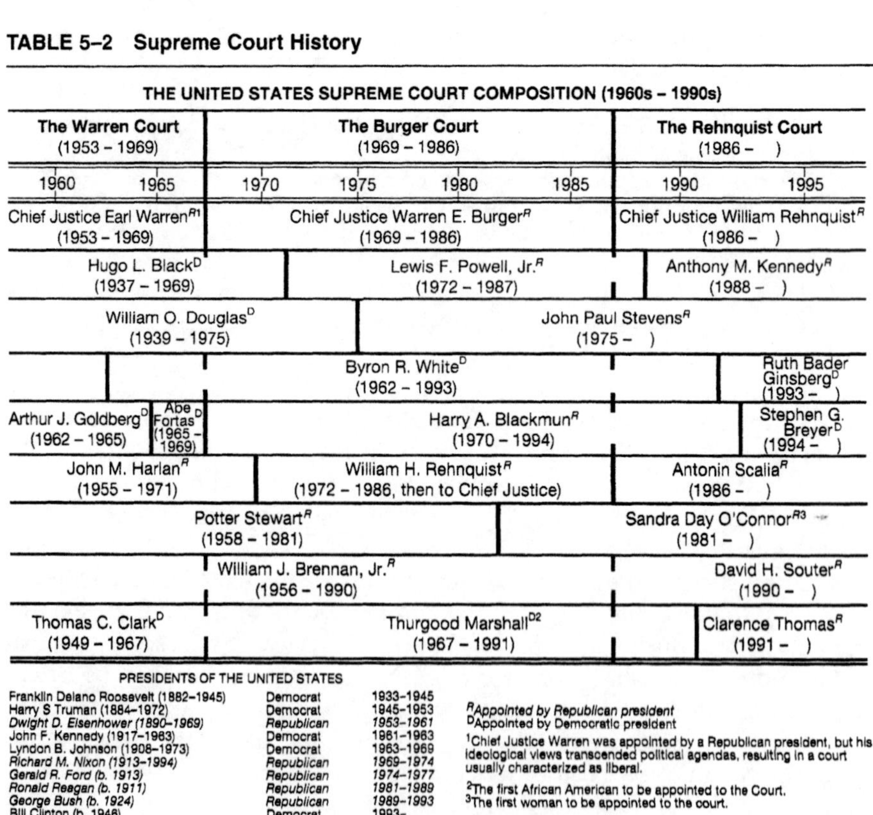

when John Jay was appointed the first Supreme Court justice. Table 5–2 identifies the justices who served on the Supreme Court from the 1960s through the present. For example, the Warren Court (also mentioned in Chapter 1), during the 1950s and 1960s, was instrumental in establishing a number of criminal due process rights specifically as they relate to criminal procedural issues. Figure 5–3 outlines briefly some of the more famous cases during that time, those that established the right against self-incrimination,

FIGURE 5–3 Criminal Due Process Rights Incorporated by the Warren Court

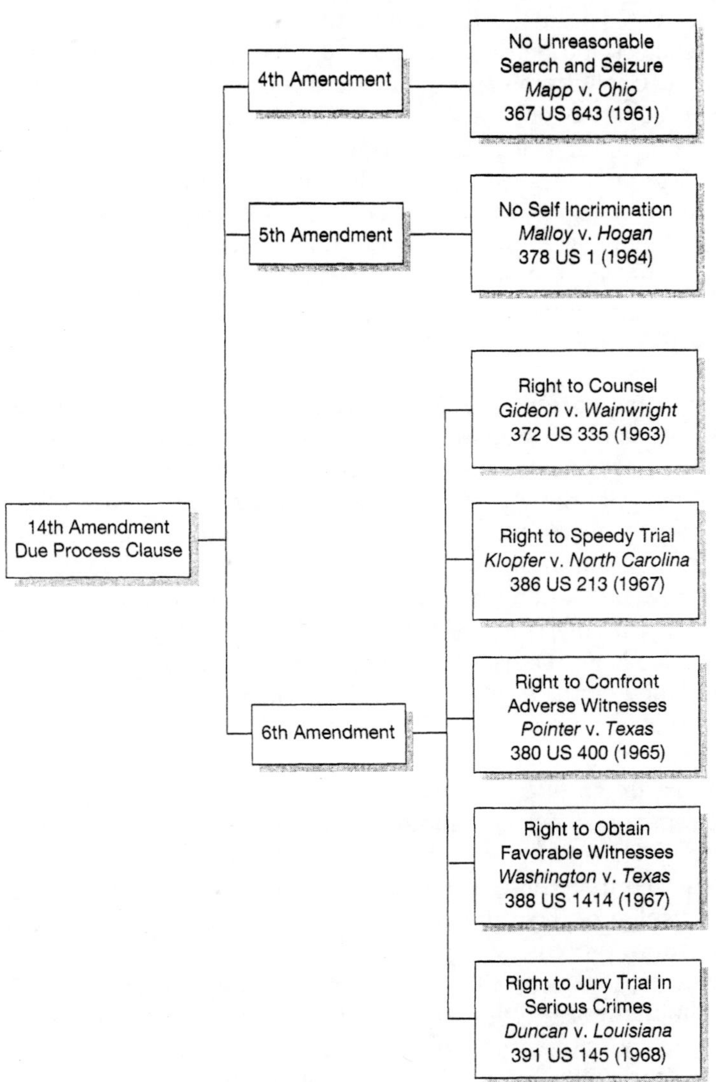

the right to a speedy trial, and the right to be free of unreasonable searches and seizure.

The Supreme Court wields a great deal of power. The justices are non-elected, lifetime appointees who can prevail over elected representatives in debates about the true meaning of the Constitution. Whether or not judicial review is *desirable*, some argue that it is not *democratic*. While we specify a representative democracy in the United States, the process of judicial review provides a mechanism for sustaining limited government. This limited government reduces the people's capacity for self-governance. Once an issue is defined as legal in nature, the number of people actually involved in deciding that issue decreases dramatically. Because the Supreme Court is required to make policy choices and political decisions, it must go beyond the technical language of the Constitution and statutes and consider the various social and political consequences of its actions. It is faced with applying nonlegal criteria to its decisions, yet its legitimacy is grounded in the belief that it uses exclusively legal criteria to make its decisions. If the Court is accepted as political, it ceases to be legitimate; if the Court actually relied solely on legal criteria, it would be unable to make decisions on key questions.

THE FLOW OF LITIGATION

In criminal cases, a high degree of discretion is involved. At any point in the process, the discretion of the legal practitioners (see Chapter 6) plays a major role in the outcome of the case. The process begins when a crime is defined by a legislative body, outlining unacceptable behavior. Once a law is violated, the next step in the process is the apprehension of the alleged offender. If the prosecutor's office has sufficient evidence, charges are filed and a preliminary hearing is set; in most cases, bail is set. The ability to meet this economic bond is a highly controversial issue; the major criticism leveled against this practice is its classist nature. Once an individual is charged by the state (represented by the prosecutor's office), she or he may be offered a plea arrangement. *Bargain justice* is utilized in approximately 54 to 97 percent of all criminal cases in the United States. Only 3 percent of criminal cases go to trial (U.S. Department of Justice, 1990). Table 5–3 indicates that in 1992 between 47 percent and 79 percent of individuals arrested were actually convicted of a crime. Those who were detained following arrest were more likely to be convicted than those who were released on bail. Figure 5–4 provides a visual display of this criminal arrest and trial process. Figure 5–5 shows the corrections process.

Legislative bodies also produce rules that guide decisions in a variety of civil cases. Guidelines for divorce settlements and child support are two such examples. Furthermore, if individuals violate rules of conduct or have some form of conflict with one another (a neighbor who builds a fence on

TABLE 5–3 Adjudicated Outcome for Felony Defendants

By released/detained status and most serious original arrest charge, 1992[a]

PERCENT OF FELONY DEFENDANTS

			Convicted			**Not Convicted**		
Most serious original felony arrest charge	Number of defendants	Total	Total convicted	Felony	Misdemeanor	Total not convicted	Dismissed/ acquitted	Other nonconvictions
Released defendants	27,212	100%	61%	45%	16%	39%	31%	7%
Violent offenses	6,567	100	47	33	15	53	48	5
Property offenses	9,420	100	65	44	21	35	28	7
Drug offenses	8,853	100	65	54	11	35	24	11
Public-order offenses	2,371	100	69	54	15	31	27	4
Detained defendants	17,985	100	79	70	9	21	20	1
Violent offenses	5,217	100	72	64	8	28	28	1
Property offenses	6,447	100	83	72	11	17	16	1
Drug offenses	4,852	100	81	73	8	19	16	3
Public-order offenses	1,469	100	79	70	9	21	20	1

Note: Ten percent of all cases were still awaiting adjudication at the conclusion of the one-year study period. Information on adjudication was available for 90 percent of all cases that were adjudicated within one year. Convictions for local ordinance violations are included under the misdemeanor category.

[a]Details may not add up to total because of rounding.

Source: U.S. Department of Justice, Bureau of Justice Statistics, *Pretrial Release of Felony Defendants, 1992*, Bulletin NCJ-148818 (Washington, DC: U.S. Department of Justice, November 1994), p. 14, Table 18.

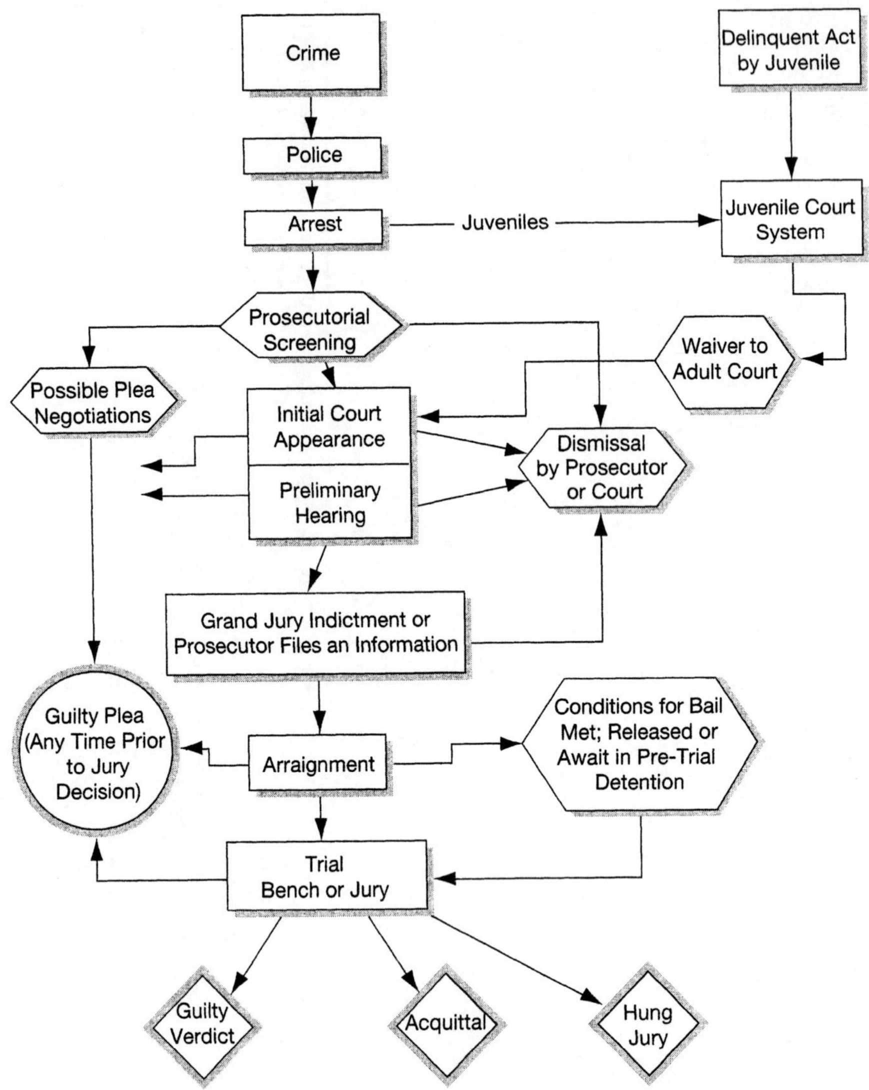

FIGURE 5–4 Criminal Justice Process—Arrest to Trial

another neighbor's property, for example), a case is filed by the plaintiff's attorney. The relief requested is called *damages*, and the award sought generally determines which court will have jurisdiction. Pretrial negotiations ideally govern the proceedings, although many civil proceedings grind to a halt because of an inability or unwillingness to negotiate. If satisfactory settlement cannot be reached through mediation or arbitration, the case goes to either a bench (only a judge hears the case) or a jury trial.

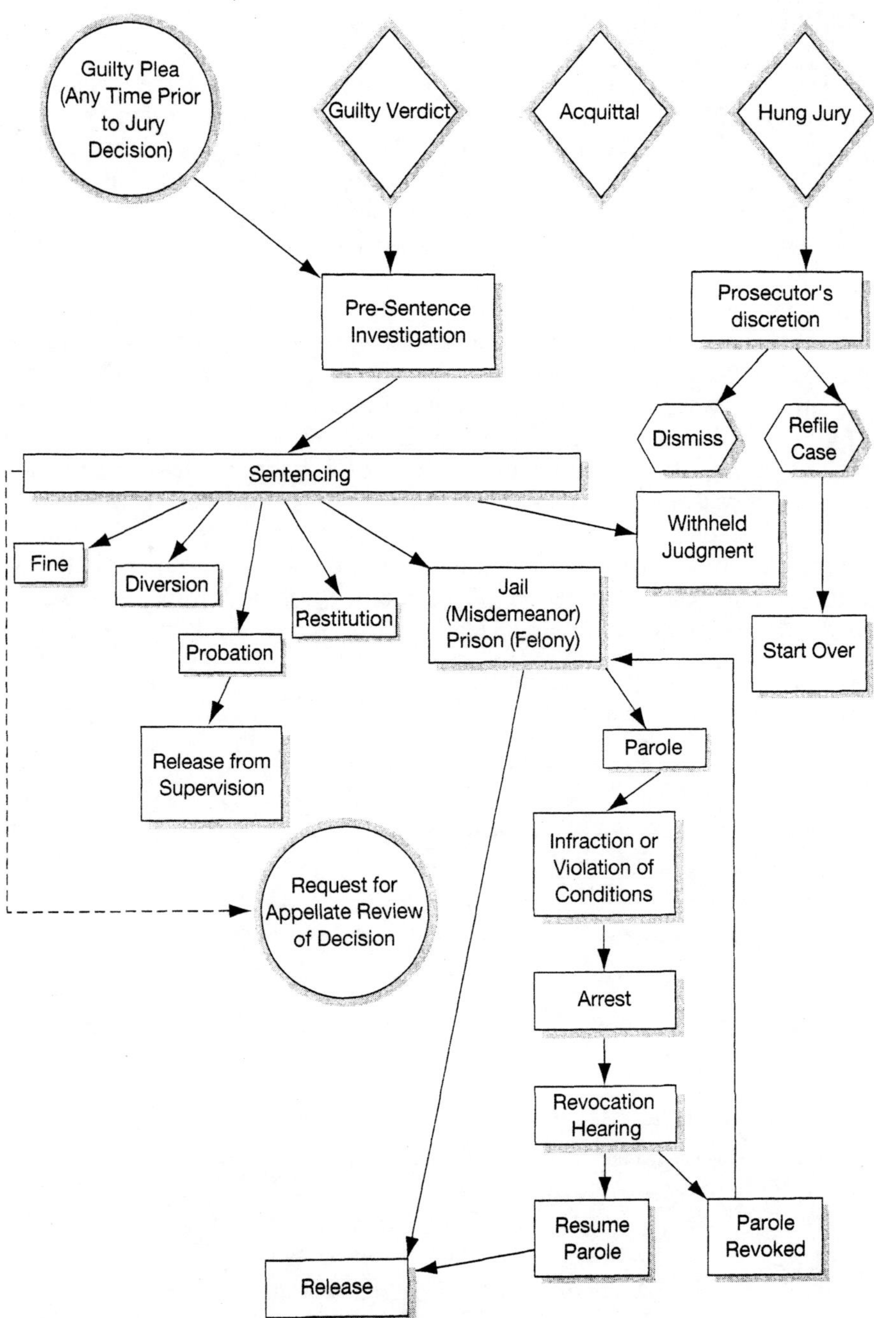

FIGURE 5–5 Criminal Justice Process—Sentencing to Corrections

CASE ATTRITION

The statistic that 90 percent of all cases end in plea arrangements (Eisenstein and Jacobs, 1977) has taken on the force of truth among practitioners in the field, the media, and the general public. This number remained immutable across time and, inevitably, was coupled with a commentary about the collapse of the criminal justice system. The U.S. Department of Justice addressed this issue in 1990 as part of an exhaustive study of the final disposition in felony cases.

Their findings, as illustrated in Figure 5–6, indicated that for every one hundred felony arrests made by police, eighteen were rejected at initial prosecutorial screening, five were diverted or referred (e.g., to juvenile court), and an additional twenty were dismissed at a later phase in the process. Fifty-four of the remaining fifty-seven cases (94.7 percent) resulted in convictions from guilty pleas to either a felony or a charge reduced to a misdemeanor. Only three cases (5.3 percent) actually went to trial, with a subsequent two-to-one ratio of guilty verdicts to acquittals. One can choose to interpret the functionality of the criminal justice system as seen in this study from two perspectives, based either on the one hundred original arrests or on the fifty-seven that remained after pretrial screening. From the former

FIGURE 5–6 Case Attrition

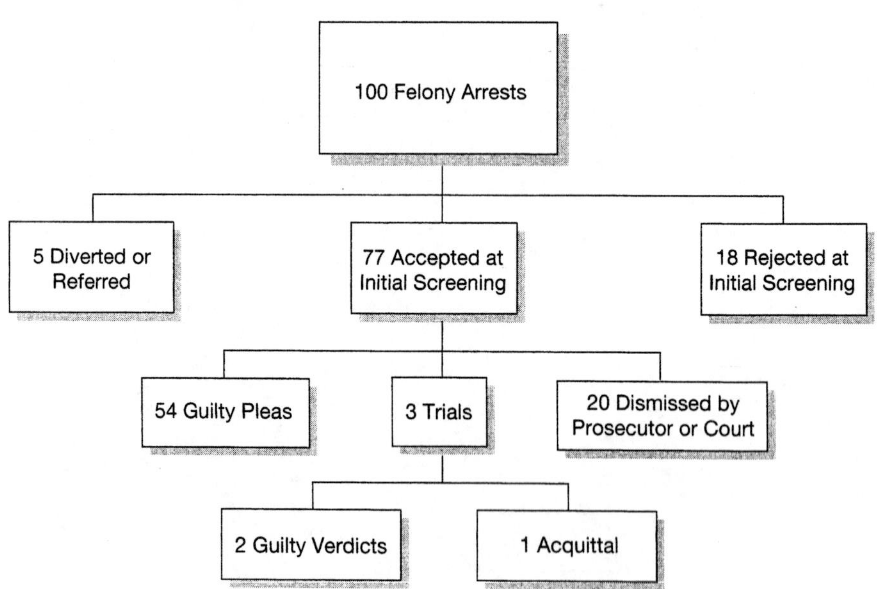

Source: Data from U.S. Department of Justice, Bureau of Justice Statistics. *The Prosecution of Felony Arrest* (Washington, DC: U.S. Government Printing Office, 1990).

perspective, 56 percent of the arrests resulted in findings of guilt, with 54 percent the result of plea negotiations and 2 percent as actual verdicts. The latter view, based on the fifty-seven cases not dismissed, is the only approach that approximates the original presumptive 90 percent plea-bargain truism. We could generalize that 95 percent of this population *plea out,* 5 percent go to trial, and less than 2 percent are acquitted.

REGULATORY AND ADMINISTRATIVE AGENCIES

Regulatory and administrative agencies have a variety of titles: commissions, bureaus, authorities, offices, departments, administrations, and divisions. These are agencies that are given the power to make regulations and implement statutes. Because statutory law is rarely self-implementing and because legislators have a limited amount of time and expertise in these usually highly specialized and technical areas, government agencies are often created to monitor administrative law. As with criminal and civil law, administrative law also contains substantive and procedural components, as well as a defined appeal process.

At the federal level, all administrative and regulatory agencies derive their power from Congress, with substantial variation in responsibilities, functions, operations, and power. More than thirty federal agencies have been created to implement statutes, and more than 1,100 federal judges hear cases. The influence of regulatory agencies on our lives is enormous. Everything from our food to our phones to our computers to our cars is regulated by laws that are overseen by such agencies.

RELIANCE ON THE COURT AND LEGAL SYSTEM IN THE UNITED STATES

As a sign of the changing times, individuals in the United States have turned to the legal system to solve problems in record numbers. This reliance on law has resulted in increased dockets all over the country, not only for civil suits, but for criminal cases as well. The states and the federal government prosecute an increasing number of cases, and the laws enacted by legislators, such as the *three strikes and you're out* rule, also have overburdened the system. Efforts to relieve this congestion in the legal system have promoted innovative dispute-resolution alternatives, which are implemented in both civil and criminal cases. Mediation and arbitration are used to reduce the need for court litigation. In the criminal justice system, alternatives in case disposition, such as community service and electronic home monitoring, are becoming more common, especially for nonviolent offenses and first-time offenders.

There are several reasons for this increased reliance on law, particularly on the judicial branch. First, a strong natural law tradition (discussed in Chapter 2) in the United States orients individuals toward the notion of *rights*. The Declaration of Independence talks about inalienable rights; the Constitution guarantees a series of rights (see the Appendix). Second, the enactment of law by legislative bodies is a slow process, and courts are perceived to expedite the proceedings through a legal solution. For example, a citizens' lobbying effort to change the law on a particular issue could take years of building coalitions with legislators and interested members of the community. Similarly, ballot initiatives consume a large amount of time and economic resources. A successful petition for injunctive relief to a judge, however, enjoys immediate implementation and can require parties to refrain from particular activities. Third, the success of ideas associated with such movements as civil rights has symbolically communicated to people that successful challenges to oppressive situations could more rapidly be brought in the courts than in legislative arenas. Figure 5–7 illustrates the dramatic increase in cases before the Supreme Court since 1976.

The vast majority of cases brought to the Supreme Court receive a certiorari denied ruling, indicating that either the specifics of the case were insufficient to be heard before the U.S. Supreme Court and/or four justices were not willing to hear the case—the *rule of four*. The Supreme Court uses

FIGURE 5–7 Total Cases on Docket from 1976 to 1998 in the U.S. Supreme Court

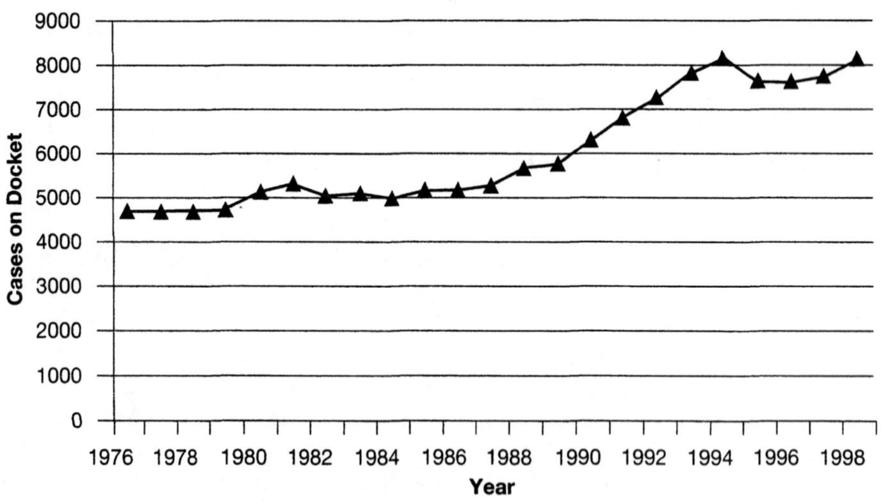

Sources: U.S. Department of Justice, *Sourcebook of Criminal Justice Statistics 1999*, Tables 5.73 and 5.74. *Sourcebook* information from Administrative Office of the United States Courts, *Annual Report of the Director, 1981*, p. A-1; *1986*, p. 135; *1999*, p. 83 (Washington DC: U.S. Government Printing Office); and Administrative Office of the United States Courts, *Annual Report of the Director, 1991*, p. 161; *1996*, p. 82 (Washington, DC: U.S. Government Printing Office).

"the writ of certiorari as a discretionary device to choose the cases it wishes to hear" (Black's Legal Dictionary, 1991: 156).

Therefore, although the number of cases on the docket has increased significantly since 1976, the number of cases actually decided by the Court has actually decreased. Of the cases that have been heard, Table 5–4 specifies a twenty-year history of the Supreme Court's activity. Actions in these cases will entail one or more of the following:

- Argued during the term,
- Disposed of by final opinions,
- Disposed of by per curiam opinions,
- Set for reargument,
- Granted review this term,
- Reviewed and decided without oral arguments, or
- Continued for argument at outset of the following term.

In 1978, 168 cases were argued before the Supreme Court during the term compared with 90 cases in 1998, even though there were 8,083 cases on the docket in 1998 compared with 4,731 cases on the docket in 1978. Although individuals and groups today are more likely to seek a resolution in the Supreme Court, they are actually less likely to be successful in their pursuit than in the past.

Per curiam opinions refer to dispositions where the Court decides a case but it is not accompanied by a full opinion. It can also denote an opinion written by the Chief Justice. These opinions are rare and represented only 8 cases in 1978 and 4 cases in 1998.

Table 5–5 gives a fifteen-year history between 1983 and 1998 of government participation in Supreme Court cases that were argued or decided on merit. Historically the government has participated in the majority of Supreme Court cases, and this participation rate has increased over the years. In 1983, the government participated in 64 percent of the cases argued before the Supreme Court. This figure rose to 84 percent by 1998. Where the government participated, in 1998, in 49 percent of the cases the government submitted an *amicus*, friend of the court, brief. The government was an appellee in 34 percent of the cases and an appellant 17 percent of the time.

Of the cases decided on merit, 57 percent involved the government in 1983 compared with a 66 percent participation rate in 1998. Of these cases, in 1983, 83 percent were decided in favor of the government's position and in 1998, 67 percent were decided in favor of the government.

CONCEPTUALIZING THE LEGAL SYSTEM

Because the law touches all of us, it is helpful to understand the assumptions that fuel the legal system. In this section, we will discuss two conceptual models, the systems model and the stimulus-response model, which attempt

TABLE 5–4 Twenty-Year History of Supreme Court Activity, 1978–1998

	CASES FILED, DISPOSED OF, AND PENDING			CASE ACTIVITY						
Year	Cases on Docket	Cases Disposed	Remaining on Docket	Argued during Term	Disposed of by Final Opinions	Disposed of by Per Curiam Opinions	Set for Reargument	Granted Review This Term	Reviewed and Decided without Oral Arguments	Total Available for Argument at Outset of Following Term
1978	4,731	4,017	714	168	153	8	8	163	110	79
1983	5,100	4,140	960	184	174	6	4	149	86	80
1988	5,657	4,911	746	170	156	12	2	147	110	81
1993	7,786	6,721	1,065	99	93	6	0	99	70	40
1998	8,083	7,045	1,038	90	84	4	2	81	59	30

Note: "Per curiam" refers to disposition of a case by the Court that is not accompanied by a full opinion.

Sources: U.S. Department of Justice, *Sourcebook of Criminal Justice Statistics 1999,* Tables 5.73 and 5.74. *Sourcebook* information from Administrative Office of the Unites States Courts, *Annual Report of the Director, 1981,* p A-1; *1986*, p. 135; *1999*, p. 83 (Washington, DC: U.S. Government Printing Office); and Administrative Office of the United States Courts, *Annual Report of the Director, 1991*, p. 161; *1996,* p. 82 (Washington, DC: U.S. Government Printing Office).

TABLE 5–5 Fifteen-Year History of Supreme Court Cases Argued and Decided on Merits, 1983–1998

	ARGUED						DECIDED ON MERITS[a]					
Year	Total Cases	Cases Government Participated in	Government as Petitioner or Appellant[b]	Government as Respondent or Appellee[b]	Government as Amicus[c]	Cases Government Did Not Participate in	Total Cases	Government Participating	Decided in Favor of Government's Position[b]	Decided Against Government's Position[b]	Not Classified as For or Against[b]	Government Not Participating
1983	184	118	46	33	39	66	262	150	124	23	3	112
1988	170	91	25	25	41	79	265	122	86	25	11	143
1993	99	70	11	20	39	29	157	97	56	37	4	60
1998	90[d]	76	13	26	37	14	143	94	63	25	6	49

Note: These data represent actions taken during the annual terms of the U.S. Supreme Court. "Amicus" refers to a party who is not involved directly in the suit, but who demonstrates an interest in the case by filing a supportive brief. "Decided on merits" refers to a reassessment and resolution of the substantive issues presented in the case, but that does not involve active participation of the litigants through the filing of written and oral arguments.

[a]Includes cases summarily affirmed, reversed, or vacated on the In Forma Pauperis Docket.

[b]Percents based on the total cases in which the government participated.

[c]Includes cases in which the government filed briefs as amicus curiae but did not participate in the argument.

[d]Includes 43 cases that were vacated and remanded for further consideration in light of *Bailey v. U.S.*, 94-7448. The case involved the review of two convictions under 18 USC 924 (c)(1), which imposes a mandatory prison term on anyone using or carrying a firearm during the commission of a drug trafficking crime.

Source: Adapted from U.S. Department of Justice, *Sourcebook of Criminal Justice Statistics 1999*, Table 5.76 (Washington, DC: U.S. Department of Justice, 2000). Original *Sourcebook* table adapted from tables provided by the U.S. Department of Justice, Office of the Solicitor General.

to explain how an organized legal system operates (Weinberg and Weinberg, 1980). The models are similar; both emphasize that law must be viewed as a social product *and* a social force within a working legal system. They differ in how that process works and how the participants in the system engage in their work. Both models illustrate the role of people and groups and ideas, as well as that of social conditions. Regardless of the language used or the process discussed, the three constructs affect what occurs in the legal system.

Systems Model

As a systems model, a legal system is defined by how it handles what is put into it. The legal system's function is to authoritatively distribute justice. It does so by converting various demands, or system inputs, into legal decisions, or system outputs. Thus, three things occur: inputs go into the system, the system uses a conversion structure to regulate the inputs, and then decisions are produced (see Figure 5–8). A legal system can continue to function only if its decisions are authoritative and perceived as binding.

The systems model operates at numerous levels. It operates at the law enforcement level when a police officer decides whether or not to make an arrest. It operates at the court level when the courts decide whether or not to hear a case. It operates at a corrections level when the parole board decides whether or not to grant parole. All three of these examples are parts of the legal system that deal with the implementation and working of law. For our purposes, we will limit our analysis to the court and legal arena.

In this model, inputs are of two types: demands and supports. Demands are the raw materials fed into the system. Without demands, the legal system would have nothing to do. Demands can take many forms but typically consist of a complaint filed by A against B (civil demand) or a complaint filed by the state against a lawbreaker (criminal demand).

Supports are necessary for the legal system to do its job. The concept of support can best be illustrated by answering this question: "Why do people support the legal system?" There are several answers. First, people support

FIGURE 5–8 Systems Model

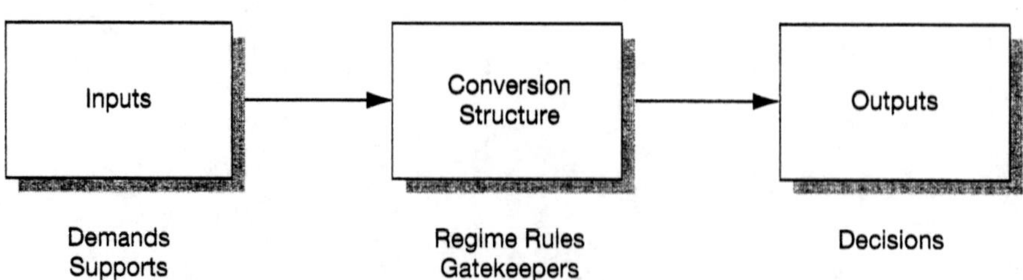

Source: L. S. Weinberg and J. W. Weinberg, *Law and Society: An Interdisciplinary Introduction* (Washington, DC: University Press of America, 1980).

the legal system because they fear the consequences if they do not. If people do not comply with legal threats, they may face the coercive power of the state through arrest and incarceration. Second, they support the legal system because they are satisfied with its decisions. Third, legal socialization accounts for the bulk of support. Legal socialization is the human process of acquiring, early in life, strongly held attitudes and beliefs about the legal system. Often the assessments are favorable, but even when individuals are critical of the system, they often support it. While we may try to fight city hall, we do it within the constraints of city hall.

The conversion structure of the legal system regulates the inputs coming into the system, in general by restricting access to its working mechanisms. While anyone can attempt to enter the legal arena, only a few people will actually be allowed to play. In the parlance of systems theorists, this restrictive component operates through two factors: regime rules and gatekeepers.

Regime rules are those that specify who can use the legal system and under what circumstances. For example, one cannot sue someone unless one has suffered a wrong. Gatekeepers are participants who deliberately work to screen and reduce the demand on the system. Lawyers who press for out-of-court settlements and prosecutors who plea-bargain are performing gatekeeping functions.

After the conversion structure deals with the inputs into the system and processes those demands in some way, the system produces decisions, which are the results, or outputs, of the system. The final stage of the systems model is its feedback function; current decisions affect the legal arena and will, at some point, affect new input.

The systems model emphasizes the dynamic quality of the legal system. Inputs affect outputs, which in turn affect inputs. Furthermore, once the legal system has acknowledged that demands are legitimate, more demands may come as a result. For example, the desegregation ruling in *Brown v. Board of Education* (1954), led to more rulings, not fewer. The systems model focuses on law as decisions made in response to demands and the effects of those decisions on future demands. The value of the model lies in the questions it causes us to ask about the legal system: who institutes litigation and thus makes demands? How frequently do people make demands? Are some types of litigants more successful than others? What happens when individuals no longer support the system; or the regime rules; or the gatekeepers? How do court decisions affect the perception and legitimacy of the courts? Who complies and under what conditions?

Stimulus-Response Model

The stimulus-response model employs slightly different concepts to achieve the same basic results. In this model, legal policies must be viewed as responses to prior stimuli in the system and, likewise, must be recognized as future stimuli to subsequent responses. We see again that three things occur:

prior stimuli, which influence the system; legal policies, which influence the system; and subsequent responses, which result in legal actions (see Figure 5–9).

Prior stimuli are affected by two variables: normative standards and empirical facts. Normative standards are the rules a social system expects its people to follow. These rules may be the government's formal laws (e.g., statutes and other regulations) or the culture's informal expectations (e.g., customs and shared values). Empirical facts are bits of information that the system uses to make decisions. They may be legally admissible evidence for a trial or less tangible (and often inadmissible) "factors," such as race, gender, and social status. Empirical facts are intended to bolster the decision-making process by providing information. Both normative standards and empirical facts are filtered through courtroom participants. Lawyers, judges, and law enforcement personnel have their own set of attitudes and characteristics, which influence their perceptions of the normative standards and empirical facts.

Prior stimuli affect the legal policies of the system. These are amenable to change and influenced by previous laws and cultural standards. Various inhibiting and facilitating factors, such as the role of the media in reporting court decisions and the reactions of public officials, also affect legal policies. The various facilitating and inhibiting factors are again filtered through the policy's appliers (judges, police, administrators) and the policy's recipients (general public). The system then produces new legal policies, which are subject to public reaction.

This public reaction is called the subsequent response. Subsequent responses to legal policies manifest themselves either as change or stability in behaviors and/or attitudes. Legal policies may change behavior but not attitudes (or vice versa), or they may change behavior and attitudes.

FIGURE 5–9 Stimulus-Response Model

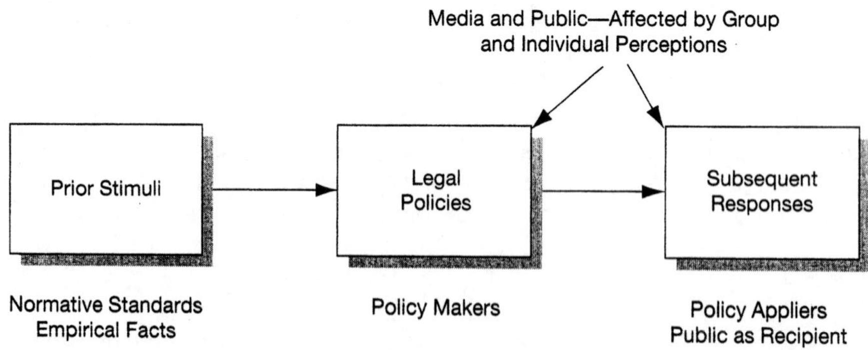

Source: L. S. Weinberg and J. W. Weinberg, *Law and Society: An Interdisciplinary Introduction* (Washington, DC: University Press of America, 1980).

Furthermore, changes in behavior and/or attitude may stimulate further policy changes. This process is continually influenced by the policy makers.

The stimulus-response model also emphasizes the ongoing dynamic quality of the legal system. However, the questions raised by this conceptual model of how the legal system works are different from those raised by the systems model. This model causes us to ask questions like these: who decides what *facts* can be used by policy makers? Who decides the role of nonsystem participants (such as the media)? How often is policy made simply because of policy makers' external motives, such as seeking reelection?

Applying the Models

To acquire a better understanding of how these conceptual models work in the real world, we will illustrate their points by discussing the 1976 Supreme Court decision in the case of *Craig v. Boren* [429 U.S. 190 (1976)]. In this case, the constitutionality of an Oklahoma statute was in question. As the law stood, women aged eighteen and older could buy alcohol, but men had to be twenty-one or older to do the same. The case was presented before the Supreme Court as a violation of the Fourteenth Amendment's equal protection clause.

Systems Model The input demand made was the constitutionality question regarding different drinking ages for women and men. The input support was the primary belief in equal protection under the law. The legal system socializes people to believe that everyone should be treated fairly, and this did not appear to be the case in this situation. The conversion process began when the Supreme Court decided to hear the case; the regime rules allowed for the admittance of the issue under the equal protection clause. The case was not kept back by the gatekeepers, although several gatekeepers along the way tried to limit its advancement. The output of the case was the Court's decision that this Oklahoma statute was indeed unconstitutional. The decision provided feedback for future equal protection cases.

Stimulus-Response Model The prior stimulus affecting this case was the current law that regulated drinking as part of Oklahoma's statutes, as well as the public's perception of this law. It is important to understand that this law was influenced by policy makers' perceptions about alcohol and gender at that time. These ideas were part of the normative standards of this case. The empirical facts that were presented included the *evidence* that there was an incremental difference between women and men in arrests for driving under the influence. The Court ruled that this evidence was not strong enough to support the differential treatment. The legal policy that came out of these standards and facts was the declaration of the unconstitutionality of the law. The subsequent response to this finding was the public's opinion about the change in the statute, as well as the political (i.e., policy maker) repercussions associated with the change. Media coverage of the decision was also a significant player in this legal process. The change in law had the feedback effect of becoming the new prior stimuli for future decisions.

Summary of Legal System Models

Both of these models are based on the beliefs and perceptions of the participants involved in them. It is important, therefore, to point out that the people involved at any given time, regardless of their particular conceptualization of how the system works, will bring their own ideas into the arena. These ideas will affect the end results (whether they are formulated as decisions or as legal policies and subsequent responses).

Furthermore, it is not just people and their ideas that significantly affect the social context of law. We need to recognize that prevailing social conditions also are important. During war or peace, good or bad economic times, liberal or conservative eras, these conditions will and do influence how the system processes the law and justice and its end result. *Craig v. Boren* reflects both the women's movement for equality under the law, and men's assertion that if they were old enough to fight for their country in Vietnam, they were old enough to have a drink.

CONCLUSION

In this chapter we have examined the operation of the legal system in the United States: how the courts are organized, the flow of litigation, and such issues as case attrition. We have also considered two separate models that attempt to explain the operation of the legal system. In the next chapter, we will examine more closely the role of those who participate in the system of law on a daily basis, the practitioners of law.

NOTES

1. See 42 U.S.C. (1983), in which claims against individuals and city governments were expanded via *Monell v. New York City Social Services* [436 U.S. 658 (1978)]. Also see Bivens' claims against federal employees established in *Bivens v. Six Unknown Named Agents of the Federal Bureau of Narcotics* [403 U.S. 388 (1971)].

6 Practitioners of Law

Many individuals in addition to lawyers practice law; in this chapter we will discuss four such groups. We will examine legislators, who make the law, as well as the professionals who enforce it, police officers. We will look at individuals responsible for interpreting the law, judges and lawyers, and those responsible for the sanctions associated with it, correctional officers. Although we investigate these practitioners separately, the jobs they do are closely related. Legislative activity affects police activity, which affects the cases lawyers present and judges decide, which affect those dealt with by correctional personnel. We will also examine here the role that social conditions, social ideas, and groups of people have on these professions.

LAWMAKERS—LEGISLATORS

The primary job of a legislator is to make law. While legislators also engage in other tasks, such as supporting executive decisions, their chief function is to legislate on behalf of the people, making laws to guide and inform the behavior of their constituency. Legislative bodies operate at both the state and federal level and are generally made up of two separate houses. At the federal level, Congress includes the House of Representatives, with 435 members, and the Senate, with 2 representatives from each of the 50 states.

The figure of 435 was set by the 1910 census count and has remained unchanged since that time. To qualify as a representative, one must be at least twenty-five years of age, a citizen of the United States, and a resident of the state in which he or she runs for office. Senate members must be at least thirty years of age, a U.S. citizen for at least nine years, and a resident of the state she or he represents. Of the two senators representing each state, the one elected first is the senior senator. The state of Nebraska is the only exception to the two-house legislature. Nebraska's legislative body is commonly referred to as a unicameral legislature; it has only one house, whereas the U.S. Congress and all other states have bicameral legislatures.

A legislature, whether at the state or federal level, has a set of informal and formal rules to help it accomplish its job. The federal Congress is required by law to assemble at least once a year, at noon on the third day of January. A Congress lasts for two years and is divided into two sessions. During each session, the primary work is to examine bills and make laws.

The passage of bills into law is a concessionary and compromise-laden process. Some of the concessions and compromises legislators make take place on the house floor during public debate. Others take place outside of the house. Public or private discussions engaged in by legislators, their aides, lobbyists, and others all serve to influence the legal system in the United States. This process is an integral part of the reciprocal relationship between law and society.

There are a number of sources of legislation, as well as a number of forms of congressional action. Legislators and their constituents can and do attempt to generate legislation. The president or the president's cabinet, as well as the many agencies and departments in the government, also propose or draft legislation. Lobbying agencies and political action committees (PACs), representing both business and grassroots interests, have become increasingly important collateral sources of legislation since the 1960s.

The following brief outline shows the legislative process at the *federal* level (Goehlert, 1979:2–3):

1. A bill is introduced by a member of Congress, either a senator or a representative.
2. The bill is assigned a number and referred to the committee or committees with jurisdiction over the subject matter.
3. The bill is either considered or refused further study. While in committee, the bill may be amended or entirely rewritten. Hearings may be held concerning the bill.
4. After committee deliberation, the bill is submitted to the full chamber. Bills favorably recommended by a committee are accompanied by a report.
5. The bill is submitted to the chamber floor for possible debate on its merits.
6. If the bill is passed, it is then sent to the other chamber for consideration. Much legislation, however, starts as similar bills in both houses.
7. The bill undergoes the same process in the other house.
8. If the House and Senate versions differ, a compromise is worked out.
9. If the bill is passed by Congress, it becomes an act and is sent to the president.
10. The president either signs the bill into law or vetoes the bill.

A majority of two-thirds is necessary in both federal houses to override a veto. The president has ten days, not counting Sunday, to act on a bill. If the president fails to act within ten days, the bill becomes law without a signature, providing Congress is in session. If Congress adjourns before the ten-day limit, the bill does not become law. This is referred to as a *pocket veto.* Table 6–1 illustrates the number of regular and pocket vetoes of each president since George Washington.

Congressional resolutions are of three types: joint, simple, and concurrent. A joint resolution is, in effect, similar to a bill. The term *joint* does not signify a simultaneous introduction and consideration of the resolution in both houses. A joint resolution that originates in the House is designated "H.J. Res.," and a joint resolution that originates in the Senate is designated "S.J. Res." Numbers identify the resolution throughout the process. Concurrent and simple resolutions are not in fact legislation. They express facts, principles, and opinions and are of limited scope.

The actual legislative process is much more complex than the simplified version presented here. Each legislator has his or her own agenda, philosophy, viewpoint, and set of attitudes and beliefs. The process involves working out these ideas among individuals and coalitions. And whereas this discussion has outlined the federal process, the process of lawmaking at the state level is similar.

At both the state and federal level, newly elected legislators go through an introductory period in which they learn the formal and informal workings of the legislative process. Legislators are expected to identify issues that they feel are important and to become knowledgeable about them. All legislators work on a variety of subcommittees. In the federal Congress, there are currently nineteen House and sixteen Senate standing subcommittees. Appointment to subcommittees is a political process, with more prestigious or powerful appointments going to senior members.

Legislators follow, as mentioned, a set of expected normative behaviors. Some of these include refrain from personal attacks, reciprocation through compromise, and upholding the integrity of the house to which they have been elected. Because legislators are usually elected, a great deal of their time is taken up in campaigning and fund-raising. Some scholars suggest that the ambiguous, confusing, and contradictory nature of much legislation is the result of the constant reelection process. Ambiguity may win office, and the result is that courts must often interpret the laws that legislators have enacted.

Who Are the Legislators?

The majority of elected legislators are males from middle- and upper-class backgrounds. This class background is significant. Parents in the upper and middle classes, for many reasons, tend in socializing their children to prepare them for publicly active lives. A higher social class generally goes hand

TABLE 6–1 Presidential Vetoes (1789–1992)

PRESIDENT	REGULAR VETOES	POCKET VETOES	TOTAL VETOES	VETOES OVERRIDDEN
George Washington	2		2	
John Adams			0	
Thomas Jefferson			0	
James Madison	5	2	7	
James Monroe	1		1	
John Q. Adams			0	
Andrew Jackson	5	7	12	
Martin Van Buren		1	1	
W. H. Harrison			0	
John Tyler	6	4	10	1
James K. Polk	2	1	3	
Zachary Taylor			0	
Millard Fillmore			0	
Franklin Pierce	9		9	
James Buchanan	4	3	7	
Abraham Lincoln	2	5	7	
Andrew Johnson	21	8	29	15
Ulysses S. Grant	45	48	93	4
Rutherford B. Hayes	12	1	13	1
James A. Garfield			0	
Chester A. Arthur	4	8	12	1
Grover Cleveland	304	110	414	2
William McKinley	6	36	42	
Theodore Roosevelt	42	40	82	1
William H. Taft	30	9	39	1
Woodrow Wilson	33	11	44	6
Warren G. Harding	5	1	6	
Calvin Coolidge	20	30	50	4
Herbert Hoover	21	16	37	3
Franklin D. Roosevelt	372	263	635	9
Harry S Truman	180	70	250	12
Dwight D. Eisenhower	73	108	181	2
John F. Kennedy	12	9	21	
Lyndon B. Johnson	16	14	30	
Richard M. Nixon	26	17	43	7
Gerald R. Ford	48	18	66	12
Jimmy Carter	13	18	31	2
Ronald Reagan	39	39	78	9
George H. W. Bush	29	16	45	1
TOTAL	1448	1066	2514	104

Source: Office of the Secretary of the Senate, *Presidential Vetoes, 1789–1991*. (Washington, DC: U.S. Government Printing Office, 1992). Update by Gregory Harnes, head reference librarian, 1993.

in hand with more formal education, and most elected officials are well educated. Higher education generally translates into occupations that are mental rather than manual, and thus individuals are trained in and used to thinking about the world in which they live. Generally, the upper classes read, travel, listen, and participate more in society than other classes (Rossides, 1997:326–327). The previous occupations of many legislators are as professionals and executives in industry, commerce, finance, law, medicine, and university teaching and research; many are lawyers. Legislators generally have incomes in excess of the U.S. mean. In recent years, there has been an increase in the number of women in legislative bodies. Undoubtedly this is the result of changing social ideas about the roles of women in society. While it illustrates that law is indeed a part of a social context, the socio-economic class background generalization still applies. In the 1996 elections, ten women were elected to the Senate and forty-nine to the House.

Effects of Social Conditions, Ideas, and Groups on Lawmakers

Part of the election experience is the match between a candidate's philosophies, attitudes, and beliefs and those of his or her constituency. As with most of us, legislators develop ideologies and philosophies that closely mirror their life experiences. These experiences reflect their class position, including their education and the occupations of their parents, their gender, age, race, and other factors. As they attempt to gain and keep office, legislators are influenced by the electorate. The force and effect of the electorate's opinions and ideas must be meshed with the candidate's own philosophies, opinions, and ideas. It is only in this way that candidates maintain support.

Past and current social conditions also influence what a legislator proposes to a congressional body. Tax breaks may provide relief for economic hardship, for example. Public attitudes and outcry over crime rates bring legislative responses. The philosophical and political background of executives, either governors or the president, also influence the work of a congressional body. Some legislatures work well and closely with their executives; others do not.

The social context of law may also be examined within the context of the debate over liberal and conservative politics. Discussions about the philosophies of legislators has been deemed important in many contemporary elections by much of the voting public. A distinction is often made in candidates' viewpoints about an issue, e.g., hard or soft on crime, for or against spending on social problems, or support of special privileges or of equal rights. The importance of the language used by lawmakers cannot be stressed too much. Language communicates lawmakers' views about important issues and how to address them. Labels such as conservative, liberal, or moderate, are attached to legislators' ideas. For example, the idea that getting tough with offenders will solve the problem of rising crime rates is generally associated with conservative politics.

LAW ENFORCERS—POLICE OFFICERS

According to the U.S. Department of Justice, Federal Bureau of Investigation, there were 13.9 million Index Offenses reported in the United States in 1995. This represents 5,278 crimes for every 100,000 inhabitants. Property valued at $15.6 billion was stolen. To keep order, there were an average of 2.4 full-time officers for every 1,000 inhabitants.

Professionals who deal every day with the decisions made by law-makers are law enforcement personnel, or police officers, who have several functions in law enforcement. They maintain public order, engage in a variety of community services, and deal with the paperwork necessary to complete their tasks. Research findings vary, but they suggest that the active pursuit of criminals is a small proportion of all law enforcement operations.

Law enforcement agencies, like the court and legislative systems, operate at the federal level (e.g., Internal Revenue Service, Drug Enforcement Administration, and Federal Bureau of Investigation), state level (e.g., California Highway Patrol and Minnesota State Patrol), county level (sheriff's departments), and local levels (city police departments). Officers' tasks vary significantly, depending on their level and the type of agency.

Types of Law Enforcers

There are over 17,000 law enforcement agencies in the United States. Of these, the vast majority are found at the local (city and county) level. These local agencies may have just one officer or thousands. Jurisdictional questions arise frequently and are not always settled to everyone's satisfaction.

The training that law officers receive varies considerably. Officers in the federal ranks of law enforcement (IRS, FBI, etc.) are generally required to have a college degree. State and local law officers may or may not have college degrees, and there is much controversy surrounding the necessity and/or importance of a degree for police work. In many police departments, higher education can lead to better promotional opportunities—but that is not always the case. The suggested benefits of higher education for law enforcement personnel are better communication skills, better writing abilities, greater skills in dealing with people, and greater initiative. The suggested negatives of higher education are that officers may get bored with their work more quickly, may question the authority in the department more frequently, and may feel animosity toward the less educated in the field. In some jurisdictions, college programs offer the training necessary for law enforcement personnel; in other jurisdictions, individuals who want a career in law enforcement must complete a separate program. The program in the state of Minnesota, for example, is the Peace Officers Standards and Training Certification.

The profession of law enforcement in the United States has not always been open to women and nonwhite individuals. This profession has been identified as male-dominated since its beginning; the male norms of aggression, brotherhood, and toughness have made law enforcement an unfriendly place for women, who may be seen as not tough enough or not able to support their partners in tight situations. Such stereotypes are often cited as reasons for women's underrepresentation in police departments. Given the nature of most policing these days, this reasoning is not relevant. See Table 6–2 for proportions of officers by gender, race, ethnicity, and place of employment.

While we find more officers of color on the job now than in years past, we also find that they are often ethnically segregated by region. In 1992, 36.3 percent and 34.2 percent of the officers in San Antonio and Albuquerque, respectively, were Hispanic, and 53.3 percent and 67.8 percent of the officers in Detroit and Washington, D.C., respectively, were black (Maguire, Pastore, and Flanagan, 1993:49–50). These statistics are in stark contrast to the general distribution of officers by color (in departments with over one hundred officers).

In general, it takes a police officer a mean of six years to reach the maximum salary level. This statistic varies by a city's size and geographic region of the country. Entrance salaries tend to be highest on the West Coast and lowest in the Southeast (Maguire and Pastore, 1994:56).

Effects of Social Conditions, Ideas, and Groups on Law Enforcement Personnel

Law enforcement personnel are public servants. Whether they work for the federal, state, or local government, their ultimate responsibility is to enforce the law on behalf of the public they serve. Numerous issues have been discussed concerning the behavior of individuals in law enforcement. One

TABLE 6–2 Race, Ethnicity, and Gender of Officers by Job Level, 1993

LEVEL	WHITE	BLACK	HISPANIC	WOMEN
County	79%	11%	3%	10%
Municipalities	82	10	7	8
Sheriff	85	9	5	14
State	89	7	3	5

Note: Data are for law enforcement agencies with 100 or more officers.

Source: U.S. Department of Justice, Bureau of Justice Statistics, *Law Enforcement Management and Administrative Statistics, 1993: Data for Individual State and Local Agencies with 100 or More Officers*, NCJ-148825 (Washington, DC: U.S. Department of Justice, 1995), p. ix, Table C.

major issue is the amount of discretionary power they have for decision making on the job. Discretionary power has been linked to a police officer's ability to search people and property, conduct interviews and investigations, write tickets, and make arrests. Some writers acknowledge that the police are the gatekeepers to the criminal justice system (see the systems model discussed in Chapter 5), in that they make on-the-spot decisions about alleged offenders and their offenses.

Other issues concerning police performance are: the use of deadly or unreasonable force; the hostility of citizens to arrest; search and seizure; the types of patrol strategies officers use; and the degree of racism, cynicism, sexism, and homophobia among officers. Issues of job stress, divorce, and suicide have also caused concern. Numerous writers have discussed the emergence of a law enforcement subculture and personality, suggesting that officers find themselves in special circumstances as law enforcers. However, it should be noted that many individuals besides police officers socialize almost exclusively with people they work with and, therefore, develop their own subcultures.

The public's ideas about how law enforcement personnel do their job is important. When situations develop, such as the case in Waco, Texas, with the Branch Davidians, the nature of the response of law enforcement may create a great deal of negative publicity for police personnel everywhere. When allegations were made by the defense team of O. J. Simpson regarding law enforcement incompetence and racism, there was a public outcry.

LAW INTERPRETERS—JUDGES AND LAWYERS

Judges

Judges perform a variety of tasks in a courtroom. They are considered the authority on law and facts, except when juries are seated, and then they are considered the authority on facts. They also have courtroom administrative responsibilities such as overseeing bailiffs and court reporters. In criminal courts, judges can order warrants and search documents, impose sentences, and conduct probation revocation hearings (Abadinsky, 1991:172). Judges must constantly interpret written precedent and statutes to make decisions in the cases before them.

It is most common for a judge to come to the bench after years of litigation practice. Unlike judges in other legal systems (see Chapter 3 for a discussion of Japan, for instance), judges in the United States receive no formal training before taking the bench. They must quickly acquire the ability to be objective, neutral participants in the courtroom process. After years of litigation and arguments for one side or the other, this may be a difficult task. Indeed, sometimes we hear people refer to a judge as a "defendant's judge," indicating that the judge was a defense attorney before taking the bench.

Trial judges spend as much time (sometimes more) in chambers, engaging in mediation and conciliation, as they do on the bench. As Abadinsky (1991:171–172) notes, the trial judge is the referee responsible for enforcing the rules that govern criminal and civil cases. He or she is responsible for ensuring that a case has been argued fairly "according to codes of procedure, applicable statutes, case law and common law."

Who Are the Judges? In the United States a judge does not have to be an attorney, although most are. Most also are white, male, well educated, and come from the middle and upper classes. National income data for 1995 show that general trial court judges earned $85,699, while the highest appellate court judges earned $95,660 (Maguire and Pastore, 1994:78). The Chief Justice of the United States earned $171,500, and associate justices on the Supreme Court earned $164,100 (p. 65). The bench hardly reflects the diversity of the U.S. population. As noted by Pollock and Adler (1992:1, 4), in 1992 only 5.3 percent of the 837 federal judges and 4.2 percent of the 356 judges on the states' highest benches were African American. There was one Hispanic in the latter group. Women account for approximately 8 percent of circuit court judges and 14 percent of district court judges.

Table 6–3 illustrates the personal characteristics of presidential appointees to U.S. district court judgeships. It is clear from these data that the philosophy of the presidential administration can have a dramatic effect. For example, President Clinton appointed 30.2 percent females to judgeships, whereas President Ford appointed 1.9 percent. President Carter appointed 13.9 percent African Americans, and President Clinton appointed 19.5 percent; President Reagan appointed 0.8 percent in his first term, and President Bush appointed 6.8 percent.

Differences between Courts and Legislatures

A comparison of the roles of judges and legislators will help illustrate these roles more clearly. Both judges and legislators make decisions that affect people's lives, but there are differences. The separation of powers designed by the framers of the Constitution was intended to provide a set of checks and balances. However, it was also deliberately made less than airtight.

Judicial selection. About 50 percent of judges are appointed and 50 percent are elected. All legislators are elected (except in special circumstances, such as the death of an incumbent). There are problems with both systems. Appointments create the danger of political connections, but election depends on voters' knowledge of a candidate. As mentioned in Chapter 5, some authors argue that the most important judicial selection is a U.S. Supreme Court justice. However, Article III of the Constitution says very little about a justice's background, and there is no requirement to be a judge prior to sitting on the Supreme Court. As discussed in Chapter 2, judges are products of their social, economic, and political background. Moreover, their

TABLE 6–3 Characteristics of Presidential Appointees to U.S. District Court Judgeships by Presidential Administration, 1963–1998[a]

	PRESIDENT JOHNSON'S APPOINTEES 1963–68 (*N* = 122)	PRESIDENT NIXON'S APPOINTEES 1969–74 (*N* = 179)	PRESIDENT FORD'S APPOINTEES 1974–76 (*N* = 52)	PRESIDENT CARTER'S APPOINTEES 1977–80 (*N* = 202)	PRESIDENT REAGAN'S FIRST-TERM APPOINTEES 1981–84 (*N* = 129)	PRESIDENT REAGAN'S SECOND-TERM APPOINTEES 1985–88[b] (*N* = 161)	PRESIDENT BUSH'S APPOINTEES 1989–92 (*N* = 148)	PRESIDENT CLINTON'S APPOINTEES 1993–98 (*N* = 248)
Sex								
Male	98.4%	99.4%	98.1%	85.6%	90.7%	92.5%	80.4%	71.8%
Female	1.6	0.6	1.9	14.4	9.3	7.4	19.6	28.2
Ethnicity								
White	93.4	95.5	88.5	78.7	93	91.9	89.2	73.8
Black	4.1	3.4	5.8	13.9	0.8	3.1	6.8	19.0
Hispanic	2.5	1.1	1.9	6.9	5.4	4.3	4	5.2
Asian	0	0	3.9	0.5	0.8	0.6	0	1.6
Native American	NA	NA	NA	0	0	0	0	0.6
Education undergraduate								
Public-supported	38.5	41.3	48.1	57.4	34.1	36.6	44.6	43.6
Private (not Ivy League)	31.1	38.5	34.6	32.7	49.6	50.9	41.2	42.3
Ivy League	16.4	19.6	17.3	9.9	16.3	12.4	14.2	14.1
Not indicated	13.9	0.6	0	0	0	0	0	0
Occupation at nomination or appointment								
Politics or government	21.3	10.6	21.2	4.4	7.8	16.8	10.8	10.9
Judiciary	31.1	28.5	34.6	44.6	40.3	34.8	41.9	46.8
Law firm, large	2.4	11.2	9.6	14	11.6	22.4	25.7	15.7
Law firm, moderate	18.9	27.9	25	19.8	25.6	14.3	14.9	15.3
Law firm, small	23	19	9.6	13.9	10.8	9.9	4.7	8.5
Professor of law	3.3	2.8	0	3	2.3	1.9	0.7	1.6
Other	0	0	0	0.5	1.6	0	1.4	1.2

Occupational experience								
Judicial	34.4	35.2	42.3	54.5	50.4	43.5	46.6	51.2
Prosecutorial	45.9	41.9	50	38.6	43.4	44.7	39.2	40.7
Other	33.6	36.3	30.8	28.2	28.7	27.9	31.8	29.8
Religion								
Protestant	58.2	73.2	73.1	60.4	58.9	60.9	64.2	NA
Catholic	31.1	18.4	17.3	27.7	34.1	27.3	28.4	NA
Jewish	10.7	8.4	9.6	11.9	7	11.2	7.4	NA
Political party								
Democrat	94.3	7.3	21.2	92.6	3.1	6.2	5.4	89.1
Republican	5.7	92.7	78.8	4.4	96.9	90.7	88.5	4.8
Independent	0	0	0	3	0	3.1	6.1	5.7
Other	NA	NA	NA	0	0	0	0	0.4
American Bar Association rating								
Exceptionally well/ well qualified	48.4	45.3	46.1	50.9	50.4	57.1	57.4	58.1
Qualified	49.2	54.8	53.8	47.5	49.6	42.9	42.6	40.7
Not qualified	2.5	0	0	1.5	0	0	0	1.2

Note: Percent subtotals for occupational experience sum to more than 100 because some appointees have had both judicial and prosecutorial experience. Data have been revised by the Source and therefore may differ from previous editions of SOURCEBOOK.

[a]Percents may not add to 100 because of rounding.

[b]One appointee classified as non-denominational.

Source: Sheldon Goldman, "Reagan's Judicial Legacy: Completing the Puzzle and Summing Up," *Judicature* 72 (April-May 1989), pp. 320, 321, Table 1; and Sheldon Goldman and Elliot Slotnick, "Clinton's First Term Judiciary: Many Bridges to Cross," *Judicature* 80 (May-June 1997), p. 261. Table adapted by SOURCEBOOK staff. Reprinted by permission.

very appointment, or election, to the bench is a highly politicized process. Each judge has an ideology that informs her or his legal decision making. While some judges and justices write postcareer treatises that explain the subtext of their ideology, others are more candid on this matter from the bench.

Limitations on judicial decision making. It is necessary to understand the differences between the methods used in judicial and legislative decision making. Judges are far more limited in what they can decide than are those who serve in a legislative body. The first limitation judges face is that of the case at hand. Judges decide only what is placed before them. Legislators may involve themselves in a variety of issues and get information from a variety of sources. The second limitation is the scope of applicability: a judge's decisions are aimed at litigants in the case before them, whereas a legislator's decisions are written to apply to everyone. Finally, judges are bound by the specific language of the law and the Constitution; legislators cannot enact legislation that violates the Constitution, but they are free to change any law.

Judicial activism versus judicial restraint. Judges, on the one hand, are supposed to act as objective, neutral observers rather than activists for a cause. They are expected to engage in self-restraint and not to allow their individual preferences and ideologies to influence their decisions. Legislators, on the other hand, are expected to become advocates for issues and to become experts in an area to demonstrate their commitment to it.

The power of the judiciary. Unlike the other two branches of government, the courts cannot *initiate* action. Judges are dependent on other branches and agencies to enforce their decisions. A judge's decision can be overruled or rewritten. Some argue that the judiciary is the branch least accountable to the public.

Statutory interpretation. One of a court's duties is to interpret statutes that are vague or unclearly written. Judges do not write statutory law, but they have the power to interpret it.

Judicial Selection and Removal The process by which judges take the bench and are removed from it are politically and socially important. Three basic methods of selection are used:

1. *Appointment by a chief executive* (mayor, governor, or president). This method, which applies to all federal judgeships, holds the executive accountable and indirectly reflects voters' interests through their participation in the election of the executives.
2. *Partisan or nonpartisan election by the electorate.* The election result is often influenced by the position of a candidate's name on the ballot, as well as by an ethnic-, racial-, or religious-sounding surname. A candidate is often unopposed; even if there is more than one candidate, this is a characteristically dull election since the candidates cannot state their positions.
3. *Merit system.* A notable example is the Missouri Plan, a tripartite system: first there is a nominating commission; then the governor's selection; and then, a

year later, a retention ballot. This method is an attempt to get past the negative aspects of the first and second methods.

Judges may be removed from the bench by impeachment and conviction, which is the only way to remove a federal judge; by legislative resolution, which requires a two-thirds vote of both houses; by the governor, if ratified by a majority vote in both houses, a system used in more than half the states; by recall, which requires the circulation of a petition, followed by placement of the judge's name on a ballot; and by the commission system, wherein a state commission on judicial conduct may remove a sitting judge (Abadinsky, 1991:182–184).

Lawyers

Lawyers, in understanding and utilizing precedent, also act as law interpreters. Legal practices and lawyers' work experiences vary. According to Vago (1997:331–338), there are three general categories of lawyers: private practitioners, about 74 percent; lawyers in government practice, 12 percent; and lawyers in private employment, 12 percent. Judges are included as the remaining 2 percent. There are more lawyers in the United States than anywhere else in the world. As Friedman (1977:24) notes, "The number of lawyers in any society is a function of the social role assigned to lawyers," which indicates their importance in the United States.

The legal profession has been one of the fastest growing professions in the United States for the last three decades. Commitment to justice, an avenue into politics, social status, and wealth are just some of the possible reasons for this growth. However, although for decades lawyers have enjoyed high occupational prestige, they have also often been mistrusted and maligned throughout history. (How many lawyer jokes do you know?) The criminal lawyer, for example, is often tainted with guilt by association. Corporate lawyers, those most respected by the legal profession itself, may be perceived as the tools of heartless capitalists.

Who Are the Lawyers? Historically, lawyers have been white, privileged, and male; earlier, the legal profession and law schools themselves did not admit people of color, Catholics, Jews, or women. These practices have changed in the last thirty years, but in most large firms the majority of the managing elite is still white, male, and middle and upper class. Entry into the profession depends on social class and academic standing. While approximately 75 percent of those who apply to law school eventually find placement, not all schools offer equal opportunity. Table 6–4 lists the top twenty-five law schools in 1999, according to *U.S. News and World Report.* The more prestigious schools offer more opportunities for higher salaries and better jobs for their graduates.

TABLE 6–4 Top Twenty-Five Law Schools

RANK	SCHOOL	OVERALL SCORE	REPUTATION SCORE BY ACADEMICS	REPUTATION SCORE BY LAWYERS/ JUDGES	1999 UNDERGRAD GPA 25TH-75TH PERCENTILE	1999 LSAT SCORE 25TH-75TH PERCENTILE	1999 ACCEPTANCE RATE	1999 STUDENT/ FACULTY RATIO	1998 GRADS EMPLOYED AT GRADUATION	EMPLOYED 9 MONTHS AFTER GRADUATION	SCHOOL'S BAR PASSAGE RATE IN JURISDICTION	JURISDICTION'S OVERALL BAR PASSAGE RATE
1	Yale University (CT)	100.0	4.9	4.8	3.80–3.95	167–174	8.2%	83	99%	100%	95.0% NY	76%
2	Stanford University (CA)	92.0	4.8	4.9	3.65–3.90	165–170	12.4%	14.7	99%	99%	88.4% CA	63%
3	Harvard University (MA)	91.0	4.9	4.9	3.73–3.93	167–173	14.7%	18.6	98%	98%	94.0% NY	76%
4	New York University	87.0	4.7	4.5	3.50–3.76	167–171	22.6%	12.8	96%	100%	96.0% NY	76%
5	Columbia University	86.0	4.8	4.8	3.43–3.75	166–171	18.7%	13.8	98%	99%	89.3% NY	76%
6	University of Chicago	84.0	4.8	4.8	3.45–3.81	165–171	29.6%	10.9	97%	9.8%	97.3% IL	82%
7	University of Michigan-Ann Arbor	83.0	4.7	4.7	3.44–3.76	163–167	36.4%	13.8	93%	99%	94.4% NY	76%
8	University of California-Berkeley	82.0	4.7	4.6	3.68–3.90	161–169	18.4%	16.0	93%	98%	93.0% CA	63%
9	University of Virginia	82.0	4.6	4.6	3.54–3.83	162–168	28.9%	14.7	92%	98%	84.0% VA	71%
10	Cornell University (NY)	79.0	4.3	4.3	3.33–3.73	163–166	38.4%	10.9	88%	96%	94.0% NY	76%
11	Duke University (NC)	79.0	4.4	4.4	3.33–3.75	162–168	27.9%	16.1	94%	99%	95.0% NY	76%
12	Northwestern University (IL)	78.0	4.2	4.2	3.25–3.71	164–168	18.1%	13.8	90%	99%	95.7% IL	82%
13	University of Pennsylvania	78.0	4.5	4.4	3.42–3.71	163–167	29.2%	15.0	95%	98%	95.0% NY	76%
14	Georgetown University (DC)	77.0	4.2	4.3	3.33–3.76	163–168	25.8%	15.9	91%	98%	92.0% NY	76%
15	University of Texas-Austin	74.0	4.3	4.1	3.45–3.81	158–164	33.1%	18.2	84%	97%	88.0% TX	81%
16	University of California-Los Angeles	73.0	4.1	4.0	3.50–3.75	161–166	19.2%	16.3	80%	98%	93.0% CA	63%
17	University of Southern California	70.0	3.7	3.4	3.30–3.78	160–165	22.4%	15.4	89%	99%	82.5% CA	63%
18	Vanderbilt University (TN)	69.0	3.9	3.8	3.35–3.78	160–165	31.8%	17.9	88%	99%	77.0% IN	78%
19	University of Minnesota-Twin Cities	68.0	3.8	3.6	3.31–3.81	160–165	38.0%	14.6	73%	99%	95.0% MN	87%
20	Washington and Lee University (VA)	67.0	3.4	3.5	3.14–3.72	161–166	38.1%	11.3	72%	97%	88.0% VA	71%
21	University of Iowa	66.0	3.7	3.5	3.18–3.73	155–161	34.6%	13.0	76%	99%	89.0% IA	85%
22	University of North Carolina-Chapel Hill	65.0	3.7	3.7	3.38–3.79	157–164	25.0%	16.6	74%	98%	89.0% NC	77%
23	Boston College	63.0	3.4	3.5	3.30–3.68	159–164	26.5%	13.6	84%	94%	92.0% MA	77%
24	George Washington University (DC)	63.0	3.5	3.6	3.27–3.61	160–163	17.1%	18.2	85%	97%	90.3% NY	76%
25	University of Illinois-Urbana Champaign	63.0	3.6	3.5	3.14–3.68	157–163	37.9%	16.6	82%	96%	88.2% IL	82%

Source: U.S. News and World Report, web page http://www.usnews.com/usnews/edu/beyond/gradrank/gdlawnf.htm, accessed 12/2000. Copyright, April 9, 2001, U.S. News & World Report.

The resources necessary to support a student through four years of college and three years of law school are readily available only to the upper classes, creating a class bias within the profession. Since many legislators are lawyers, there is overrepresentation of the middle and upper classes among law interpreters and lawmakers.

Hierarchy of the Legal Profession *The school.* Several hierarchies exist within the legal profession, one of which is the law school itself. A clear hierarchy of law schools is evident (see Figure 6–1), and the lawyer's career path depends in large part on his or her school.

The firm. As seen in Figure 6–2, there are generally three strata of firms. Stratum I consists of elite Wall Street firms and large national firms. The most prestigious employ over two hundred lawyers. About fifty such firms exist in the United States, and half of them qualify as elite firms; the largest firms are based in Chicago and have more than one thousand lawyers and hundreds of support staff. Stratum II law firms are made up of the corporate attorneys, such as attorneys for Fortune 500 firms, attorneys for large corporations, and some government attorneys (like federal judges, U.S. attorneys, and legal counsel to the president). Stratum III law firms are best described as attorneys, that is, all others who don't fit in the first two levels. These are lawyers in solo practice, in small firms, and in small corporations and other government attorneys (such as public defenders and county district attorneys).

The specialty. Some lawyers, particularly those in private practice, are generalists who handle a variety of cases. Within firms, however, lawyers concentrate on litigation, tax law, probate law, corporate law, criminal law, family law, international law, estate law, or other specialized segments. Criminal law appears at the bottom of the legal hierarchy, and corporate law

FIGURE 6–1 Stratification of Legal Education

Stratum I

Elite Law Schools

Stratum II

National Law Schools

Stratum III

Regional Law Schools

Stratum IV

Local Law Schools

Source: H. Abadinsky, *Law and Justice: An Introduction to the American Legal System* (Chicago: Nelson-Hall, 1995).

Stratum I

Elite Law Firms

Wall Street Law Firms

Large National Law Firms

Stratum II

Corporate Attorneys

Fortune 500 Firms

Large Corporations

Government Attorneys[a]

Stratum III

Lawyers

Solo Practitioners

Small Law Firms

Attorneys for Small Corporations

---

[a]A relatively small number of government attorneys, for example, federal judges, U.S. attorneys, legal counsel to the president, and other ranking officials are in Stratum II.

Source: H. Abadinsky, *Law and Justice: An Introduction to the American Legal System* (Chicago: Nelson-Hall, 1995).

FIGURE 6–2 Stratification of Legal Profession

is at the top. Criminal lawyers often must work with the least-advantaged elements of society, many of whom cannot even pay their legal bills. Corporate attorneys work in a world of money and power.

What Lawyers Do Only a small proportion of all lawyers engage in actual litigation. Most spend their time counseling clients, negotiating with opposing sides, researching the law, investigating, and writing briefs. Some lawyers choose careers in which their legal background and knowledge of the law is important, such as tax collectors, credit investigators, FBI agents, insurance adjusters, and probation officers.

The polar extremes in the legal world are the private practitioners and the Wall Street firms. Private practitioners are not well respected in the legal community; they generally must work hard to maintain a client base and are underpaid relative to their colleagues in other types of practice. Private practitioners of color often have a clientele of color and earn more respect within their community than in the legal profession itself.

In Wall Street firms, the favored client is the corporation. There is a hierarchy in the large firms, and family background often plays an important part in a lawyer's placement. Attorneys in large firms are expected to be totally dedicated to the interests of their clients, expending an unlimited amount of time and effort on the client's behalf. Most Wall Street firms do their best to avoid litigation, which represents failure of negotiation. The practice of preventive law avoids the uncertainty of the trial courts. However, because of the changing face of corporate America, due to multicompany takeovers, class action suits, and an increasingly litigious society, even Wall Street firms must litigate. It is estimated that about one-third of the work of these firms now involves litigation.

Heinz and Laumann (1994) suggest that the best distinction between lawyers is not private practitioner or Wall Street practitioner but rather the distinction made between lawyers who represent large organizations and lawyers who represent individuals. This distinction forms a great divide, a form of social stratification that creates two systems of justice, separate and unequal. In our analysis, stratum I and stratum II firms represent large organizations; stratum III practitioners represent individuals. The divide is rarely crossed, either by lawyers or by clients.

Effects of Social Conditions, Ideas, and Groups on Lawyers and Judges

People, conditions, and ideas affect the worlds of both judges and lawyers. Judges, whether elected or not, are influenced by public opinion, even though we suggested earlier that the judicial branch is the least accountable in the legal system. Media coverage and even television cameras in the courtroom have made judges more aware of their responsibility to the public.

Lawyers, too, are aware of the public's perception of their work. The people, conditions, and ideas in society that define crime and criminals affect who lawyers work for and how and why. When the public redefines law so that drunk drivers are treated as criminals, a lawyer's client load shifts. New social ideas about battered women, sexual harassment, and the death penalty all affect the job of the law interpreter. As players in the justice game, lawyers and judges must adapt to the changing nature of the law.

LAW SANCTIONERS—CORRECTIONAL OFFICERS

The correctional worker's job is to mete out the sanctions that the legal system has specified to offenders who have been convicted and sentenced. The conditions under which correctional officers work are influenced by current social philosophies. How corrections, as an arm and institution of the legal system, operates has much to do with whom individuals and society think are the criminals and what should be done with them.

We can discuss six general goals of incarceration and the correctional system:

1. *Rehabilitation,* or reform of the sanctioned offender
2. *Deterrence,* both specific and general
3. *Incapacitation,* either permanent or temporary
4. *Moral education and normative reinforcement,* or use of punishment to define and establish the idea that the act is wrong
5. *Restitution,* material compensation to society and/or the victim
6. *Retribution through punishment and atonement,* called *justice* by proponents and *revenge* by detractors.

Each of these philosophies plays a role in how correctional personnel do their jobs. If rehabilitation is the current, primary social idea in penology, corrections officers work to implement programs for rehabilitation. If the prevailing social idea is punishment, corrections officers respond by focusing on retribution and restitution. At this writing, there is a notable increase of people incarcerated in the United States. Table 6–5 indicates the focus on incarceration as a primary sanction for violators, showing increases ranging from 165 percent to 260 percent since 1980.

Correctional Officers—Who They Are and What They Do

Individuals who work in corrections have diverse backgrounds. Some come from the community to work in community correctional institutions, and others have acquired college degrees in some area applicable to corrections.

TABLE 6–5 Number and Rate (per 100,000) of Adults in State and Federal Prisons and Jails

UNITED STATES, 1985, 1990–1996

	Total Custody	Federal Prisons	State Prisons	Local Jails	Total Rate
1985	744,208	35,781	451,812	256,615	313
1990	1,148,702	58,838	684,544	405,320	461
1991	1,219,014	63,930	728,605	426,479	483
1992	1,295,150	72,071	778,495	444,584	508
1993	1,369,185	80,815	828,566	459,804	531
1994	1,476,621	85,500	904,647	486,474	567
1995	—	89,538	989,007	—	—
1996 (June 30)	**1,630,940**	**93,167**	**1,019,281**	**518,492**	**615**
		Annual average increase			
12/31/85–6/30/96	7.8%	9.5%	8.1%	6.9%	X
12/31/90–6/30/96	6.6%	8.7%	7.5%	4.6%	X

Source: U.S. Department of Justice, Bureau of Justice Statistics, *Prison and Jail Inmates at Midyear 1996,* NCJ-162843 (Washington, DC: U.S. Department of Justice, 1997), p. 2, Table 1.

Numerous schools around the country offer A.A., A.S., B.A., B.S., and M.S. degrees in fields considered appropriate for corrections careers: criminal justice, law enforcement, and criminology. Other social science fields such as sociology and social work also contribute.

Correctional officers engage in a variety of tasks. They guard inmates in both federal and state institutions; search the premises; inspect security; direct inmates during work assignments; and keep track of inmates' whereabouts, work assignments, health, and well-being. At times they may find it necessary to use weapons and force to maintain peace in correctional facilities (*Dictionary of Occupational Titles,* 1989:29).

As of June 1994, approximately 59.4 percent of correctional officers in adult systems in the United States were white males, 15.9 percent were African-American males, and 5.3 percent were Hispanic males. Women have gained minimal entrance into the field. The same report notes that white women accounted for 9.6 percent of all workers, African-American women 6.7 percent, and Hispanic women .09 percent. More women worked in juvenile facilities (35.3 percent) than in adult facilities (29.8 percent) (Maguire and Pastore, 1995).

However, as with elsewhere in the labor force, the majority of both supervisors and wardens are male, approximately 86 percent for both (Maguire and Pastore, 1994:94, 96). The salaries of correctional officers vary, depending on their rank in an institution and the jurisdiction in which they work. Entry-level officers earn from approximately $15,000 to $38,000, and wardens and chief administrative officers generally have salaries in the upper $30,000s.

Organization of Correctional Systems

The correctional system is organized in a fashion similar to the court system. There are both state and federal correctional systems. Within the state systems are local and county jurisdictions, often referred to as the city or county jail. In theory, the federal correctional system incarcerates individuals who have violated federal laws. These people have been processed through the federal court system before going to federal correctional institutions. Individuals punished for state violations go to state correctional institutions. Generally, felons are placed in prisons and those convicted of misdemeanors are sent to jails. Jails also serve as holding areas. At any given time, approximately 50 percent of jail inmates are awaiting trial.

Effects of Social Conditions, Ideas, and Groups on Correctional Officers

In the last fifteen years in the United States, prison populations have almost doubled. This has created a larger workforce in corrections, as well as numerous problems. New facilities must be built to relieve severe overcrowding, and individuals must be trained to work in them. As the legal system responds to crime by locking up more prisoners, officers in institutions must deal with the population growth. When prisons are overcrowded and problems with propinquity arise, it is officers who must deal with increased tensions and violence. The brief on *Ruiz et al. v. Estelle* clearly illustrates the kinds of problems that face correctional institutions today. What the public is thinking, what legislators are passing, and what lawyers are arguing and judges are hearing, all affect the day-to-day life of these professionals. Correctional officers must face the hardest cases in the American legal system.

Ruiz et al. v. Estelle
679 F.2d 1115 (5th Cir., 1982)

The Texas state prison system was the largest in the United States in 1980 (by 1990 it was third, behind California and New York), with more than 33,000 inmates confined in 10,000 cells and dormitories in 22 units, most of which were maximum security. The system, operated by the Texas Department of Corrections (TDC), was operating minimally at 230 percent of rated capacity because of the imposition of a number of mandatory sentencing statutes in the 1970s. The inmates alleged that the overcrowded conditions bred violence and that lack of access to legal and medical services constituted cruel and unusual punishment, in violation of the Eighth Amendment.

In June 1972, *Ruiz v. Estelle*, a joinder of eight suits alleging cruel and unusual conditions in the Texas prison system, was instituted as a class action suit on behalf of all past, present, and future TDC inmates against W. J. Estelle, the director of TDC. In April 1974, as the scope of the investigation into conditions expanded, the U.S. District Court for the Southern District of Texas ordered the United States to participate in this case with the full rights of a party (1134). The case finally came to trial in October 1978 before U.S. District Chief Judge William Wayne Justice (503 F. Supp. 1265). The trial lasted 159 days, with 349 witnesses and 1,565 exhibits received into evidence. Justice found that the conditions of confinement violated the Constitution and appointed monitors to supervise the implementation of and compliance with the specified reforms (1115).

The TDC filed an appeal with the Court of Appeals, vehemently objecting to Judge Justice's bias in favor of the inmates; the participation of the U.S. government as a party to the suit; and the intrusive nature of the district court's decree, which violated the sovereign immunity of the State of Texas (1116–1126). Circuit Judge Alvin B. Rubin held that (1) those portions of the district court's decree requiring TDC to report the number of inmates and the space per inmate (a minimum of 40 square feet per confinee); to reduce the *overall* number of inmates; to preserve a record of disciplinary hearings; to provide regular exercise to segregated inmates and mandatory access to courts, counsel, and public officials were proper. (2) Portions requiring TDC to take steps relating to good time, parole, work conditions, and furloughs impermissibly interfered with prison administration. (3) The portion of the decree requiring TDC to improve a state prison hospital was invalid. (4) The appointment of monitors was proper, but a hearing process prior to action by the U.S. district court was necessary.

AFFIRMED IN PART AND REVERSED IN PART

CONCLUSION

Each of the professions discussed in this chapter plays a specific part in the justice process and legal system. The workers' training, education, and background may differ, but their participation as policymakers or gatekeepers (see Chapter 5 for a discussion of the models of law) is important to the smooth operation of the system. These groups of individuals also are affected by the social conditions, ideas, and people of their time. Again, the social context of law is significant, especially for those who work in the system.

7 The Purpose and Usefulness of Law

Law exists solely because members of society believe it is useful and purposeful. Over time, the uses and purposes of law have changed because of changing social conditions and attitudes. However, the underlying principles of law remain generally constant. As we continue our discussion, we find that the law is used to settle conflicts, to bring about social change, and to act as a means of social control.

LAW AS A FORM OF INFORMAL AND FORMAL SOCIAL CONTROL

Social control is the way in which societies secure conformity among their members (Rush, 1994:315). Because of this social control process, most of us have internalized a sense of right and wrong. If, as members of society, we act in positive ways, our behavior is positively sanctioned, or rewarded. Behavior contrary to socially defined norms is punished with a variety of negative sanctions, ranging from ostracism to imprisonment.

Social controls operate at formal and informal levels. Informal social controls are the unwritten rules that are vital to the smooth functioning of society. These control mechanisms are most effective in small groups, which involve face-to-face interaction, and inform most of our daily activities. When we climb up the right-hand side of a staircase, we engage in an informal control process. There is no rulebook that teaches us to walk on the right side, but informal controls in society have taught us to do so. Walking on the socially approved side is rewarded by a smooth traffic flow. If we choose to go against the flow of traffic, we could be met with the negative social sanctions of dirty looks or pushing and shoving. There is no formal sanction, such as a ticket, for walking up the wrong side of the stairs, merely negative social pressures.

Formal social controls, on the other hand, are those rules of society that are important enough to be written down. Statutory law, for example, guides interpersonal behaviors, driving a motor vehicle, and many other activities. When we violate these formal social controls, the negative sanctions, criminal and civil, are generally more severe than when we violate informal social controls.

The internalization of informal and formal social controls is an ongoing socialization process, which itself is a form of social control. This process controls members of society by conferring a definition of self. It also defines the world and our place in it. Through socialization, we learn not only who we are but also how we should relate to society as a whole. Furthermore, the socialization process defines our relationship to other people. As individuals we learn to interact with, think about, and deal with others. Sanctions in the socialization process control the individual by encouraging or discouraging the acquisition of certain skills and knowledge; these sanctions, or the lack of them, often depend on the individual's gender, race, social class, and other factors.

Depending on the way in which socialization takes place, the individual discovers aspirations, as well as limitations. Socialization instills a set of beliefs about oneself that allows for possibilities, as well as constraints. As the individual learns self-definition, his or her place in society is also defined. If, for example, the individual's idea of ultimate success is becoming a university professor and then that goal is achieved, this person sees the achievement as a positive sanction and feels secure in the respect of colleagues and students. In contrast, if the individual's vision includes becoming a university president, the fact that he or she is merely a professor may be seen as a negative sanction. Individuals learn, through socialization, to admire and even love some members of society, as well as to fear or hate others. The individual may learn to accept authority unquestioningly or to distrust and reject authority, depending on the type and severity of sanctions brought to bear during the individual's formative years. Many sanctions, both positive and negative, occur because of gender, race, or social status and deeply affect the knowledge and social skills of the individual.

LAW AS DETERRENCE

Currently, social scientists and others discuss two primary forms of deterrence. *Specific deterrence* is achieved by intimidating a specific individual. *General deterrence* attempts to inhibit behavior in large categories of people. Cesare Beccaria (1963) and Jeremy Bentham (1789) postulated that the effectiveness of deterrence was influenced by three variables: (1) the severity of the punishment for the offense, (2) the certainty of punishment for the offense, and (3) the swiftness, or speed, of punishment. This idea, generally associated with classical theory, is one of the most frequently discussed topics in the discipline of criminology. Most contemporary opinion, however, suggests that legal sanctions are not effective deterrents.

Some concepts and terms need to be clarified. When legislative bodies prohibit certain conduct, such as robbery, and specify a punishment for violators, this is a *legal threat* and a formal social control. The ability of the legal threat to deter behavior varies because individuals' responses to the threat vary. Some people may cease to engage in that behavior because of the legal threat. Others may respond by changing the style and/or frequency of the behavior. Most individuals never engage in the negatively sanctioned behavior—but some may do so simply because they have been told not to. These responses to the legal threat are referred to as *channeling effects*.

While deterrence is intended to restrain specified behavior, it enjoys only varying degrees of success. *Net deterrent effect* is a term used to describe how well deterrence is working; it is the total number of threatened behaviors prevented minus those that have occurred. The reality is that while some legal threats may deter behavior, they may not have a net deterrent effect (Weinberg and Weinberg, 1980).

Individuals are acted on by factors that cause them to be more or less deterrable. For instance, present-oriented people tend to be less deterrable than those who are *future*-oriented. Optimists tend to be less deterrable than pessimists—because they believe that they will not get caught. Authoritarian personalities tend to be more deterrable because of their belief in and respect for authority.

When societies use the law and create legal threats, the law becomes a formal avenue of social control. Indeed, many of us see the prime purpose and use of law as a mechanism of social control. If societies did not identify certain behaviors as negative and then attach punishments to violations, there would be no purpose to law. It is useful and purposeful because it acts as a guide.

LAW AS A METHOD OF CONFLICT RESOLUTION

In addition to the control of behavior, another use and purpose of law is to settle conflicts or disputes. Disputes are a form of social conflict involving two or more parties who have incompatible goals. Disputes vary in scope, intensity, duration, mode of settlement, outcomes, and consequences. *Conflict resolution, conflict regulation, conflict management, dispute processing, dispute settlement,* and *dispute resolution* are all terms that refer to a process whereby individuals and parties settle the issues between them (Vago, 1997:234).

Conflict resolution in one form or another has existed for centuries. Throughout history, means of settling disputes have varied enormously. Simon Roberts (cited in Vago, 1997:236–238) argues that in some parts of the world, direct, interpersonal violence, such as assault, feuding, and dueling, is an approved method of dispute settlement. Conflict resolution also has been accomplished through shame, ridicule, public harangue, and public sacrifice, as well as through supernatural forces—religion, witchcraft, and sorcery. Not all parties in conflict deal directly with its resolution. Inaction is one method of resolution: the issue that gave rise to the conflict is ignored, and the relationship to the offending party continues as before. Avoidance refers to limiting the relationship with other disputants so that the dispute is no longer salient. Exit behavior is that in which one party simply withdraws or terminates the relationship. However, these more passive approaches to conflict resolution are not always viable.

Causes of disputes are too numerous to list here. Individual disputes may involve money, relationships, land rights, or a host of other issues. When individuals have a dispute with an organization, the issue may be property and money, damages and restitution, civil rights or organizational actions, or procedures and policies. Disputes between organizations also occur. When the state is in dispute with an individual or organization, the issue revolves around a violation of a law or a regulation.

Stages in the Dispute Process

Nader and Todd (1978:14–15) identify three stages in the dispute process, although these are not always clear-cut or sequential:

1. *Grievance or preconflict stage.* This involves situations that an individual or group perceives as unjust; it is monadic and may erupt into conflict, or it may wane.
2. *Conflict stage.* An aggrieved party confronts the offending party by communicating resentment or a sense of injustice. This is dyadic, involving only two parties. If the conflict is not settled at this point, it evolves into the third stage.
3. *Dispute stage.* The conflict is made public, and legal resources are utilized. This stage is triadic, that is, characterized by the involvement of a third party.

Structurally, the *law* resolves only the *legal* components of the conflict. The law is not capable or prepared to deal with the underlying causes. People and parties still may be antagonistic and aggrieved toward one another even after the dispute is legally settled. Consider, for example, a marital dissolution when children are involved. During the divorce proceedings, child custody and child support are *settled*—but in reality, the parents often find themselves in continuing conflictive roles as their children grow and as new partners enter the picture.

Methods of Conflict Resolution

In the United States, two important forms of dispute resolution are commonly used. Parties may determine the outcome through negotiation between themselves, or the conflict may involve the participation of a third, impartial body (Vago, 1997:238–245).

Two-Party Process—Negotiation Negotiations take place when disputants seek to resolve their disagreement without the help of a neutral third party. This is a two-party arrangement, which involves debate and bargaining. The basic requirement is that both parties want the conflict to be settled. In the United States, inaction, avoidance, and negotiation (discussed earlier in the chapter) are the three ways disputes are usually resolved.

Three-Party Processes Some writers refer to three-party processes of conflict resolution as forms of *negotiated justice* (Abadinsky, 1995:331). Disputes involving a third party vary in their level of formality, their degree of openness, their perception of relevance, and their decision-making style.

Mediation Mediation is a process that utilizes a neutral third party. The basic tenet of mediation is cooperation and reconciliation, not competition. A mediator is a facilitator who works with both parties to settle the issues in everyone's best interests. Ideally, both parties in the conflict have confidence in the mediator. Mediation is a nonadversarial process that is devoid of the attempt to determine right or wrong; its goal is to settle the dispute. This is the least formal of all three-party processes. The mediator tries to help the parties adjust their differences regardless of who is right.

Arbitration In arbitration, a final and binding decision is made for the disputants by an individual who is perceived as neutral and competent. Disputants agree beforehand to allow the arbitrator to perform this function. Unlike a court case, these proceedings may remain private, informal, and simple. The arbitrator, although acting like a judge, is not a professional judge. Arbitration tends to be lower in cost and quicker than adjudication. Most collective bargaining contracts contain a provision for final and binding arbitration.

Use of Ombudsman Another third-party process, involving both mediation and investigation, is the use of an ombudsman. In the United States, this process is employed primarily by corporations, hospitals, and universities. A major criticism of this process is the belief that the ombudsman often has vested interests in favor of one party or the other. For example, if the ombudsman is employed by the university, it stands to reason that he or she may be biased in favor of the university. This lack of objectivity is offset by the need for heightened expertise in technical areas, such as health-care delivery. In the corporate sector, a dispute over intellectual property would necessitate someone well versed in the field to determine the merits of each side's argument. When this knowledge is derived from previous participation in the same industry, a phenomenon occurs called the *capture thesis*, based on real or philosophical alliances. This phenomenon occurs when the only individuals capable of investigating, evaluating, and mediating a complex dispute are those who participate in the industry.

Adjudication Adjudication is the court process, and the emphasis is on the legal rights and duties of the disputants. In the United States, adjudication is a zero-sum process, involving an either/or outcome. The process is adversarial, and therefore one of the parties must be prepared for a total loss. In contrast to arbitration, adjudication requires a professional judge. Adjudicated outcomes are legally binding decisions.

Small-Claims Courts Small-claims courts are processes of adjudication in which the filing process is simple and the rules of evidence are less stringent than in other courts. Judges, legal referees, or panels of lawyers sit on these benches. While individuals may appear without an attorney, it may be advantageous to retain one since these courts have become a collection agency for businesses. Studies suggest that 85 to 93 percent of small claims involve businesses that are filing as plaintiffs.

Plea Bargaining Plea bargaining is a negotiated, third-party form of criminal justice. In the United States, plea bargaining was well entrenched by the 1880s. In the 1920s, it began to draw criticism for allowing preferential treatment of more highly regarded or connected citizens. Criticism again surfaced in the 1950s and focused on the issue of coercion. Today, both criticisms are common. While one of the advantages of the plea-bargaining process is its measure of predictability, the questions and arguments for and against plea bargains have existed for decades. The importance of voluntary agreement by the defendant is central to the process, but some legal critics argue that the choice between pleading guilty or going to trial does not represent a voluntary decision. Another discussion is the class bias of plea bargains. On the one hand, persons of limited means may feel they have no choice if they cannot afford bail. On the other hand, if a person is highly regarded in the community, which almost always relates to class standing, more options will be available to that defendant, including release on bail.

The plea-bargaining process involves negotiations between a defendant's lawyer and the prosecutor to reduce in seriousness or number the charges against the defendant in exchange for a plea of guilty or no contest.

When discussing case attrition in Chapter 5, we pointed out the contemporary controversy about the prevalence of plea bargains. Regardless of jurisdictional use and differences, it is believed that the process of *bargain justice* reduces the burden on court dockets by eliminating the expense and time of a trial. A number of variables affect the decision to use or not to use this negotiated process.

Figure 7–1 lists the variables that influence a prosecutor in deciding whether or not to charge a case. The key variables are the seriousness of the charges and the prosecution's likelihood of winning the case, based on its strengths and weaknesses. Quadrant I shows a case in which the charges are not serious and the evidence is weak; this case will usually not be prosecuted.

FIGURE 7–1 Variables Influencing a Prosecutor's Changing Decision

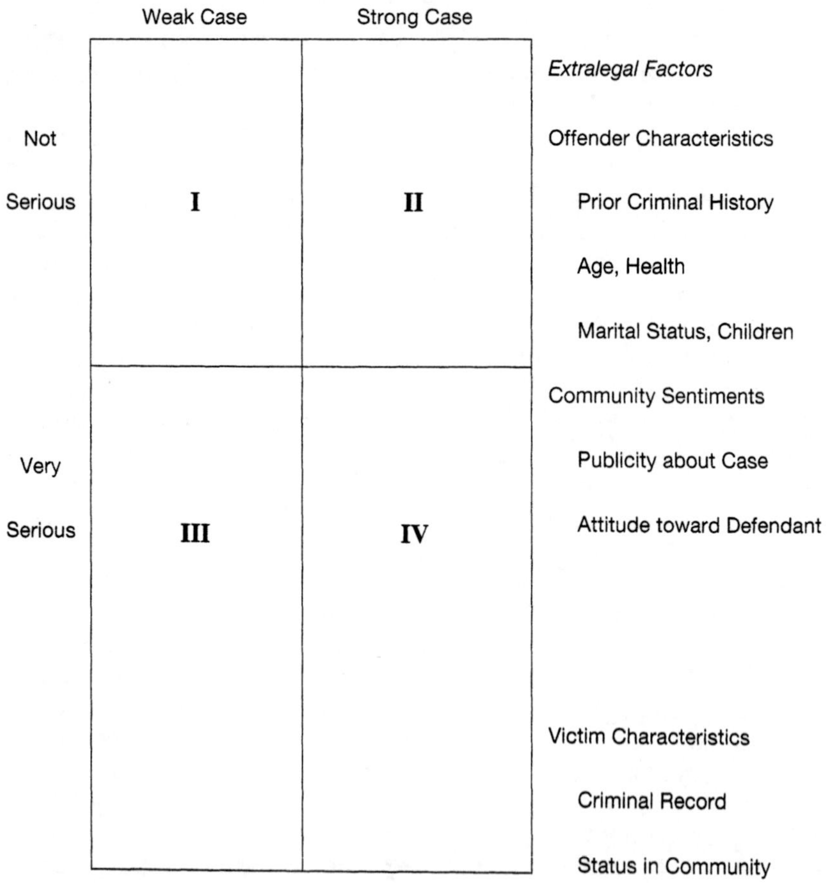

	Weak Case	Strong Case
Not Serious	I	II
Very Serious	III	IV

Extralegal Factors

Offender Characteristics

- Prior Criminal History
- Age, Health
- Marital Status, Children

Community Sentiments

- Publicity about Case
- Attitude toward Defendant

Victim Characteristics

- Criminal Record
- Status in Community

Source: H. Abadinsky, *Law and Justice; An Introduction to the American Legal System* (Chicago: Nelson-Hall, 1995).

Quadrant II contains a case in which the charges are not serious but the evidence is strong; this case is a good candidate for a plea bargain. Quadrant III contains a case in which the charges are serious but the evidence is weak; this kind of case will most often be rejected, dismissed, or plea-bargained. Quadrant IV contains the type of case that is vigorously prosecuted.

While a plea bargain provides a predictable outcome for the accused rather than the vagaries of a trial, many critics argue that there is no justice when there is no trial. Research has found that, in general, plea bargaining results in more lenient sentences than if an individual went to trial and was found guilty. It should also be noted that sentencing, which is an integral part of the process of a plea bargain, is not the function of a trial. In a trial, guilt must be ascertained before a sentence becomes necessary. The plea bargain circumvents the entire process by offering an accused person the knowledge of a sentence in exchange for a plea of guilty.

LAW AS A PUNISHMENT AND REMEDY

A discussion of the usefulness and purpose of law would not be complete without noting how the law actually resolves the problems associated with conflicts. *Remedies* and *punishments* are of central importance in the common law system in the United States. They are the legal system's tools to settle issues; they enforce legally recognized rights and redress injuries.

Punishment occurs because an individual has violated the rules, written or otherwise, of society. Therefore, societies punish people by incarcerating them, making them pay fines, requiring them to engage in certain kinds of behavior, or some combination of the three. Punishment is a form of social control—it can occur informally, as when parents punish their children, or formally, as with the previous examples.

Damages

Damages are monetary settlements, meant to compensate for harm caused by the violation of legal rights or the occurrence of injury, including personal injury. There are several kinds of compensation for damages.

Nominal damages are token damages, awarded when a plaintiff's legal rights have been violated but where there is not significant or material loss or injury.

Compensatory damages are the most frequently sought and awarded legal remedy. The purpose of this award is to make the injured parties *whole* again, that is, to restore them to the position they would have been in had they not been injured. The damages in these cases must be real, direct, and substantial, and they can be awarded, for example, for personal injury and breach of contract.

Punitive damages are awarded not as compensation for injury but as punishment to a defendant. Because the purpose of punitive damages (also called *exemplary damages*) is twofold, to punish for past wrongdoings and to deter future wrongdoings, the focus is not on the extent of damages per se but on the outrageousness of the defendant's behavior. Punitive damages may be awarded only in cases in which the defendant has demonstrated *malice.*

Equitable Remedies

Early in common law systems, the basic remedy available to individuals was damages. Because of those limited remedies, however, when some individuals felt that they had a legal claim, they also felt that they had nowhere to turn. To deal with this problem, the common law system eventually established two courts: equity courts (to deal with claims that were not addressed by existing laws or precedent) and legal courts (for damage cases). Historically, a litigant who seeks resolution in an equity court must have had no other remedy available, must not have waited too long to seek a remedy, must have requested a remedy that was practical, and must not have acted in any way that would have made the injury (as claimed) worse. Although these two courts existed side by side for decades, today no distinction is made between them.

Injunctions

Injunctions, which are court orders that require a certain kind of behavior, were originally established in equity courts. The instructed behavior, the injunction, required an individual either to engage in a certain behavior or not to engage in a certain behavior. The aim of an injunction is directed toward the prevention of future harm rather than redressing issues in the past. Over time, various kinds of injunctions have been developed.

Temporary injunctions are used to maintain the status quo until the parties' issues can be settled in court.

Permanent injunctions are long-term injunctions and involve a behavior order that has been established through litigation.

Mandatory injunctions are direct orders to do something.

Temporary restraining orders and *orders for protection* are additional kinds of ex parte orders; that is, they may be granted without prior hearing or minimal notice to the other party. Generally a plaintiff must show cause for either of these two injunctions.

Declarative Judgments

Declarative judgments are another type of evolved equity remedy. These are court decrees that articulate the legal rights of two parties involved in a dispute. The judgment is simply a statement of outcome; it does not require either party to do anything but simply declares a legal situation.

Criminal Remedies

Remedies for criminal violations are more familiar than are civil remedies. Criminal remedies include imprisonment, probation, fines, community service, and a variety of new types of punishment tactics meted out by judges and juries. The discussion of plea bargains, for example, is associated with criminal remedies.

LAW AS A METHOD OF SOCIAL CHANGE

Social change is the transformation of culture and social institutions over time. In Chapter 2 we introduced the ideas of Roscoe Pound and his belief that law should be used as a tool of social change (Pound, 1959). Social change is a product of many factors and has four key characteristics (Macionis, 1996:412–414):

1. It occurs in all societies and cultures, although the rate of change varies.
2. It may be intentional or unintentional.
3. It usually generates controversy.
4. Some social changes matter more than others.

Law, as we have pointed out, is both an independent and dependent variable in and of social change, a cause and an effect. In the United States, for example, enacted laws have given or taken away the rights of women and people of color, forced native populations off tribal lands, and granted civil rights and ownership of property to select groups at the expense of others. Segregation laws were eventually supplanted by desegregation laws, both the result and cause of changing social ideologies. Changing patterns of domestic relationships caused changes in divorce law, which further changed society's view of marriage. These examples suggest that law responds to the social environment, but we must remember that the relationship between law and social change is not always so direct or positive.

Resistance to Social Change

As Vago (1997) notes, change in society is rarely accomplished without resistance, and the more dramatic the change, the greater the resistance. Those with a vested interest in the status quo may fear loss of power, prestige, or wealth if change comes about. Some individuals may oppose change for class, ideological, or organizational reasons. In addition to these social factors are psychological factors of resistance. Habit, motivation, ignorance, and selective perceptions of possible benefits of change also cause resistance, as do cultural factors like fatalism, ethnocentrism, and superstition. Finally, economic factors may hinder change. For instance, equal access laws that require aisles in all movie theaters to be accessible to wheelchairs were less than welcome by theater owners, who bore the cost of refitting their theaters.

William Evan (1965:288–291) suggests that law is likely to be an effective impetus to change when the following seven conditions are met:

1. Law must come from an authoritative or prestigious source.
2. Law must be rational in terms that are understandable and compatible with existing values.
3. Advocates of any change in the law must show that it has worked in other countries.
4. Enforcement of new laws should be immediate.
5. Those enforcing new laws must be supportive and committed to the change.
6. The implementation of the law should include positive and/or negative sanctions.
7. The enforcement of the law should be equitable to those who stand to lose because of its enforcement.

A law is likely to gain acceptance only when it meets the above conditions because it then appears to be fair, to have worked, and to be as equitable as possible. If laws aimed toward social change appear to be based on nothing, people will not endorse them.

The Advantages and Disadvantages of Using Law to Create Social Change

Vago (1997:296–306) suggests that there are both advantages and disadvantages in using law to create social change. The three primary advantages are these:

Law as a legitimate authority. The major advantage of law as an instrument of social change is the perception in society that legal commands and prohibitions ought to be observed. Weber's ([1914] 1954) analysis of law (mentioned in Chapter 1) highlights this point by discussing traditional authority, rational-legal authority, and charismatic authority. Research suggests that legitimate authority greatly affects both actions and attitudes.

The binding force of law. Law is considered binding for several reasons. Some individuals see law as ordained by nature and/or a deity. Many people believe that it is their obligation to obey the law, sometimes at the expense of morality. Laws represent order and predictability, aid in the socialization process, and represent consensus.

The use of sanctions. Law has the power to impose negative sanctions, which have the effect of overcoming resistance to change. This effect may be seen in laws for affirmative action and equal employment opportunity. Negative sanctions are the consequence of resistance to legally mandated behaviors.

The three primary limitations are these:

Conflicts of interest. Laws designed to further social ends but that inflict collateral damage on a society's established mode of access to scarce resources meet with great resistance.

Divergent views on the law as a tool for directed social change. The views of the most powerful negate or neglect the views of the oppressed.

Prevailing values and morality. If the law comes into conflict with these, its effectiveness is lessened. As stated by William Graham Sumner (1906), "Stateways cannot change folkways."

LAW AND PUBLIC POLICY

Law is a means of social change and social control because it is through law that society enacts public policy, which is "a goal directed or purposive course of action followed by an actor or set of actors in an attempt to deal with a public problem" (Anderson, Brady, and Bullock, 1978:5). As such, public policies are developed by government institutions and their legitimate authorities. It is what governments do, for example, to control inflation, maintain the environment, or manage immigration, and it may be intentionally action-oriented or laissez faire in nature. In other words, many of the legal practitioners we discussed in Chapter 6 are public policy makers and implementers.

The civil rights movement, *glasnost*, and the abolition of slavery are all examples of changes in, or the introduction of, public policy that resulted in social change. New or changed laws or public policies that require individuals to wear seat belts or to minimize their alcohol consumption before driving are attempts by policy makers to control people's behavior.

Public policy decisions are made within a historical, political, public (opinion), social system, and economic context. When goal-directed, purposive decisions are introduced, implementers of law do so within the historical and political context of their time. This is not new information to us, but given the goal of this chapter, it seems like a perfect time to reemphasize this reality.

Most changes in public policy, as may be discernible from the discussion on social change, are incremental in nature (Anderson et al., 1978:394–395) for two reasons. First, because there are often numerous social problems to be dealt with at any one time, policy makers simply do not have the time, money, or knowledge to address every issue. Second, because political power is fragmented, coalition building is required, which is a slow process. While there may be a desire for political expedience, the reality is that political wheels often turn slowly, partly because of the resistance to social change that we noted above.

Public policies, or the laws that are passed, often fail to exhibit their intended effect. Lawmakers may get elected on a specific public policy platform, and administrative agencies may be created to carry out policy decisions—but sometimes policies simply fall short. The reasons for this are numerous: inadequate resources or solutions that are too costly; the existence of other problems, which distract a practitioner's attention; the inadequate administration of the policy guidelines; the reaction of people affected by the policy, which may nullify it or lessen its impact; and the fact that policies from different eras sometimes conflict with one another. Some policy problems are so huge they simply are not solvable. And just as the courts rarely have the last word, the adoption of a public policy only marks the end of one stage and the beginning of another (Anderson et al., 1978:403–405). Citizens who complain that laws do not work often fail to recognize the limitations of public policy implementation.

CONCLUSION

When we consider the role of law in our lives, we realize it has many different uses and purposes. Social ideas, social conditions, and people all play a part in the perception of the usefulness and purpose of law. Whether we consider Prohibition, affirmative action, injunctions on behavior, or deterrence measures, why we judge these issues important and how we accomplish them varies according to the social conditions of society, the ideas then current, and the people who are participating in the process.

8 | Gender, Race, Social Class, and Law

One of the best ways to illustrate the social context of law is to examine *social variables*. Because dominant beliefs are often codified into laws, understanding the influence of social conditions, people, and ideas can help us to understand how laws have affected gender, race, and social class. While we choose to separate these variables to study them, it is very important to understand that in reality they are very much intertwined. The interconnection of gender and class or gender and race is a strong influence on how a person is affected by the law. We begin our discussion with gender.

GENDER AND THE SOCIAL CONTEXT OF LAW

Social ideas about gender have always played a part in how women have been treated by the law. Such ideas as those exemplified by the "true womanhood" ideology (Welter, 1966) have certainly influenced lawmakers. That ideology, prevalent originally in the eighteenth century among the middle and upper classes in Great Britain, the United States, and elsewhere, posited that "true" women should demonstrate four values: purity, piety, submissiveness, and domesticity. This idea caused lawmakers to make women the legal property of men. If women should be domestic and submissive, the objects of that domesticity and submissiveness are men and their families.

This notion has best been illustrated through the implementation of *coverture*, a concept defined by Sir William Blackstone (the individual most commonly cited as the author of a unified common law system; see Chapter 3): "Women and men are one, and that one is the husband" (Blackstone, 1993). Although coverture no longer exists legally, its legacy still is felt.

The reality of coverture meant that married women could not own their own property, sign contracts, sue on their own behalf, or execute a will. Marriage was considered a *civil death* for women in the United States in the eighteenth and early nineteenth centuries; it was actually advantageous for women not to get married (although not getting married was considered against women's *nature*). Even today, a divorced woman may have trouble securing credit in her own name, a legacy of coverture.

The first real loosening of coverture came in 1839 with the passage of the first Married Women's Property Act in the state of Mississippi. Many states followed suit shortly thereafter. These acts were passed largely through the influence of early feminists, after circuitous discussions about the ability of women to own and manage their own property. Unfortunately, historians tell us that even so, the acts were often implemented, not because of a true concern for women's rights, but rather to protect the property (particularly slaves) of landowners. By placing property in women's names, creditors had a more difficult time collecting debts. The social fabric had not changed enough in the early 1800s to allow women to own property because of their own merit.

For centuries, the notion that women were men's familial property allowed for the battery of women in the household. Many authors believe that the phrase "rule of thumb" came from a common law tradition which asserted that men were allowed to beat their wives with sticks no bigger around than their thumb. Certainly this idea illustrates the relationship between social ideas of particular eras and how they affect the law. The battering of women is as old as time, and attitudes about it have changed only recently. Not until 1913 did the courts, in *Bailey v. People*, make it abundantly clear that a husband had no right to use threats or violence to compel some desired behavior from his wife. The *Bailey* case strictly specified that the rule of thumb "is a relic of barbarism that has no place in an enlightened civilization."

Labor is another area where the social construction of law has affected women's lives. Historically (and, many argue, today) women's labor was often overlooked, and the conditions under which they worked were not considered important. Both of these thoughts have been challenged. First, *women have always worked*. Women have always, at a minimum, engaged in unpaid work. Women's domestic duties are only now being recognized as necessary and important tasks of labor. Second, women have always engaged in some kind of paid labor as well, whether for a wage or by barter. Thus women's position in the paid labor force needs to be examined more thoroughly.

Laws pertaining to women's paid labor were strongly influenced by such ideas as the "true womanhood" ideology, which resulted in the passage of one of the most famous reviews of labor legislation, *Muller v. Oregon* [208 U.S. 412 (1908)]. In 1903, the state of Oregon passed this piece of labor legislation (Session Laws 1903, p. 148), which was upheld by the U.S. Supreme Court. Thus, the legal principle that women's labor must be controlled and overseen was verified. Judicial discussions about women's nature and stature led to the passage of this law, which ideologically protected women but also limited and restricted the type of paid employment they *were allowed* to engage in. Nineteenth-century feminists discussed the notion of *protecting* women, and contemporary feminists continue the discussions. Does protecting women amount to a form of gender equality or gender discrimination? This question and others like it are among the key issues for feminist legal theory and scholars (as mentioned in Chapter 2). The flip side of the coin during the *Muller* era was that indeed some women did work in paid employment that was dangerous and unhealthy—and not viewed as overly laborious. Women could get jobs in textile mills since weaving had long been viewed as women's work. Thus women toiled in unhealthy working conditions while being kept out of other areas of employment.

The issue of low pay is another topic of consideration. Women in the U.S. paid labor force have historically been paid less money than men. The Equal Pay Act of 1963 recognized that women should receive equal pay for comparable work. The passage of this act could only have occurred in the social conditions of the 1960s. But even with its implementation, women still do not earn the same wages as men. Numerous studies have found that the pay gap still stands around 67:100. One of the reasons the Equal Pay Act has not eradicated differences in pay is that women and men do not do *equal* work, or at least work that is so defined. The segregation of the labor force continues to keep women in traditionally women's jobs, which pay less, and their work, consequently, is not considered equal to the work men do at traditionally men's jobs.

The workplace environment for women is a relatively new topic of discussion. Contemporary laws against sexual harassment are new and controversial. The act of sexual harassment is not new; women have experienced harassment since the beginning of a market environment. What is new is that society and the legal system now recognize how the work environment can affect one's work life. On November 10, 1980, the Equal Employment Opportunity Commission, then chaired by Eleanor Holmes Norton, issued the current guidelines defining sexual harassment. The guide was brief and to the point—just one page long. Since then, two primary forms of harassment have been routinely discussed and recognized: quid pro quo (a favor for a favor) and a hostile environment. Because people tend to understand the former, the hostile environment charge was initially met with greater resistance. Both kinds of harassment have been tried in the courts and have been ruled illegal forms of behavior.

Bailey v. People
130 P. 832 (Colorado Supreme Court) (1913)

Eugene H. Smith had a reputation in his neighborhood of being quarrelsome and dangerous, particularly when he was drunk. The usual focus of his ill temper was his wife, with "repeated and continued acts of brutality," as well as threats to take the life of both his wife and her entire family if they attempted to intervene. On July 15, 1910, Smith, in a drunken rage, "jumped up on the abdomen of his wife and caused hemorrhages, which afterwards necessitated an operation." Mrs. Smith and her two children went to her mother's house for protection, "as she had done oftentimes before" (836). Mrs. Smith's brother-in-law, R. L. McDonald, attempted to convince Eugene to stop battering his wife, at which time Eugene Smith said, "Well, if she will come back and live with me and do just what I say, I will live with her; and if she won't, God damn her, I will kill her" (834).

On July 18, 1910, Eugene Smith approached the home of his mother-in-law in a violent rage. According to Mrs. Smith, "He was just plunging. . . . It frightened me so. I could see . . . he was in a very angry, bad mood, and I ran to my brother's bedroom. . . . I said, 'For God's sake, don't let him come in here. If you do, he will kill the whole family. He will kill Mother and me.'" (833). Her brother, Joseph E. Bailey, secured a revolver and called out to Eugene at least four times, warning him not to try to enter the house. Smith said, "I will come in and get the whole God damned push of you." Bailey implored him to stop for the fifth time. "I tell you for God's sake, don't try to enter this side porch or this house. If you do, I will shoot you" (834). Smith, a very large and powerful man, much larger than Bailey, entered the door and was shot, subsequently dying of the wound. Joe Bailey was indicted, tried, and convicted of murder in the first degree. The jury relied on the trial court's instructions in reaching the verdict:

> If you believe . . . that Eugene H. Smith, attempted to enter the house of Joseph E. Bailey or his mother . . . and feloniously intended to assault or kill any of the inmates thereof, then you are instructed that the doctrine that every man's house is his own castle would apply. . . . But upon the other hand, if you believe that said Smith attempted to enter the house . . . to exercise a reasonable supervision and control over his wife and her conduct, then you are instructed that there is no self-defense in this case, and no justifiable killing. (834)

Bailey appealed his conviction, assigning numerous errors by the trial court. Justice Scott wrote the opinion for the Colorado Supreme Court on March 3, 1913, clearly indicating that the district court of the city and county of Denver had made egregious legal and moral errors in convicting Bailey. In a scathing commentary on the conduct of the deputy district attorney and the court being "unusual, uncalled for, and manifestly unfair, at least, if not reprehensible" (836–837), Justice Scott enumerated nine distinct violations of Bailey's rights under both constitutional and common law:

> [The trial court's] instructions are the equivalent of a denial of the very right of self-defense. . . . It strikes at the very foundation and sanctity of home life. . . . It would destroy the moral, constitutional, statutory, and

> common-law right of defense of habitation. Even more shocking . . . the jury are [*sic*] told that a husband . . . over the protest of the wife . . . has a right also to use such force . . . as may be necessary to cause the wife to leave the house of her mother and come back to his home with him, and that no person, not even her brother, has the right to interfere with . . . his force to secure the possession, control and abduction of the person of the wife, and all this as against her will, her fear and even the apparent danger of her life. . . . Such is not, and can never be, the law in a civilized country. (835)

Justice Scott reviewed case law from both England and the United States, concluding that there never was any process of law for seizing a wife at common law. Furthermore, he cites *Fulgham v. State*, 46 Ala. 143, that stated a wife is entitled "in person and in property, to the fullest protection of the laws. Her sex does not degrade her below the rank of the highest in the commonwealth" (835). Scott affirms the abrogation of the "rule of thumb" as stated in *State v. Oliver*, 70 N.C. 61: "Indeed, the courts have advanced from that barbarism until they have reached the position that the husband has no right to chastise his wife under any circumstances" (836). And citing *Commonwealth v. McAfee*, 108 Mass. 459, Justice Scott reiterates,

> Under modern legislation, as well as judicial opinions, that fiction of legal unity by which the separate existence of the wife in a legal sense is denied is exploded. Her person is as sacred as that of the husband. . . . To say that a court of law will recognize in the husband the power to compel the wife to obey his wishes, by force if necessary, is a relic of barbarism that has no place in an enlightened civilization. (836)

The Colorado Supreme Court concluded that Bailey's actions constituted justifiable homicide.

REVERSED AND REMANDED

Even though it took the Colorado Supreme Court until 1913 to render the *Bailey* decision, women in that state had already secured voting rights by the turn of the century, even before the passage of the Nineteenth Amendment in 1920. Women's suffrage was common in the West because it increased the population count and counterbalanced the more densely inhabited states of the East and South. The motivation was largely political, not progressive; a woman's vote was seen as an extension or doubling of her husband's vote. The social ideas of the day about the role of women were still in transition. There were conflicting notions of women's emerging rights and the assumed supremacy of husbands.

Laws about rape also demonstrate changing social ideas and conditions. Originally, rape laws were implemented in common law systems as a way to punish the assailant and to provide compensation to the raped woman's father, brother, or husband. Indeed, these early legal ideas about rape had more to do with the perceived violation of the victim's family than of the victim herself. Because women were the property of men, when women were violated, their husbands were violated. It is only recently that rape laws have recognized that women themselves are indeed the victims of the crime.

RACE AND THE SOCIAL CONTEXT OF LAW

The interrelationship between race and the law is still relevant in the United States. Historical and contemporary ideas about racial and ethnic inferiority, savagery, and inability have resulted in the passage of many pieces of legislation designed to keep people in an inferior position. While many racial and ethnic groups could be included in this discussion, for brevity and clarity we will focus on Native Americans and African Americans.

Native Americans

The attitude of the U.S. government toward Indians has been at best paternalistic, at worst savage. Two central facts need to be emphasized: the Indians discovered America, and they had developed a diverse set of societies and cultures long before Europeans arrived (McLemore and Romo, 1998:49). Among the earliest legal statements made by white Europeans about Native Americans was the Proclamation of 1763: (1) all land west of the crest of the Appalachian Mountains was "Indian country"; (2) any settlers west of the Appalachians who did not have legal title to their land from the Indians must return to the colonies; (3) all future land purchases from the Indians must be conducted in public with a representative of the king (pp. 322–323). This proclamation was further elaborated by the Northwest Territory Ordinance of 1787: "The utmost good faith shall always be observed toward the Indians; their lands and property shall never be taken from them without their consent; and their property, rights, and liberty, they shall never be invaded or disturbed, unless in just and lawful wars authorized by Congress" (Jackson and Galli, 1998:323). There is no reliable count of the just and lawful wars waged against Native Americans, and once ideologies such as Manifest Destiny took hold, the idea that Indians were *in the way* was at the forefront of federal policy.

As described in Chapter 4, a number of unique circumstances define the legal system as it pertains to Native Americans. First, there is no single, definable legal system since there are more than five hundred separate societies of indigenous peoples in the United States, each with distinct, complex sociopolitical, economic, and historical cultures. Tribal law refers to the philosophy of law within and among indigenous nations, tribes, and bands. U.S. Indian law, on the other hand, refers to the laws and legal interactions between Native Americans and the government.

Indian Law and Tribal Sovereignty Since the era of Chief Justice John Marshall, the Supreme Court has grappled with the doctrine of tribal sovereignty, that is, the right of indigenous nations to govern and rule their people with a degree of autonomy. According to the U.S. Constitution, the president is the only person who has the power to enter into treaties, and Congress has the power to regulate commerce with the Indian tribes. The Indian Commerce Clause (Article I, Section 8, clause 3) is the main source of federal power over the tribal nations; it has been used by Congress to recognize and define tribal sovereignty (Prygoski, 1995). Legislation was passed in 1871 that ended U.S. treaties with Indian tribes. Tribal sovereignty has become a critical issue for the Supreme Court, as it attempts to balance the rights of Native-American nations with the powers of the Congress and the president. Three significant cases, known as the *Marshall trilogy*, established the basis for interpreting federal Indian law and thereby defining tribal sovereignty (Prygoski, 1995: *Johnson v. McIntosh* [21 U.S. (8 Wheat.) 543 (1823)], *Cherokee Nation v. Georgia* [30 U.S. (5 Pet.) 1 (1831)], and *Worcester v. Georgia* [31 U.S. (6 Pet.) 515 (1832)].

In 1823, in *Johnson v. McIntosh*, Justice Marshall ruled that Indian tribes did not have the right to dispose of their land without the approval of the federal government. This ruling diminished the sovereignty of the tribes. In 1831, in *Cherokee Nation v. Georgia*, it was ruled that the Cherokee nation was not a "foreign state" and was therefore allowed to sue the state of Georgia. The Court ruled that Indian tribes were "domestic dependent nations," existing "in a state of pupilage." Underlying this ruling was the belief that tribes were not capable of handling their own affairs, and it was assumed that it was the responsibility of the federal government to protect them from state and local encroachments (Spicer, 1983). In 1832, *Worcester v. Georgia* established that the state of Georgia could not impose laws in Cherokee territory. This ruling established the principle that states cannot exercise regulatory or taxing jurisdiction on tribal land. Three basic principles arose from the Marshall trilogy (Prygoski, 1995):

1. Indian tribes possess some incidents of preexisting sovereignty.
2. Only the federal government could reduce or eliminate this sovereignty.
3. The United States imposed a trust responsibility on the tribes because of their limited inherent sovereignty and corresponding dependency.

These principles continue into modern times, guiding the Court in its decisions about the relationships between the tribes and the federal and state governments.

The Indian Removal Act of 1830 resulted in the mass relocation of Indian nations so that white Europeans could settle the lands east of the Mississippi River. This decade-long deportation resulted in what many Indians have called the "trail of tears." Because treaty making with the Indians was becoming ever more problematic and burdensome to the federal government, the Appropriations Act of 1871 ended that task. A rider to this act stated that all treaties with Indians currently in force would stand, but from then on all new arrangements between tribes and the federal government would be decided by Congress through legislation rather than through negotiation (McLemore and Romo, 1998:332)

A major change occurred with the passage of the Major Crimes Act by Congress in 1885 (18 U.S.C. 1153). This act, in response to the verdict in *Ex Parte Crow Dog* [109 U.S. 556 (1883)], defined seven major crimes that were removed from tribal responsibility and placed under the jurisdiction of the federal courts. Crow Dog had been convicted in a federal court of murdering another Indian on tribal land. The Court ruled that because of tribal sovereignty, the federal court did not have jurisdiction. To gain jurisdiction, tribal sovereignty must be specifically addressed by an act of Congress. Therefore, the Court overturned Crow Dog's conviction, and in 1885, Congress passed the Major Crimes Act.

The constitutionality of the Major Crimes Act was upheld in *U.S. v. Kagama* [118 U.S. 375 (1886)], a case in which two Indians were convicted of murdering another Indian on a reservation. The case centered on the issue of whether or not Congress had the power, through its right to regulate commerce, to pass the Major Crimes Act. The Court agreed that Congress did not have the power within the commerce regulation to impose this law; however, it ruled that the trust relationship between the federal government and the tribes gave Congress not only the power but also the duty to regulate tribal concerns. In the series of cases that have occurred between 1886 and today, the Court has continued to move away from the idea of intrinsic tribal sovereignty toward a view of tribal sovereignty as an entitlement given to tribes by Congress, which can be changed, expanded, or diminished by Congress.

In 1887, the General Allotment Act, also known as the Dawes Act, allocated to each Indian family a piece of land. The government established a blood quantum test, still in use today for some situations, to decide if a family was truly Indian; then, based on this evaluation, families were allotted plots of land for a twenty-year period. The U.S. government, influenced by, and a participant in, an ideology that espoused the inferiority and savagery of native peoples, used the Dawes Act to applaud its own kindness and generosity. Indians in the United States were not considered U.S. citizens until 1924. Previously, their legal status was nebulous as far as the U.S. government was concerned.

During the Great Depression, the Indian Reorganization Act (IRA), or Wheeler-Howard Act, of 1934, was implemented in response to calls for change in Indian and government relations. This act sought to assist Indians so they could "lead self-respecting, organized lives in harmony with their aims and ideals, as an integral part of American life" (McNickle, 1998:337). The IRA restored the right of Indian tribes to govern themselves as long as they adopted the American model of representative government. The act encouraged Indians to develop their native languages, renew their crafts, and revive their cultures.

In 1953, Congress adopted House Concurrent Resolution 108, which declared Indians free from any and all federal supervision and control. This policy, officially called "termination" (McLemore and Romo, 1998:337), was analogous to responses in years past, in which promises were made through treaties (see Chapter 1) that were rarely enforced. Instead, a series of acts was passed that whittled away at the rights of the Indian nations. Termination was meant to relieve the federal government of the dependency of tribal communities.

In response to tribal concerns, on April 24, 1994, in a White House memorandum to the heads of executive departments and agencies, President Clinton raised the issue of tribal sovereignty and the need to philosophically and procedurally address the needs of tribal communities in intergovernment relationships:

> The United States Government has a unique legal relationship with Native American tribal governments as set forth in the Constitution of the United States, treaties, statutes, and court decisions. As executive departments and agencies undertake activities affecting Native American tribal rights or trust resources, such activities should be implemented in a knowledgeable, sensitive manner respectful of tribal sovereignty.

President Clinton further stated that he was "strongly committed to building a more effective day-to-day working relationship reflecting respect for the rights of self-government due the sovereign tribal governments."

As mentioned earlier, many issues center on tribal sovereignty, from hunting and fishing rights to taxation, gambling, and adoptions. We will use the Indian Child Welfare Act of 1978 (ICWA) to illustrate one contemporary conflict.

Indian Child Welfare Act of 1978 (92 Stat. 3069, 25 U.S.C. §§ 1901–1963) In the 1970s, research by social scientists produced evidence that cross-racial adoptions and foster care placements were bad for the children involved. Indian children placed in non-Indian homes were not growing up in a culture that supported and taught the children's heritage. The U.S. Senate held oversight hearings in 1974, which produced an extensive volume of case histories, statistical analyses, and expert testimony concerning the large numbers of Indian children being removed from their tribal communities and Indian families. At the time, estimates indicated that 25 to 30 percent of all Indian children had been separated from their families at one time or another and placed with adoptive families, in foster care, or in other care institutions (Indian Child Welfare Program, 1974). A large proportion were placed in adoptive families, and tribal and parental rights were terminated.

During the 1974 hearings, statistics from the state of Minnesota revealed that one in eight Native-American children under the age of eighteen had been placed in adoptive homes. Of these, approximately 90 percent were placed in non-Indian homes. During 1971–1972, 25 percent of Indian infants were placed in adoptive homes. The rate of adoption of Indian children was eight times higher than the rate for non-Indian children.

Joseph Westermeyer, a social psychologist from the University of Minnesota, reported that adolescent Indian children who had been placed in non-Indian homes knew virtually nothing about their Indian culture or Indian behavior and had no viable Indian identity. In addition, members of the non-Indian communities believed that the Indian children did not belong there and used "derogatory name calling in relation to their racial identity" (Indian Child Welfare Program, 1974:46). "Society put on them an identity which they didn't possess, while taking from them the identity they did not possess" (p. 46).

Additional hearings were held in 1977 and 1978, focusing on the ethnocentrism inherent in the government agencies charged with child welfare and protective services (Hearing on Senate 1214, 1977, 1978). Calvin Isaac, tribal chief of the Mississippi Band of Choctaw Indians and a member of the National Tribal Chairman's Association, gave the following testimony at the 1978 hearings:

> One of the most serious failings of the present system is that Indian children are moved from the custody of their natural parents by non-tribal governmental authorities who have no basis for intelligently evaluating the cultural and social premises underlying Indian home life and childrearing. Many of the individuals who decide the fate of our children are at best ignorant of our cultural values, and at worst contemptful of the Indian way and convinced that removal, usually to a non-Indian household or institution, can only benefit an Indian child. (pp. 191–192)

According to Isaac, the removal of children from the tribal communities prevents them from transmitting their cultural heritage to new generations: "These practices seriously undercut the tribes' ability to continue as self-governing communities" (p. 193).

Following the hearings, the Indian Child Welfare Act of 1978 (ICWA) was passed. There are two primary objectives in the law. First, jurisdiction over the custody of children entitled to tribal membership and domiciled on tribally held lands was the exclusive province of the tribes. Second, when the tribe chose or circumstances compelled a state court to consider placement of an Indian child, it must conform to ICWA standards for placement in strict preferential order. Noting the importance of the extended family in tribal cultures and societies, Congress established the placement order as (1) extended family members of the child; (2) the tribe itself; and if a home could not be found in the tribe, (3) another Indian tribe. Congress also provided for mandatory notification of the tribe. Tribal rights to retain custody of the child took precedence over the rights of individual parents, who could terminate their own parental role but not that of the tribe.

Indian Gaming Regulatory Act In 1988, Congress passed the Indian Gaming Regulatory Act to define and control gambling on reservations. The Act referred to the tribes as sovereign nations, but then regulated almost all aspects of the industry on tribal land, further eroding tribal sovereignty. Full casino-type gambling on reservations is not possible without a compact with the state where the casino is located, which resulted in more state intervention in tribal affairs. Only a small number of tribes, those whose location is in proximity to populations of potential gamblers, are able to open viable commercial gambling sites. In order to bring money onto the reservation, the non-Native-American public must be invited onto the reservation. The price of gambling revenue is non-Native-American presence and influence on Native Americans who live on the reservation. Outside designers, contractors, and developers usually are needed to build the physical plant for gaming. A large-scale operation requires employees from outside the Native-American community, and some tribes hire non-Native-American companies to operate their casinos under tribal oversight.

The impact of casino revenues on reservations has been an increase in employment, improvements in reservation infrastructure, and a better standard of living for many Native Americans, but only for those communities who are able and willing to endure further non-Native-American encroachment into their cultures. The gaming buildings themselves represent acculturation; crowds of non-Native-American visitors bring with them the possibility of extensive and costly legal interaction with the outside in the form of claims and suits against the casino; factional differences over the distribution of wealth created by the casinos upset relationships within the community and contribute to the potential destruction of tribal values and institutions. Casino operations are undertaken generally by tribal communities already acculturated and proximate to mainstream U.S. society, while the more isolated and traditional bands are often left out. The more isolated communities are more likely to struggle with poverty and would most benefit from a large infusion of revenue, and they are the most resistant to cultural intrusion (Mezey, 1996).

Other forms of industry and commerce have been attempted on Native American land, with little success in most cases. Manufacturing jobs on the reservation require worker relocation and disrupt family ties. The pay usually is minimum wage, with little room for advancement, and no guarantee of continued employment, so there is small incentive to invite further encroachment on Native American sovereignty (Vinje, 1985).

One Native American group that is trying to bring industry to their land is the Goshutes tribe of Skull Valley Indian Reservation in Utah. Once a band of thousands who roamed the Great Basin, the Goshutes were forced into a tiny parcel of desert by Mormon settlers during the nineteenth century. Only 30 members of the community remain in Skull Valley. The reservation is surrounded by an Army nerve-gas test site, a hazardous-waste incinerator, a bombing range, a chemical-weapons destruction depot, and a magnesium plant that tops a list of the nation's biggest air polluters. Huge metal sheds for testing rocket engines sit empty on the reservation, testimony to an industrial project that didn't work. Nothing is left for the Goshutes except gaming, or radioactive-waste storage. Their plan, as explained by tribal chairman Leon Bear, is to turn a square mile of the reservation into storage space for used nuclear-reactor fuel. Jobs at the storage facility and lease payments from the storage company, Private Fuel Storage, will bring cash to the reservation, and may save the Goshutes tribe from extinction (Wolfson, 2000). The cost, however, is high, not only in terms of human health and ecological risk, but in turning a nominally sovereign dependent nation into just one more waste site in the Great Basin hazardous-industry zone.

The negative sociological impact of foreign encroachment on Native Americans cannot be minimized. Rich, vibrant cultures have been reduced to mementos in museums and shreds of oral history. As always, the conquerors' culture has supplanted that of the conquered. Although regret for the arrogant destruction of a different way of life is now stylish, it is doubtful that Native-American law, as practiced before colonization, ever will be practiced again.

Summary Generalizations concerning indigenous peoples in the United States are extremely difficult and prone to error. There are more than five hundred official U.S. tribal communities, all with unique cultural identities. Although, as always, social conditions, ideas, groups, and people will influence the law both within the tribal community and in the relationships between the tribe and the United States government, the unique legal and cultural dualism of tribal communities is a more complex and intricate model.

African Americans

African Americans also have been treated harshly by U.S. laws. According to Article I, Section 2, of the U.S. Constitution, blacks ("Negroes") in the United States were to be counted as three-fifths of a person for census purposes (this was called the Three-fifths Compromise and no longer holds true today). Attitudes about African Americans were clearly stated by the founders of the country. The first Africans were brought to this country as early as 1526, and many of them retained the status of indentured servant. However, within a few decades, individual states began to pass legislation that changed that status to slavery (e.g., Maryland in 1640; Massachusetts in 1641; Virginia in 1661). By the time the Declaration of Independence was signed, there were 600,000 slaves in the colonies (Rothenberg, 1988).

While the issue of slavery was important in the Civil War, the survival of the nation was crucial. Abraham Lincoln himself saw unification of the states as the central issue and favored deportation as the answer to the (so called) Negro problem. Even so, Lincoln signed the Emancipation Proclamation on January 1, 1863, and the slaves were freed (it also allowed them to enlist in the army). Shortly thereafter, the Civil War amendments to the Constitution (Thirteen, Fourteen, and Fifteen) were ratified (see Appendix), abolishing slavery, providing equal protection, and extending the vote to black men.

However, because ideas seldom change with the laws, *black codes* were passed by several southern legislatures. These were attempts to keep blacks in an inferior status by hindering their access to land and land ownership, curtailing their right to work and to hold apprenticeships, limiting their ability to move from state to state, and making criminal the appearance of vagrancy or unemployment (DuBois, 1988).

Congress's response to the black codes was the Civil Rights Act of 1866. Based on the Thirteenth Amendment and passed over President Johnson's veto, the act declared blacks to be citizens of the United States and gave them equal civil rights. The Ku Klux Klan, organized in 1866, attempted to force blacks back into their traditional servant or slave position. The Klan was also concerned with what it saw as the erosion of white political power (McLemore and Romo, 1998:263). As the Klan's activities became more terroristic, some states and the federal government responded by passing anti-Klan laws.

For many years, the primary conflicts between blacks and whites, particularly in the South, concerned the right to vote and the segregation of public transportation. Jim Crow laws were originally implemented to deal with these two issues but were eventually expanded to include schooling, housing, religion, jobs, the courts, recreation, and health care (McLemore and Romo, 1998:265). Although the Fifteenth Amendment extended the right to vote to black men, many southern legislatures attempted to block their votes. In 1890, the Mississippi legislature changed its voting requirements to keep blacks out of the voting booths, using literacy tests, poll taxes, and other ploys. Other states soon followed suit.

Perhaps the biggest blow to the freedom of blacks was the U.S. Supreme Court decision *Plessy v. Ferguson* (1896). *Plessy*, discussed in Chapter 1, implemented "separate but equal" institutions and reflected the strongly held racist attitudes that still existed in the country. *Plessy* was not overturned until six decades later by *Brown v. Board of Education* (1954). *Brown* declared the "separate but equal" notion illegal. The following decade brought an era of civil rights reform, which eradicated many forms of legal and social discrimination. Again, people, ideas, and social conditions influenced the laws.

SOCIAL CLASS AND THE SOCIAL CONTEXT OF LAW

The upper classes enjoy an advantage when dealing with the legal system in the United States. For example, the country's bail system is criticized because of its inherent class bias. Individuals who can afford to pay bail can get out of jail; those who can't, don't. This class distinction extends to the caliber of lawyers people are able to hire, such as the team of attorneys who defended O. J. Simpson.

The Sixth Amendment to the Constitution affords the right to counsel and jury trial to everyone, regardless of ability to pay. The case of *Gideon v. Wainwright* (1963) established the right to counsel for indigent defendants in state felony trials; in 1972, *Argersinger v. Hamlin* expanded the right to counsel for indigent defendants to all cases in which it was possible for the state to deprive an individual of his or her liberty, regardless of whether the case was a misdemeanor or a felony.

The case of Clarence Earl Gideon was particularly important to the Warren Court's (see Table 5–1) agenda in extending similar protections afforded to criminal defendants in federal courts to those being prosecuted in state courts. The case has been discussed in hundreds of legal essays; a major book, *Gideon's Trumpet* by Anthony Lewis (1964); and the 1979 Samuel Goldwin production of the same name, in which Henry Fonda portrayed Gideon. The romanticized portrayals of Gideon perhaps lent support for this particular Supreme Court decision, which never attracted the backlash experienced by both the *Mapp* and *Miranda* rulings in 1961 and 1966, respectively. Rights derived from these cases, the former extending the exclusionary rule to the states; the latter being the genesis of the Miranda warning, have experienced significant erosion over the course of two decades, since our society has apparently come to a consensus that the preferred response to rising crime rates is to *get tough* on criminals. Perhaps the distinction lies in the players themselves. Mapp had an apparent penchant for pornography, and Miranda was convicted of heinous crimes in his second trial. Neither was a particularly sympathetic figure, which caused rumblings that the liberal Warren Court was "letting criminals get off." But Clarence Earl Gideon was a bittersweet enigma, a petty career criminal who would not hurt a fly. We should recognize that by 1963 all but a handful of states had already provided counsel to indigent defendants. In addition, the attorneys general of twenty-eight states submitted amicus briefs on behalf of Gideon. Whatever the dynamics that shape the social response to Supreme Court rulings, *Gideon v. Wainwright* was a vital legal leap, perceived as a significant advancement in achieving parity for the poor.

As illustrated in Table 8–2, 74 percent of prisoners in state prisons charged with violent offenses were represented by assigned counsel. These figures increase to 85 percent for property offenses and 75 percent for public-order offenses. A higher percentage of blacks rely on assigned counsel than whites. Table 8–3 shows the number of white-collar crimes prosecuted

Gideon v. Wainwright 372 U.S. 337 (1963)

Clarence E. Gideon was a drifter who frequently supported himself either by gambling or, when the dice "ran cold," by occasional petty thefts. He never committed a violent act but had four prior felonies. Gideon was charged with breaking and entering into the Bay Harbor Pool Room in Panama City, Florida, with the *intent* of committing a misdemeanor. A peculiar provision of Florida statutory law enhanced the petty larceny crime to a felony offense. On August 4, 1961, Gideon was tried in the Bay County Circuit Court before Judge Robert L. McCrary, Jr. The defendant, in a colloquy that has been frequently cited in many contexts, asked the judge to appoint counsel for him because he didn't have any money to hire a lawyer. Judge McCrary explained that the state of Florida can only appoint indigent counsel when a capital crime is charged. "I'm sorry, but I will have to deny your request to appoint Counsel to defend you in this case" (336–337). The mild-mannered, fifty-one-year-old defendant, calmly informed the judge, "The United States Supreme Court says I am entitled to be represented by Counsel" (they hadn't, but they would) (337).

Gideon conducted his own defense before a jury, and perhaps because of prior experience on the "wrong side" of the bar, did "about as well as could be expected from a layman. He made an opening statement to the jury, cross-examined the State's witnesses, presented witnesses in his own defense, declined to testify himself, and made a short argument 'emphasizing his innocence to the charge contained in the Information filed in this case'" (337).

Despite his lay legal efforts, he was convicted of the crime charged and sentenced to five years in the state prison. Gideon filed a habeas corpus petition in the Florida Supreme Court, attacking his conviction and sentence on the ground that the trial court's refusal to appoint counsel denied him rights "guaranteed by the Constitution and the Bill of Rights by the United States Government" (337). In footnote 1, the observation is made that the petition for habeas corpus was signed and apparently prepared by the petitioner himself, who stated, "I, Clarence Earl Gideon, claim that I was denied the rights of the 4th, 5th, and 14th amendments of the Bill of Rights" (337). Although Gideon missed the fundamental Sixth Amendment right to counsel in his litany of amendments, he was nevertheless astute in mentioning the Fourteenth Amendment (the due process clause being the prime vehicle for incorporation of federal rights to state actions). After being denied any relief by the Florida Supreme Court, a petition was filed with the U.S. Supreme Court, who granted certiorari.

> Since 1942, when *Betts v. Brady*, 316 U. S. 455, was decided by a divided Court [always used as a foundation when a precedent is about to be overturned; i.e., less consensus means a less weighty decision], the problem of a defendant's federal constitutional right to counsel in a state court has been a continuing source of controversy and litigation in both state and federal courts. To give this problem another review here, we granted *certiorari.* Since Gideon was proceeding in forma pauperis, we appointed counsel to represent him. (337–338)

The counsel appointed to represent Gideon was Abe Fortas, who would soon be appointed to the Supreme Court. The move underscored the Court's resolve to overturn the *Betts* decision. Since Supreme Court case law can never be dismissed lightly, the Court's carefully structured language is particularly noteworthy. Justice Black wrote,

> Treating due process as a "concept less rigid and more fluid than those envisaged in other specific and particular provisions of the Bill of Rights," the Court held that refusal to appoint counsel under the particular facts and circumstances in the *Betts* case was not so "offensive to the common and fundamental ideas of fairness" as to amount to a denial of due process. Since the *facts* and *circumstances* of the two cases are *so nearly indistinguishable*, we think the *Betts v. Brady* holding *if left standing* would *require us to reject* Gideon's claim that the Constitution guarantees him the assistance of counsel. Upon full reconsideration we conclude that *Betts v. Brady* should be overruled. (339; emphasis added)

In conclusion Justice Black affirmed,

> In our adversary system of criminal justice, any person haled into court, who is too poor to hire a lawyer, cannot be assured a fair trial unless counsel is provided for him. . . . From the very beginning, our state and national constitutions and laws have laid great emphasis on procedural and substantive safeguards designed to assure fair trials before impartial tribunals in which every defendant stands equal before the law. This noble ideal cannot be realized if the poor man charged with crime has to face his accusers without a lawyer to assist him. (344)

REVERSED

in 1995. A simple comparison with the Index Offenses (described in Chapter 4) indicates that our criminal justice system is primarily geared toward prosecuting *traditional* crimes, that is, crimes more likely to be committed by individuals in poor and working-class environments, and less likely to prosecute white-collar crimes, the access to which requires a certain class standing.

SOCIAL CONTEXT OF THE DEATH PENALTY

Capital punishment is the most severe sentence possible for an individual who has been convicted of a crime. In the United States, the death penalty is reserved for only the most heinous crimes, usually some form of homicide. Ninety-four other countries and territories have some form of death penalty for ordinary crimes, which are crimes differentiated from military crimes or wartime crimes and include such offenses as rape or murder. Fifty-seven nations have abolished all uses of capital punishment, and fifteen additional nations use the death penalty only for military crimes or crimes committed in exceptional circumstances such as wartime (Doan, 1997). In the United States, the use and administration of the death penalty is determined by the individual states. Thirty-eight states have capital punishment statutes, although four of them have not imposed sentences. Each state determines its own method of execution. As illustrated in Table 8–1, lethal injection is the most frequent method of execution. Electrocution and lethal gas are also options in a number of states. Three states still list hanging as an option, and two states, Utah and Idaho, allow for a firing squad, as well as lethal injection.

The use of the death penalty varies greatly from state to state. Between 1977 and 1994, Texas executed more inmates (85) than any other state (Florida was the next highest, with 33 executions). During that same period, Texas sentenced 624 inmates to death (Florida sentenced 702 inmates), while Virginia sentenced 96 inmates.

In 1996 there were 3,122 inmates on death row and 328 have been executed in the United States since 1976 (NAACP Legal Defense Fund, 1996). This year is significant because in 1976 the Supreme Court ruled, in *Gregg v. Georgia*, that the death penalty was constitutional if applied in a fair and nonarbitrary manner. Since the death penalty has been reinstated, along with a number of due process protections to avoid its uneven application, the numbers increased to a peak of 56 executions in 1995. The United States has averaged 30 executions a year between 1990 and 1995.

Two key Supreme Court cases have shaped the nature and use of the death penalty in the United States. First, in *Furman v. Georgia* (1972), the Supreme Court temporarily curbed the death penalty by finding its application to be arbitrary and capricious. Justice Potter Stewart stated in his concurring opinion that the death penalty had been "wantonly and so freakishly imposed." In *Gregg v. Georgia* (1976), the Supreme Court narrowly defined the range of cases in which the death penalty could be imposed. According to James Acker, two structural legislative changes occurred after *Furman v. Georgia*:

1. Some crimes, such as rape, burglary, kidnapping, and robbery, were eliminated as capital offenses, and the range of criminal homicides that allowed for the death penalty was narrowed.
2. Capital trials became bifurcated (guilt v. punishment) in all jurisdictions. (Ryan, 1997:4)

The proceedings to determine guilt or innocence in a capital offense trial is separated from the sentencing proceedings, which can result in the imposition of the death penalty.

Since the 1972 decision in *Furman*, public opinion has been strongly in favor of the death penalty. Public support has never fallen below 57 percent, climbing to 66 percent in 1981 and reaching an all-time high of 80 percent in 1994 (Maguire and Pastore, 1995). Much support of the death penalty is related to perceptions of the criminal justice system as ineffective and slow. When asked in 1994, "In your view, what should be the penalty for murder—

TABLE 8–1 Methods of Execution by State, 1998

LETHAL INJECTION	ELECTROCUTION	LETHAL GAS	HANGING	FIRING SQUAD
Arizona[a,b]	Alabama	Arizona[a,b]	Delaware[a,c]	Idaho[a]
Arkansas[a,d]	Arkansas[a,d]	California[a]	New Hampshire[a,e]	Oklahoma[a,f]
California[a]	Florida	Missouri[a]	Washington[a]	Utah[a]
Colorado	Georgia	North Carolina[a]		
Connecticut	Kentucky[a,g]	Wyoming[a,h]		
Delaware[a,c]	Nebraska			
Idaho[a]	Ohio[a]			
Illinois	Oklahoma[a,f]			
Indiana	South Carolina[a]			
Kansas	Tennessee[a,i]			
Kentucky[a,g]	Virginia[a]			
Louisiana				
Maryland				
Mississippi				
Missouri[a]				
Montana				
Nevada				
New Hampshire[a,e]				
New Jersey				
New Mexico				
New York				
North Carolina[a]				
Ohio[a]				
Oklahoma[a,f]				
Oregon				
Pennsylvania				
South Carolina[a]				
South Dakota				
Tennessee[a,i]				
Texas				
Utah[a]				
Virginia[a]				
Washington[a]				
Wyoming[a,h]				

Note: The method of execution of Federal prisoners is lethal injection, pursuant to 28 CFR, Part 26. For offenses under the Violent Crime Control and Law Enforcement Act of 1994, the method is that of the State in which the conviction took place, pursuant to 18 USC 3596.

[a]Authorizes two methods of execution.

[b]Arizona authorizes lethal injection for persons whose capital sentence was received after Nov. 15, 1992; for those who were sentenced before that date, the condemned prisoner may select lethal injection or lethal gas.

[c]Delaware authorizes lethal injection for those whose capital offense occurred after June 13, 1986; for those whose offense occurred before that date, the condemned prisoner may select lethal injection or hanging.

[d]Arkansas authorizes lethal injection for those whose capital offense occurred after July 4, 1983; for those whose offense occurred before that date, the condemned prisoner may select lethal injection or electrocution.

[e]New Hampshire authorizes hanging only if lethal injection cannot be given.

[f]Oklahoma authorizes electrocution if lethal injection is ever held unconstitutional and firing squad if both lethal injection and electrocution are held unconstitutional.

TABLE 8–1 (continued)

[g]Kentucky authorizes lethal injection for persons whose capital sentence was received on or after Mar. 31, 1998; for those sentenced before that date, the condemned prisoner may select lethal injection or electrocution.

[h]Wyoming authorizes lethal gas if lethal injection is ever held unconstitutional.

[i]Tennessee authorizes lethal injection for those whose capital offense occurred after Dec. 31, 1998; for those whose offense occurred before that date, the condemned prisoner may select lethal injection or electrocution.

Source: K. Maguire and A. L. Pastore, eds., 1999. *Sourcebook of Criminal Justice Statistics 1998*, Table 6.96. *Sourcebook* source: U.S. Department of Justice, Bureau of Justice Statistics, Capital Punishment 1998, Bulletin NCJ-179012 (Washington, DC: U.S. Department of Justice, December 1999), p. 5, Table 3.

TABLE 8–2 State and Federal Prisoners with Assigned Counsel By Race and Offense, United States, 1994

PERCENT OF INMATES WITH COURT-ASSIGNED COUNSEL

	State			Federal		
Most serious offense	All[a]	White	Black	All[a]	White	Black
Number of prisoners	**675,659**	**334,165**	**317,889**	**52,485**	**33,228**	**16,508**
Violent offenses	**74%**	**71%**	**77%**	**72%**	**67%**	**75%**
Murder	**66**	**65**	**67**	**74**	**66**	**70**
Negligent manslaughter	**64**	**59**	**67**	[b]	[b]	[b]
Rape	**73**	**67**	**80**	[b]	[b]	[b]
Robbery	**81**	**80**	**82**	**82**	**83**	**81**
Assault	**78**	**73**	**82**	**63**	[b]	[b]
Property offenses	**85**	**83**	**88**	**53**	**44**	**70**
Burglary	**86**	**84**	**89**	**80**	[b]	[b]
Larceny	**85**	**82**	**88**	**62**	[b]	[b]
Motor vehicle theft	**89**	**87**	**93**	[b]	[b]	[b]
Drug offenses	**70**	**65**	**74**	**48**	**43**	**60**
Drug possession	**73**	**71**	**75**	**49**	**47**	**53**
Drug trafficking	**68**	**62**	**73**	**49**	**42**	**61**
Other drug	**73**	**52**	**83**	**45**	**36**	**59**
Public-order offenses	**75**	**72**	**78**	**55**	**50**	**63**
Weapon	**72**	**65**	**78**	**60**	**53**	**65**
Other	**75**	**74**	**79**	**49**	**47**	**57**
Other offenses	**83**	**81**	**84**	**45**	**39**	[b]

Note: Current offense data were available for 99.4 percent of state prisoners and 99.7 percent of federal prisoners who had legal representation for the offense for which they were serving time. These data do not include 2 percent of state and 3 percent of federal prisoners with counsel who used a combination of assigned and private counsel. Also excluded were those prisoners who said they did not have counsel. Table does not present all individual offense categories.

[a]Includes all races.

[b]Sample size was too small to yield statistically reliable results.

Source: U.S. Department of Justice, Bureau of Justice Statistics, Indigent Defense, Selected Findings NCJ-158909 (Washington, DC: U.S. Department of Justice, February 1996), p. 3, Table 4. U.S. Department of Justice, Executive Office for United States Attorneys, *United States Attorneys' Offices Statistical Report: Fiscal Year 1995* (Washington, DC: USGPO, 1996), p. 48.

TABLE 8–3 White-collar Crimes Prosecuted, 1995 (Criminal cases filed and disposed of and number of defendants handled by U.S. attorneys by offense type, United States, fiscal year 1995)

	CASES		DEFENDANTS		DISPOSITIONS				
Offense type	Filed[a]	Terminated[b]	Filed[c]	Terminated[d]	Guilty	Not guilty[e]	Dismissed[f]	Rule 20[g]	Other
White-collar crime									
Advance fee schemes[1]	123	95	234	194	170	1	11	12	0
Against business Institutions	548	449	832	672	601	8	38	24	1
Antitrust violations	17	26	19	32	26	3	2	1	0
Bank fraud and embezzlement	2,498	2,324	3,169	2,830	2,511	23	216	76	4
Bankruptcy fraud	158	126	182	153	126	2	23	2	0
Commodities fraud	10	9	14	10	9	0	0	1	0
Computer fraud	27	14	43	25	23	0	2	0	0
Consumer fraud	178	148	325	274	234	12	24	4	0
Federal procurement fraud	114	129	173	215	166	17	27	4	1
Federal program fraud	737	728	1,069	946	781	9	136	19	1
Health-care fraud	229	169	381	286	254	6	22	4	0
Insurance fraud	271	229	461	389	328	10	37	11	3
Other investment fraud	72	53	108	98	88	0	7	3	0
Securities fraud	103	62	154	113	102	3	7	1	0
Tax fraud	913	863	1,239	1,127	977	20	96	30	4
Other fraud	993	925	1,373	1,303	1,105	18	146	33	1
All other	3,849	3,663	4,952	4,629	3,646	91	772	100	20

Note: The U.S. attorney is the highest ranking law enforcement representative in each of the federal judicial districts. The attorney and staff members assist the U.S. attorney general in the enforcement of federal criminal laws, the investigation and prosecution of corrupt public officials and organized crime figures, and the initiation of environmental litigation. In addition, the U.S. attorney is responsible for the enforcement of laws pertaining to federal programs. These include violations involving Medicaid and Medicare, U.S. government contracts, the use of labor union funds, educational benefits for war veterans, and the food stamp program. The U.S. attorneys are responsible for collecting criminal fines, civil judgments, prejudgment claims, forfeitures, penalties, and other monies owed to the federal government. Beginning in fiscal year 1994, the category "bank robber" was eliminated, and these offenses are included in the "other violent crime" category. The fiscal year 1995 data presented are not comparable to previous years because of changes in offenses that make up several categories.

[a]Includes 615 cases initiated by transfer under Rule 20.

[b]Includes 572 cases terminated by transfer under Rule 20.

[c]Includes 654 defendants initiated by transfer under Rule 20.

[d]Includes 758 defendants terminated by transfer under Rule 20 (see footnote g) and 2 defendants dismissed because of superseding indictment or information.

[e]Includes 32 verdicts of not guilty by reason of insanity involving 38 defendants.

[f]Includes transfers, dismissals other than by court, pretrial diversions, and proceedings suspended indefinitely by court.

[g]Rule 20 of the Federal Criminal Rules permits the transfer of a case from one district to another for plea and sentencing. That is, if an offender is arrested in one district on an indictment or information originating in another district, the offender may plead guilty and be sentenced in the arresting district.

[1]Fraud against businesses or individuals involving the payment of a fee in advance for goods, services, or other things of value.

Source: U.S. Department of Justice, Executive Office for United States Attorneys, United States Attorneys' Offices Statistical Report: Fiscal Year 1995 (Washington, DC: USGPO, 1996), p. 48. Table adapted by SOURCEBOOK staff.

the death penalty or life imprisonment with absolutely no possibility of parole," 32 percent of the respondents favored imprisonment without parole and 50 percent favored the death penalty (Maguire and Pastore, 1995).

Illustrating the Intersection of Age, Race, Class, and Gender: The Death Penalty

The issues surrounding the *Furman* and *Gregg* cases have centered on the necessity to be consistent and nonarbitrary in the application of the death penalty. While one would hope that the imposition of such a severe penalty has undergone scrupulous review to be sure that no discriminatory factors have been involved, the issues are complex and inevitably reflect the diversity and bias inherent in society. Just as the law reflects the culture, people, and ideas of a society, the use of punishment also must be viewed in that context. Therefore, it would be unrealistic to assume that the biases and prejudices in society are somehow removed from the judicial system. Leigh Bienen (1997:4) stated, "It seems there is more uniformity in rhetoric than there is uniformity across jurisdictions."

Table 8–4 is a breakdown of the inmates who were under sentence of death between December 31, 1995 and December 31, 1998, in the United States. These data clearly indicate that men who are members of a minority group, have little education, are twenty-five to forty years of age, and have previous felony convictions are more likely to receive a death sentence.

TABLE 8–4 Demographic Characteristics of Prisoners under Sentence of Death on December 31, 1995–1998[a]

	1995 (%)	1996 (%)	1997 (%)	1998 (%)
Total number	3,054	3,219	3,335	3,452
Sex				
Male	98.4	98.5	98.7	98.6
Female	1.6	1.5	1.3	1.4
Race				
White	56.6	56.5	56.3	55.2
Black	41.7	41.9	42.2	43.0
Other	1.6	1.6	1.6	1.7
Ethnicity				
Hispanic	8.5	8.8	9.2	10.0
Non-Hispanic	91.5	91.2	90.8	90.0
Age[b]				
17 years or younger	0.0	[c]	0.0	0.0
18 to 19 years	0.8	0.5	0.4	0.4
20 to 24 years	9.7	8.7	8.2	7.7
25 to 29 years	16.1	14.9	14.9	15.0
30 to 34 years	20.9	18.5	17.3	16.9
35 to 39 years	21.6	21.8	21.8	20.6

TABLE 8–4 (continued)

	1995 (%)	1996 (%)	1997 (%)	1998 (%)
40 to 44 years	12.9	14.9	15.6	16.7
45 to 49 years	9.8	10.6	10.6	10.2
50 to 54 years	4.7	5.7	6.5	7.5
55 to 59 years	2.1	2.5	2.6	2.9
60 years and older	1.5	1.8	1.9	2.1
Education				
Grade 8 or less	14.7	14.4	14.2	14.3
Grades 9 to 11	37.2	37.5	37.6	37.6
High school graduate/GED	37.8	37.8	38.0	38.0
Any college	10.3	10.2	10.1	10.1
Marital status				
Married	25.6	24.9	24.5	24.0
Divorced or separated	21.6	21.8	21.8	20.8
Widowed	2.5	2.7	2.6	2.7
Never married	50.3	51.1	51.5	52.5
Prior felony conviction history				
Prior felony convictions	66.3	65.7	65.3	65.0
No prior felony convictions	33.7	34.3	34.7	35.0
Prior homicide conviction history				
Prior homicide conviction	[d]	8.6	8.6	8.6
No prior homicide conviction	[d]	91.4	91.4	91.4
Legal status at time of capital offense				
Charges pending	6.9	7.3	7.6	7.2
Probation	10.0	10.0	10.1	9.9
Parole	20.4	20.0	19.5	18.1
Prison escapee	1.6	1.4	1.3	1.3
Prison inmate	2.4	2.4	2.6	2.9
Other status	1.2	1.1	1.0	0.9
None	57.5	57.7	58.0	59.7

[a]Percents may not add to 100 because of rounding.

[b]The youngest person under sentence of death in 1996 was a Black male in Nevada, born in May, 1979, and sentenced to death in June, 1996. The youngest person under sentence of death in 1997 was a Black male in Alabama, born in November, 1979, and sentenced to death in October, 1997. The youngest person under sentence of death in 1998 was a Black male in Alabama, born in July, 1980, and sentenced to death in December, 1998. The oldest person under sentence of death during the years 1996 to 1998 was a white male in Arizona, born in September, 1915, and sentenced to death in June, 1983.

[c]Less than 0.1%

[d]Data on prior homicide convictions were not available for 1995.

Sources: Adapted from K. Maguire and A. L. Pastore, eds., *Sourcebook of Criminal Justice Statistics 1996*, Table 6.62. Table adapted by *Sourcebook* staff from U.S. Department of Justice, Bureau of Justice Statistics, "Capital Punishment 1995," Bulletin NCJ-162043 (Washington, DC: U.S. Department of Justice, December 1996), p. 8, Tables 6 and 7; p. 9, Table 8; U.S. Department of Justice, *Sourcebook of Criminal Justice Statistics 1999* (Washington, DC: Bureau of Justice Statistics), Table 6.84. Table adapted by *Sourcebook* staff from U.S. Department of Justice, Bureau of Justice Statistics, "Capital Punishment 1996," Bulletin NCJ–167081, p. 8, Table 7; p. 9: p. 10, Table 9; 1997 Bulletin NCJ–172881, p. 8, Table 7; p. 9; p. 10, Table 9; and 1998, Bulletin NCJ–179012, p. 8, Table 7; p. 7, p. 10, Table 9 (Washington, DC: U.S. Department of Justice).

Gender

Women are less likely to support the death penalty (74 percent) than men (80 percent) and are much less likely to be sentenced to death themselves. Of those on death row on December 31, 1994, only 1.4 percent were women. In 1998, forty-eight women awaited execution in prison. Following the brief respite in executions between 1968 and 1976, Margie Velma Barfield was the first woman to be executed. She was convicted in 1978 of first-degree murder for poisoning her fiancé. Later she admitted to killing three additional people, including her mother. She was executed on November 2, 1984, in North Carolina, the first woman to be executed in the United States since 1962 and the first in the post-*Gregg* period. A more detailed description of Margie Velma Barfield's case is seen in the brief on pages 185–186.

Since the Barfield execution, the number of women executed has slowly risen. Two women were executed in 1998, one in Texas and one in Florida. In 1998, women were awaiting execution in 17 states (see Table 8–5). California had ten women on Death Row, the most in any state. In 1997, there were 44 women awaiting execution. An additional eight received a death sentence in 1998, and four had their death sentences removed. Of these four, two were in Florida, one in New Jersey and one in Texas.

In her book, *Women Who Kill*, Ann Jones (1980) gives a historical account of women who have been convicted of murder in the United States.

TABLE 8–5 Women under Sentence of Death by State as of December 31, 1998

	NUMBER	%
Alabama	3	6.25
Arizona	1	2.1
Arkansas	1	2.1
California	10	20.8
Florida	4	8.3
Georgia	1	2.1
Idaho	1	2.1
Illinois	3	6.35
Indiana	1	2.1
Mississippi	1	2.1
Missouri	1	2.1
Nevada	1	2.1
North Carolina	3	6.25
Oklahoma	3	6.25
Pennsylvania	4	8.3
Tennessee	2	4.2
Texas	8	16.7
Total	48	100.1

Source: Adapted from U.S. Department of Justice, *Sourcebook of Criminal Justice Statistics 1999* (Washington, DC: Bureau of Justice Statistics), "Capital Punishment 1998," NCJ–179012 (Washington, DC: U.S. Department of Justice, December 1999), p. 7.

Barfield v. Woodard et al.
748 F. 2d 844 (U. S. Court of Appeals, 4th Cir., 1984)

Margie Velma Barfield was convicted on March 2, 1978, for the first-degree murder of her fiancé, Stuart Taylor, a Raleigh, N.C., tobacco planter. Margie confessed to police that she had poisoned Taylor when he threatened to expose her check forgery on his account in order to finance her long-standing addiction to Valium. She further admitted to killing three other people with poison, her mother and an elderly couple she had been hired to care for. A fifth homicide was suspected in the death of Barfield's former husband in 1969, although no charges were brought in any but Taylor's murder. Barfield's conviction was noteworthy in that she was a prolific offender relative to the normative profile of women who kill intimates. But the case of Margie Velma Barfield attracted national media frenzy because she was the first woman executed in the United States since 1962, and the first (and only as of 1997) in the post-*Gregg* [*Gregg v. Georgia*, 428 U.S. 153 (1976)] period, or "modern era" of capital punishment. The *Gregg* Court reaffirmed the constitutionality of the death penalty if states employed strictly defined procedural controls to avoid disparate imposition of sentences of death.

In accord with the Gregg ruling, North Carolina (as had most states seeking to salvage capital punishment) incorporated the Model Penal Code schema for finding at least one aggravating factor to a capital crime, as specifically enumerated by statute. The sentencing jury in Barfield's trial "found three aggravating circumstances: that the murder of Stuart Taylor (1) was committed for pecuniary gain; (2) was committed to hinder the enforcement of law; and (3) was especially heinous, atrocious or cruel" (845). Margie Barfield was originally scheduled for execution on February 9, 1979. Barfield appealed directly to the North Carolina Supreme Court [*State v. Barfield*, 298 N.C. 306 (1979)], raising fourteen issues as error. Included were (1) the admission into evidence of a bottle of rat poison and assorted allegedly forged checks; (2) denial of her motion to suppress the confessions she had given; (3) admission of expert testimony about the cause of death of Taylor, Edwards, Lee, and Jennings Barfield; and (4) the trial court's failure to submit the defense of insanity to the jury (846). Both the conviction and the sentence were affirmed by the North Carolina Supreme Court.

Although Margie had a relatively short appellate span of less than seven years (the mean is 11.8), her counsel left few appellate stones unturned. The case at bar before the Fourth Circuit Court of Appeals on the eve of her November 2, 1984, execution was the culmination of many direct and collateral legal actions (nine in state Superior Court, including six execution dates being set; twelve in U.S. District Court; fourteen in the N.C. Supreme Court; and seven petitions to the U. S. Supreme Court, and this case, the sixth in the federal circuit court). Appellate issues were expanded initially but distilled over time. The final issue to be resolved was whether Barfield had been competent to stand trial because of her ten-year addiction to prescription drugs. New scientific evidence had entered the medical literature in 1983, with withdrawal from drugs of the benzodiazepine family "B drugs" now being recognized as "interfering with a person's ability to appreciate and respond rationally to the circumstances of life" (850). Affidavits submitted by medical and pharmacological experts tended to support her request for an evidentiary hearing on her competence at the time of the original trial, but the circuit court nevertheless held that

> her conduct did not bespeak incompetence to stand trial in the legal sense. . . . When the petitioner's forecast of evidence is assessed in its best possible light . . . it simply fails to raise more than a basis for bald conjecture that if the withdrawal effects now claimed to have been discovered . . . did during the very period of her trial, and with the consequences that would establish constitutionally inadequate competence to stand trial. . . . Whatever her admittedly difficult emotional situation and possibly even somewhat impaired intellectual capacities, she was not legally incompetent to stand trial. Petitioner's claim of constitutional violation, raised at this late date, on the basis of so meager a body of inevitably disputable scientific opinion . . . simply does not suffice to require an evidentiary hearing . . . and not to justify a further stay. (851)

JUDGMENT AFFIRMED. APPLICATION FOR STAY DENIED.

Mere hours after the appeals court affirmed her conviction, Barfield's historic execution proceeded on schedule. According to the *New York Times*, November 2, 1984, she refused a final meal, instead opting to partake of "Coca-Cola and Cheeze Doodles" (A-14). Refusing to try further avenues of appeal available to her, she was strapped to a gurney, sporting pink pajamas and blue slippers. She died by lethal injection of toxins at 2:15 A.M. on November 2, 1984.

Using case histories, she illustrates that patriarchy and paternalism have characterized women's experiences in the courtroom. Women considered traditionally feminine were frequently patronized by the courts and given light sentences. Nontraditional women, particularly minority women, often received harsher sentences.

Age

In the United States there is a separate judicial system for juveniles, generally considered to be anyone under the age of eighteen. Because our criminal system requires those convicted of a crime to have mens rea, individuals must be capable of determining right from wrong and to be consciously aware of their behavior. Children, although often capable of committing the behavior, may not have a consciousness well enough formed to realize the full extent of their wrongdoing. Therefore, we have a juvenile justice system that is geared more toward rehabilitation than punishment. A juvenile, however, who commits a capital offense can be waived to adult court if it is shown that the juvenile's development is at a stage where he or she is capable of knowing the wrongfulness of the behavior.

This waiver to adult court often gives juveniles more due process and constitutional protections than are afforded in juvenile court, such as a jury

TABLE 8–6 Minimum Age for Waiver of Juveniles to Adult Criminal Court

STATES	YOUNGEST AGE BY STATE LAW
Alaska, Arizona, Maine, New Hampshire, Oklahoma, Rhode Island, South Dakota, Wyoming	None Specified
Montana	12
Georgia, Illinois, Mississippi, North Carolina	13
Alabama, California, Colorado, Connecticut, Delaware, Florida, Idaho, Indiana, Iowa, Kansas, Kentucky, Louisiana, Massachusetts, Minnesota, Missouri, New Jersey, North Dakota, Pennsylvania, South Carolina, Utah, Wisconsin	14
District of Columbia, Michigan, Ohio, Oregon, Texas, Washington	15
California,* Delaware, District of Columbia, Hawaii, Indiana, Kansas, Kentucky, Minnesota, Montana, Nevada, North Dakota, South Carolina, Tennessee, West Virginia, Wisconsin	16
Washington	17

*States that appear twice indicate different minimum ages for different types of offenses.
Source: Adapted from K. Maguire and A. L. Pastore, eds., *Sourcebook of Criminal Justice Statistics 1994.* Table 1.96.

trial. However, they also must face adult penalties, including the death penalty. Each state determines the minimum age at which a juvenile can be tried in an adult court and under what circumstances. Table 8–6 lists the minimum ages for waiver to adult criminal court by state. The conditions under which a juvenile can be waived to adult court vary by state. Most states reserve the process for more serious felony offenses, leaving most misdemeanors to be handled by the juvenile courts.

In *Stanford v. Kentucky* and *Wilkins v. Missouri* [109 S. Ct. 2969 (1989)], the Supreme Court upheld the constitutionality of the death penalty for sixteen- and seventeen-year-olds. For juveniles under the age of sixteen, the Court ruled in *Thompson v. Oklahoma* [208 S. Ct. 2687 (1988)] that the death penalty can be a viable sentence as long as it is specifically provided for by state statute. Table 8–7 shows also the minimum age and examples of restrictions for imposing the death sentence on juveniles.

In 1995, the youngest person under sentence of death was a white male from Nevada who was seventeen years old. The oldest person was a white male from Arizona who was sixty-eight years old. Forty-four percent of prisoners who are under sentence of death are between the ages of thirty and forty.

Race

African Americans are more likely than any other racial group in the United States to receive the death penalty. Of the 4,291 prisoners who were executed between 1930 and 1997, 2,016 were white, 2,228 were Black, and 47 were clas-

TABLE 8–7 Minimum Age for Imposition of Death Penalty

LOWEST AGE ALLOWED BY STATE LAW	STATES	EXAMPLES OF RESTRICTIONS
No age specified by state law	Arizona, Idaho, Louisiana, Montana, Pennsylvania, South Carolina, South Dakota, Utah	First-degree murder; aggravated kidnapping; treason
14	Arkansas	Felony murder; arson causing death; intentional murder; multiple murders; contract murders
15	Virginia	Murder during commission or attempts to commit specified felonies (abduction, armed robbery, rape, forcible sodomy)
16	Alabama, Delaware, Florida, Indiana, Kentucky, Mississippi, Missouri, Nevada, Oklahoma, Wyoming	Murder during kidnapping, robbery, rape, sodomy, burglary, sexual assault or arson; sexual battery on a child under age 12; murder by bomb or explosive; murder when the victim is a child who has been injured, tortured, or maimed
17	Georgia, New Hampshire, North Carolina, Texas	Murder; aircraft hijacking; treason; kidnapping for ransom when the victim dies; first-degree murder; murder of an individual under 6 years of age
18	California, Colorado, Connecticut, Illinois, Kansas, Maryland, Nebraska, New Jersey, New Mexico, Ohio, Oregon, Tennessee, Washington	First-degree murder; contract murder; aggravated murder, including assassination; aggravated first-degree premeditated murder

Source: Adapted from K. Maguire and A. L. Pastore, eds., *Sourcebook of Criminal Justice Statistics 1995,* Table 1.103.

sified as "Other." According to the NAACP Legal Defense and Educational Fund, Inc., 3,671 individuals were imprisoned under sentence of death in the United States on April 1, 2000. Whites accounted for 1,698, Blacks 1,574, Hispanics 321, Native Americans 47, and Asians 31. Whereas African Americans represent 12.9 percent of the overall U.S. population, they account for 43 percent of the executions. Table 8–8 compares the percentages by race of those executed between 1930 and 1997; those under sentence of death as of April 1, 2000; and the overall population of the United States as of July 1, 2000.

TABLE 8–8 Comparison of Death Row Inmates by Race, 2000

RACE	PERCENT EXECUTED BETWEEN 1930[a] AND 1997	PERCENT UNDER SENTENCE OF DEATH APRIL 1, 2000	PROJECTED PERCENT OF OVERALL U.S. POPULATION JULY 1, 2000
White	46.98	46.25 (n = 1,698)	82.12
Black	51.92	42.88 (n = 1,574)	12.91
Other	1.10	10.87 (n = 399)	4.97

[a]There were no executions from 1968 through 1976.

Sources: Adapted from U.S. Department of Justice, 2000, *Sourcebook of Criminal Justice Statistics 1999* (Washington, DC: Bureau of Justice Statistics), Tables 6.83 and 6.95. *Sourcebook* sources: U.S. Department of Justice, Bureau of Justice Statistics, *Correctional Populations in the United States, 1997*, NCJ–127613 (Washington, DC: U.S. Department of Justice, 2000), Table 7.26; NAACP Legal Defense and Educational Fund, Inc. "Death Row, U.S.A.: Spring 2000," New York: NAACP Legal Defense and Educational Fund, Inc. 2000 (mimeograph), pp. 1, 23, 24; U.S. Bureau of the Census, *Statistical Abstract of the United States: 1999*, Table No. 12.

There is much debate as to whether the application of the death penalty is racially discriminatory. Some scholars, such as James Coleman, argue that the criminal justice system is both racist and discriminatory (Ryan, 1997). The more frequent imposition of the death penalty on African Americans is seen as a reflection of the belief of U.S. citizens that African Americans deserve more severe punishment and are, in general, more threatening to the public. Coleman argues that "there is no such thing as a race neutral decision in the criminal justice system, when it affects black people and when their voice is not part of the discussion leading to the decision" (Ryan, 1997:6).

Supporters of the system argue that the behavior of the individuals involved determines the use of the death sentence and that it is not an intrinsic problem. David Baldus states that the data, which reflect the higher proportion of blacks receiving the death sentence, are misleading (Ryan, 1997). He makes the methodological argument that, when researchers control for other variables, the influence of race declines: "At best, these data are suggestive, and experience indicates that when the disparities in death sentencing rates are adjusted for legitimate case characteristics, unadjusted race disparities usually, but not always, decline" (Ryan, 1997:7).

While the arguments on both sides are certain to continue, it is clear that the controversy raises many issues related to the fair and nondiscriminatory implementation of the death penalty. The American Bar Association has called for a moratorium on the death penalty, in order to gain some perspective on the issue. Resolution 107 "calls upon jurisdictions that have capital punishment to refrain from its use until greater fairness and due process are assured" (Harris, 1997:2).

Social Class

Social class differences also determine the probability that an individual will receive the death penalty. Leigh Beinen argues that class standing and economic discrimination are key factors, weighing more heavily than all others in producing an unjust system: "I would also argue that the class and economic discrimination affecting the death penalty are 'worse,' in the sense of being more unjust, than the racial elements" (Ryan, 1997:7). Sister Helen Prejean (1993), author of *Dead Man Walking*, argues that the death penalty is a poor man's sentence and that, in fact, there are no rich men on death row.

Education plays an important role in determining one's class standing. As illustrated in Table 8–4, 62.0 percent of prisoners under sentence of death in 1998 had not completed high school nor had they passed the high school equivalency exam. This figure compares with 19.1 percent of the general population. With an overall lack of education and generally low incomes, the ability of individuals to obtain an adequate and fair criminal defense in a case that involves a death sentence is extremely limited.

CONCLUSION

We have used the death penalty to illustrate some of the themes developed throughout this book. In the social context of law, nothing stands in isolation. From development of laws through implementation and punishment, the culture of our society plays an important role in defining justice.

It is apparent that variables which affect our chances of success in this society, such as age, gender, race, and class, also influence our chances of facing a death sentence. At each of our life stages, these variables play a role and shape our opportunities—or lack of opportunities. For example, if an individual is born into poverty, his or her opportunity for higher education, adequate health and nutrition, and appropriate socialization may be limited. This person will have to deal with the circumstances of his or her birth throughout adult life. Chances and opportunities for adults are often expanded or limited by one's childhood opportunities, which are affected by race, gender, and class. Therefore, in analyzing how death sentences are applied to individuals in a society, we must first look at the complex cultural context for an accurate portrayal of the issues.

The social conditions of our times help to shape and define the legal structure. The controversies surrounding the death sentence, its constitutionality, its arbitrary use, and its potential for deterrence, are all reflections of the issues that permeate society at large. The desire for a fair and just system is often at odds with public opinion and the biases in the social structure. However, reflection of these biases in the application of the death penalty is of particular concern because it is the most extreme use of coercive force by the state.

Appendix The Constitution of the United States

WE THE PEOPLE of the United States, in Order to form a more perfect Union, establish justice, insure domestic Tranquility, provide for the common defence, promote the general Welfare, and secure the Blessings of Liberty to ourselves and our Posterity, do ordain and establish this Constitution for the United States of America.

ARTICLE I

Section 1. All legislative Powers herein granted shall be vested in a Congress of the United States, which shall consist of a Senate and House of Representatives.

Section 2. The House of Representatives shall be composed of Members chosen every second Year by the People of the several States, and the Electors in each State shall have the Qualifications requisite for Electors of the most numerous Branch of the State Legislature.

No Person shall be a Representative who shall not have attained to the Age of twenty five Years, and been seven Years a Citizen of the United States, and who shall not, when elected, be an inhabitant of that State in which he shall be chosen.

Representatives and direct Taxes shall be apportioned among the several States which may be included within this Union, according to their respective Numbers, which shall be determined by adding to the whole Number of free Persons, including those bound to Service for a Term of Years, and excluding Indians not taxed, three fifths of all other Persons. The actual Enumeration shall be made within three Years after the first Meeting of the Congress of the United States, and within every subsequent Term of ten Years, in such Manner as they shall by Law direct. The Number of

Representatives shall not exceed one for every thirty Thousand, but each State shall have at Least one Representative; and until such enumerations shall be made, the State of New Hampshire shall be entitled to chuse three, Massachusetts eight, Rhode-island and Providence Plantations one, Connecticut five, New-York six, New Jersey four, Pennsylvania eight, Delaware one, Maryland six, Virginia ten, North Carolina five, South Carolina five, and Georgia three.

When vacancies happen in the Representation from any State, the Executive Authority thereof shall issue Writs of Election to fill such Vacancies.

The House of Representatives shall chuse their speaker and other Officers; and shall have the sole Power of impeachment.

Section 3. The Senate of the United States shall be composed of two Senators from each State, chosen by the Legislature thereof, for six Years; and each Senator shall have one vote.

Immediately after they shall be assembled in Consequence of the first Election, they shall be divided as equally as may be into three Classes. The Seats of the Senators of the first Class shall be vacated at the Expiration of the second Year, of the second Class at the Expiration of the fourth Year, and of the third Class at the Expiration of the sixth Year, so that one third may be chosen every second Year; and if Vacancies happen by Resignation, or otherwise, during the Recess of the Legislature of any State, the Executive thereof may make temporary Appointments until the next Meeting of the Legislature, which shall then fill such Vacancies.

No Person shall be a Senator who shall not have attained to the Age of thirty Years, and been nine Years a Citizen of the United States, and who shall not, when elected, be an Inhabitant of that State for which he shall be chosen.

The Vice President of the United States shall be President of the Senate, but shall have no Vote, unless they be equally divided.

The Senate shall chuse their other Officers, and also a President pro tempore, in the Absence of the Vice President, or when he shall exercise the Office of President of the United States.

The Senate shall have the sole Power to try all Impeachments. When sitting for that Purpose, they shall be on Oath or Affirmation. When the President of the United States is tried, the Chief Justice shall preside: And no Person shall be convicted without the concurrence of two thirds of the Members present. Judgment in Cases of Impeachment shall not extend further than to removal from Office, and disqualification to hold and enjoy any Office of honor, Trust or Profit under the United States: but the Party convicted shall nevertheless be liable and subject to Indictment, Trial, Judgment and Punishment, according to law.

Section 4. The Times, Places and Manner of holding Elections for Senators and Representatives, shall be prescribed in each State by the Legislature thereof; but the Congress may at any time by Law make or alter such Regulations, except as to the Places of chusing Senators.

The Congress shall assemble at least once in every Year, and such Meeting shall be on the first Monday in December, unless they shall by Law appoint a different Day.

Section 5. Each House shall be the Judge of the Elections, Returns and Qualifications of its own Members, and a Majority of each shall constitute a Quorum to do business; but a smaller Number may adjourn from day to day, and may be authorized to compel the Attendance of absent Members, in such Manner, and under such Penalties as each House may provide.

Each House may determine the Rules of its Proceedings, punish its Members for disorderly Behaviour, and, with the Concurrence of two thirds, expel a Member.

Each House shall keep a journal of its Proceedings, and from time to time publish the same, excepting such Parts as may in their judgment require Secrecy; and the yeas and Nays of the Members of either House on any question shall, at the Desire of one fifth of those Present, be entered on the journal.

Neither House, during the Session of Congress, shall, without the Consent of the other, adjourn for more than three days, nor to any other place than that in which the two Houses shall be sitting.

Section 6. The Senators and Representatives shall receive a Compensation for their Services, to be ascertained by Law, and paid out of the Treasury of the United States. They shall in all Cases, except Treason, Felony and Breach of the Peace, be privileged from Arrest during their Attendance at the Session of their respective Houses, and in going to and returning from the same; and for any Speech or Debate in either House, they shall not be questioned in any other Place.

No Senator or Representative shall, during the Time for which he was elected, be appointed to any civil Office under the Authority of the United States, which shall have been created, or the Emoluments whereof shall have been encreased during such time; and no Person holding any Office under the United States, shall be a Member of either House during his Continuance in Office.

Section 7. All Bills for raising Revenue shall originate in the House of Representatives; but the Senate may propose or concur with Amendments as on other Bills.

Every Bill which shall have passed the House of Representatives and the Senate, shall, before it become a Law, be presented to the President of the United States; if he approve he shall sign it, but if not he shall return it, with his Objections to that House in which it shall have originated, who shall enter the Objections at large on their journal, and proceed to reconsider it. If after such Reconsideration two thirds of that House shall agree to pass the Bill, it shall be sent, together with the Objections, to the other House, by which it shall likewise be reconsidered, and if approved by two thirds of that House, it shall become a Law. But in all such Cases the Votes of both Houses shall be determined by yeas and Nays, and the Names of the Persons voting for and against the Bill shall be entered on the Journal of each House respectively. If any Bill shall not be returned by the President within ten Days (Sundays excepted) after it shall have been presented to him, the Same shall be a Law, in like Manner as if he had signed it, unless the Congress by their Adjournment prevent its Return, in which Case it shall not be a Law.

Every Order, Resolution, or Vote to which the Concurrence of the Senate and House of Representatives may be necessary (except on a question of Adjournment) shall be presented to the President of the United States; and before the Same shall take Effect, shall be approved by him, or being disapproved by him, shall be repassed by two thirds of the Senate and House of Representatives, according to the Rules and Limitations prescribed in the Case of a Bill.

Section 8. The Congress shall have Power To lay and collect Taxes, Duties, Imposts and Excises, to pay the Debts and provide for the common Defence and general Welfare of the United States; but all duties, Imposts and Excises shall be uniform throughout the United States;

To borrow Money on the Credit of the United States;

To regulate Commerce with foreign Nations, and among the several States, and with the Indian Tribes;

To establish an uniform Rule of Naturalization, and uniform Laws on the subject of Bankruptcies throughout the United States;

To coin Money, regulate the Value thereof, and of foreign Coin, and fix the Standard of Weights and Measures;

To provide for the Punishment of counterfeiting the Securities and current Coin of the United States;

To establish Post Offices and post Roads;

To promote the Progress of Science and useful Arts, by securing for limited Times to Authors and Inventors exclusive Right to their respective Writings and Discoveries;

To constitute Tribunals inferior to the supreme Court;

To define and punish Piracies and Felonies committed on the high Seas, and Offences against the Law of Nations;

To declare War, grant Letters of Marque and Reprisal, and make rules concerning Captures on Land and Water;

To raise and support Armies, but no Appropriation of Money to that Use shall be for a longer Term than two Years;

To provide and maintain a Navy;

To make rules for Government and Regulation of the land and naval Forces;

To provide for calling forth the Militia to execute the Laws of the Union, suppress Insurrections and repel Invasions;

To provide for organizing, arming, and disciplining, the Militia, and for governing such Part of them as may be employed in the Service of the United States, reserving to the States respectively, the Appointment of the Officers, and the Authority of training the Militia according to the discipline prescribed by Congress;

To exercise exclusive Legislation in all Cases whatsoever, over such District (not exceeding ten Miles square), as may, by Cession of particular States, and the Acceptance of Congress, become the Seat of the Government of the United States, and to exercise like Authority over all Places purchased by the Consent of the Legislature of the State in which the Same shall be for the Erection of Forts, Magazines, Arsenals, dock-Yards, and other needful Buildings;-And

To make all Laws which shall be necessary and proper for carrying into Execution the foregoing Powers, and all other Powers vested by this Constitution in the Government of the United States, or in any Department or Officer thereof.

Section 9. The Migration or Importation of such Persons as any of the States now existing shall think proper to admit, shall not be prohibited by the Congress prior to the Year one thousand eight hundred and eight, but a Tax or duty may be imposed on such Importation, not exceeding ten dollars for each Person.

The Privilege of the Writ of Habeas Corpus shall not be suspended, unless when in Cases of Rebellion or Invasion the public Safety may require it.

No Bill of Attainder or ex post facto Law shall be passed.

No Capitation, or other direct, Tax shall be laid, unless in Proportion to the Census or Enumeration herein before directed to be taken.

No Tax or Duty shall be laid on Articles exported from any State.

No Preference shall be given by any Regulation of Commerce or Revenue to the Ports of one State over those of another: nor shall Vessels bound to, or from, one State, be obliged to enter, clear, or pay Duties in another.

No money shall be drawn from the Treasury, but in Consequence of Appropriations made by Law; and a regular Statement and Account of the Receipts and Expenditures of all public Money shall be published from time to time.

No Title of Nobility shall be granted by the United States: And no Person holding any Office of Profit or Trust under them, shall, without the Consent of the Congress, accept of any present, Emolument, Office, or Title, of any kind whatever, from any King, Prince, or foreign State.

Section 10. No State shall enter into any Treaty, Alliance, or Confederation; grant Letters of Marque and Reprisal; coin Money; emit Bills of Credit; make any Thing but gold and silver Coin a Tender in Payment of Debts; pass any Bill of Attainder, ex post facto Law, or Law impairing the Obligation of Contracts, or grant any Title of Nobility.

No State shall, without the Consent of the Congress, lay any Imposts or Duties on Imports or Exports, except what may be absolutely necessary for executing its inspection Laws: and the net Produce of all Duties and Imposts, laid by any State on Imports or Exports, shall be for the Use of the Treasury of the United States; and all such Laws shall be subject to the Revision and Controul of the Congress.

No State shall, without the Consent of Congress, lay any Duty of Tonnage, keep Troops, or Ships of War in time of Peace, enter into any Agreement or Compact with another State, or with a foreign Power, or engage in War, unless actually invaded, or in such imminent Danger as will not admit of delay.

ARTICLE II

Section 1. The executive Power shall be vested in a President of the United States of America. He shall hold his Office during the Term of four Years, and, together with the Vice President, chosen for the same term, be elected, as follows

Each State shall appoint, in such Manner as the Legislature thereof may direct, a Number of Electors, equal to the whole Number of Senators and Representatives to which the State may be entitled in the Congress: but no Senator or Representative, or Person holding an Office of Trust or Profit under the United States, shall be appointed an Elector.

The Electors shall meet in their respective States, and vote by Ballot for two Persons, of whom one at least shall not be an Inhabitant of the same State with themselves. And they shall make a List of all the Persons voted for, and of the Number of Votes for each; which List they shall sign and certify, and transmit sealed to the Seat of the Government of the United States, directed to the President of the Senate. The President of the Senate shall, in the Presence of the Senate and House of Representatives, open all the Certificates, and the Votes shall then be counted. The Person having the greatest Number of Votes shall be the President, if such Number be a Majority of the whole Number of Electors appointed; and if there be more than one who have such Majority, and have an equal Number of Votes, then the House of Representatives shall immediately chuse by Ballot one of them for President: and if no Person have a Majority, then from the five highest on the List the said House shall in like Manner chuse the President. But in chusing the President, the Votes shall be taken by States, the Representation from each State having one Vote; A quorum for this Purpose shall consist of a Member or Members from two thirds of the States, and a Majority of all the States shall be necessary to a Choice. In every Case, after the Choice of the President, the Person having the greatest Number of Votes of the Electors shall be the Vice President. But if there should remain two or more who have equal Votes, the Senate shall chuse from them by Ballot the Vice President.

The Congress may determine the Time of chusing the Electors, and the Day on which they shall give their Votes; which Day shall be the same throughout the United States.

No Person except a natural born Citizen, or a Citizen of the United States, at the time of the Adoption of this Constitution, shall be eligible to the office of President; neither shall any Person be eligible to that Office who shall not have attained to the Age of thirty five Years, and been fourteen Years a Resident within the United States.

In Case of the Removal of the President from Office, or of his Death, Resignation, or Inability to discharge the Powers and Duties of the said Office, the Same shall devolve on the Vice President, and the Congress may by Law provide for the Case of Removal, Death, Resignation or Inability, both of the President and Vice President, declaring what Officer shall then act as President, and such Officer shall act accordingly, until the Disability be removed, or a President shall be elected.

The President shall, at stated Times, receive for his Services, a Compensation, which shall neither be encreased nor diminished during the Period for which he shall have been elected, and he shall not receive within that Period any other Emolument from the United States, or any of them.

Before he enter on the Execution of his Office, he shall take the following Oath or Affirmation:-"I do solemnly swear (or affirm) that I will faithfully execute the Office of President of the United States, and will to the best of my Ability, preserve, protect and defend the Constitution of the United States."

Section 2. The President shall be Commander in Chief of the Army and Navy of the United States, and of the Militia of the several States, when called into the actual Service of the United States, he may require the Opinion, in writing, of the principal Officer in each of the executive Departments, upon any Subject relating to the Duties of their respective Offices, and he shall have the Power to grant Reprieves and Pardons for Offences against the United States, except in Cases of Impeachment.

He shall have Power, by and with the Advice and Consent of the Senate to make Treaties, provided two thirds of the Senators present concur; and he shall nominate, and by and with the Advice and Consent of the Senate, shall appoint Ambassadors, other public Ministers and Consuls, Judges of the supreme Court, and all other Officers of the United States, whose Appointments are not herein otherwise provided for, and which shall be established by Law: but the Congress may by Law vest the Appointment of such inferior Officers, as they think proper, in the President alone, in the Courts of Law, or in the Heads of Departments.

The President shall have Power to fill up all Vacancies that may happen during the Recess of the Senate, by granting Commissions which shall expire at the End of their next Session.

Section 3. He shall from time to time give to the Congress Information of the State of the Union, and recommend to their Consideration such Measures as he shall judge necessary and expedient; he may, on extraordinary Occasions, convene both Houses, or either of them, and in Case of Disagreement between them, with Respect to the Time of Adjournment, he may adjourn them to such Time as he shall think proper; he shall receive Ambassadors and other public Ministers; he shall take Care that the Laws be faithfully executed, and shall Commission all the Officers of the United States.

Section 4. The President, Vice President and all civil Officers of the United States, shall be removed from Office on Impeachment for, and Conviction of, Treason, Bribery, or other High Crimes and Misdemeanors.

ARTICLE III

Section 1. The judicial Power of the United States, shall be vested in one supreme Court, and in such inferior Courts as the Congress may from time to time ordain and establish. The Judges, both the supreme and inferior Courts, shall hold their Offices during good Behaviour, and shall, at stated Times, receive for their Services, a Compensation, which shall not be diminished during their Continuance in Office.

Section 2. The judicial Power shall extend to all Cases, in Law and Equity, arising under this Constitution, the Laws of the United States, and Treaties made, or which shall be made, under their Authority;—to all Cases affecting Ambassadors, other public Ministers and Consuls;—to all Cases of admiralty and maritime Jurisdiction;—to Controversies to which the United States shall be a Party;—to Controversies between two or more States; *between a State and Citizens of another State;*—between Citizens of different States;—between Citizens of the same State claiming Lands under Grants of different States, and between a State, or the Citizens thereof, and foreign States, Citizens, or Subjects.

In all Cases affecting Ambassadors, other public Ministers and Consuls, and those in which a State shall be Party, the supreme Court shall have original Jurisdiction. In all the other Cases before mentioned, the supreme Court shall have appellate Jurisdiction, both as to Law and Fact, with such Exceptions, and under such Regulations as Congress shall make.

The Trial of all Crimes, except in Cases of Impeachment, shall be by Jury; and such Trial shall be held in the State where the said Crimes shall have been committed; but when not committed within any State, the Trial shall be at such Place or Places as the Congress may by Law have directed.

Section 3. Treason against the United States, shall consist only in levying War against them, or in adhering to their Enemies, giving them Aid and Comfort. No Person shall be convicted of Treason unless on the Testimony of two Witnesses to the same overt Act, or on Confession in open Court.

The Congress shall have Power to declare the Punishment of Treason, but no Attainder of Treason shall work Corruption of Blood, or Forfeiture except during the Life of the Person attainted.

ARTICLE IV

Section 1. Full Faith and Credit shall be given in each State to the public Acts, Records, and judicial Proceedings of every other State. And the Congress may by general Laws prescribe the Manner in which such Acts, Records and Proceedings shall be proved, and the Effect thereof.

Section 2. The Citizens of each State shall be entitled to all Privileges and Immunities of Citizens in the several States.

A Person charged in any State with Treason, Felony, or other Crime, who shall flee from justice, and be found in another State, shall on Demand of the executive Authority of the State from which he fled, be delivered up, to be removed to the State having jurisdiction of the Crime.

No person held to Service or Labour in one State, under the Laws thereof, escaping into another, shall, in Consequence of any Law or Regulation therein, be discharged from such Service or Labour, but shall be delivered up on Claim of the Party to whom such Service or Labour may be due.

Section 3. New States may be admitted by the Congress into this Union; but no new State shall be formed or erected within the jurisdiction of any other State; nor any State be formed by the junction of two or more States, or Parts of States, without the Consent of the Legislatures of the States concerned as well as of the Congress.

The Congress shall have Power to dispose of and make all needful Rules and Regulations respecting the Territory or other Property belonging to the United States; and nothing in this Constitution shall be so construed as to Prejudice any Claims of the United States, or of any particular State.

Section 4. The United States shall guarantee to every State in this Union a Republican Form of Government, and shall protect each of them against Invasion; and on Application of the Legislature, or of the Executive (when the Legislature cannot be convened) against domestic Violence.

ARTICLE V

The Congress, whenever two thirds of both Houses shall deem it necessary, shall propose Amendments to this Constitution, or, on the Application of the Legislatures of two thirds of the several States, shall call a Convention for proposing Amendments, which, in either Case, shall be valid to all Intents and Purposes, as Part of this Constitution, when ratified by the Legislatures of three fourths of the several States, or by Conventions in three fourths thereof, as the one or the other Mode of Ratification may be proposed by the Congress; Provided that no Amendment which may be made prior to the Year One thousand eight hundred and eight shall in any Manner affect the first and fourth Clauses in the Ninth Section of the first Article; and that no State, without its Consent, shall be deprived of its equal Suffrage In the Senate.

ARTICLE VI

All Debts contracted and Engagements entered into, before the Adoption of this Constitution, shall be as valid against the United States under this Constitution, as under the Confederation.

This Constitution, and the Laws of the United States which shall be made in Pursuance thereof, and all Treaties made, or which shall be made, under the Authority of the United States, shall be the supreme Law of the Land; and the Judges In every State shall be bound thereby, any Thing In the Constitution or Laws of any State to the Contrary notwithstanding.

The Senators and Representatives before mentioned, and the Members of the several State Legislatures, and all executive and judicial Officers, both of the United States and of the several States, shall be bound by Oath or Affirmation, to support this Constitution; but no religious Test shall ever be required as a Qualification to any Office or public Trust under the United States.

ARTICLE VII

The Ratification of the Conventions of nine States, shall be sufficient for the Establishment of this Constitution between the States so ratifying the Same.

done in Convention by the Unanimous Consent of the States present the Seventeenth Day of September in the Year of our Lord one thousand seven hundred and Eighty seven and of the Independence of the United States of America the Twelfth *In witness whereof We have hereunto subscribed our Names,*

	G, Washington-Presid[t]
	and deputy from Virginia
New Hampshire	John Langdon
	Nicholas Gilman
Massachusetts	Nathaniel Gorham
	Rufus King
Connecticut	W[m] Sam! Johnson
	Roger Sherman
New York	Alexander Hamilton
New Jersey	Wil: Livingston
	David Brearley.
	W[m] Paterson.
	Jona: Dayton
Pennsylvania[1]	B Franklin
	Thomas Miff lin
	Rob[t] Morris
	Geo. Clymer
	Thom FitzSimons
	Jared Ingersoll
	James Wilson
	Gouv Morris
Delaware	Geo Read
	Gunning Bedford jun
	John Dickinson
	Richard Bassett
	Jaco: Broom
Maryland	James McHenry
	Dan of S[t] Tho! Jenifer
	Dan[l] Carroll
Virginia	John Blair-
	James Madison Jr.
North Carolina	W[m] Blount
	Rich[d] Dobbs Spaight.
	Hu Williamson
South Carolina	J. Rutledge
	Charles Cotesworth Pinckney
	Charles Pinckney
	Pierce Butler.
Georgia	William Few
	Abr Baldwin

1. Spelled with one *n* on the original document.

AMENDMENTS

[*The first ten amendments were ratified December 15, 1791, and form what is known as the Bill of Rights.*]

AMENDMENT 1

Congress shall make no law respecting an establishment of religion, or prohibiting the free exercise thereof, or abridging the freedom of speech, or of the press; or the right of the people peaceably to assemble, and to petition the Government for a redress of grievances.

AMENDMENT 2

A well regulated Militia, being necessary to the security of a free State, the right of the people to keep and bear Arms, shall not be infringed.

AMENDMENT 3

No Soldier shall, in time of peace be quartered in any house, without the consent of the Owner, nor in time of war, but in a manner to be prescribed by law.

AMENDMENT 4

The right of the people to be secure in their persons, houses, papers, and effects, against unreasonable searches and seizures, shall not be violated, and no Warrants shall issue, but upon probable cause, supported by Oath or affirmation, and particularly describing the place to be searched, and the persons or things to be seized.

AMENDMENT 5

No person shall be held to answer for a capital, or otherwise infamous crime, unless on a presentment or indictment of a Grand Jury, except in cases arising in the land or naval forces, or in the Militia, when in actual service in time of War or public danger; nor shall any person be subject for the same offence to be twice put in jeopardy of life or limb; nor shall be compelled in any criminal case to be a witness against himself, nor be deprived of life, liberty, or property, without due process of law; nor shall private property be taken for public use, without just compensation.

AMENDMENT 6

In all criminal prosecutions, the accused shall enjoy the right to a speedy and public trial, by an impartial jury of the State and district wherein the crime shall have been committed, which district shall have been previously ascertained by law, and to be informed of the nature and cause of the accusation; to be confronted with the witnesses against him; to have compulsory process for obtaining witnesses in his favor, and to have the Assistance of Counsel for his defence.

AMENDMENT 7

In Suits at common law, where the value in controversy shall exceed twenty dollars, the right of trial by jury shall be preserved, and no fact tried by a jury, shall be otherwise re-examined in any Court of the United States, than according to the rules of the common law.

AMENDMENT 8

Excessive bail shall not be required, nor excessive fines imposed, nor cruel and unusual punishments inflicted.

AMENDMENT 9

The enumeration in the Constitution, of certain rights, shall not be construed to deny or disparage others retained by the people.

AMENDMENT 10

The powers not delegated to the United States by the Constitution, nor prohibited by it to the States, are reserved to the States respectively, or to the people.

AMENDMENT 11 *(RATIFIED FEBRUARY 7, 1795)*

The Judicial power of the United States shall not be construed to extend to any suit in law or equity, commenced or prosecuted against one of the United States by Citizens of another State, or by Citizens or Subjects of any Foreign State.

AMENDMENT 12 *(RATIFIED JULY 27, 1804)*

The Electors shall meet in their respective states, and vote by ballot for President and Vice-President, one of whom, at least, shall not be an inhabitant of the same state with themselves; they shall name in their ballots the person voted for as President, and in distinct ballots the person voted for as Vice-President, and they shall make distinct lists of all persons voted for as President, and of all persons voted for as Vice-President, and of the number of votes for each, which lists they shall sign and certify, and transmit sealed to the seat of the government of the United States, directed to the President of the Senate;-The President of the senate shall, in the presence of the Senate and House of Representatives, open all the certificates and the votes shall then be counted;-The person having the greatest number of votes for President, shall be the President, if such number be a majority of the whole number of Electors appointed; and if no person have such majority, then from the persons having the highest numbers not exceeding three on the list of those voted for as President, the House of Representatives shall choose immediately, by ballot, the President. But in choosing the President, the votes shall be taken by states, the representation from each state having one vote; a quorum for this purpose shall consist of a member or members from two-thirds of the states, and a majority of all the states shall be necessary to a choice. And if the House of Representatives, shall not choose a President whenever the right of choice shall devolve upon them, before the fourth day of March next following, then the Vice-President shall act as President, as in the case of the death or other constitutional disability of the President.-The person having the greatest number of votes as Vice-President, shall be the Vice-President, if such number be a majority of the whole number of Electors appointed, and if no person have a majority, then from the two highest numbers on the list, the Senate shall choose the Vice-President; a quorum for the purpose shall consist of two-thirds of the whole number of Senators, and a majority of the whole number shall be necessary to a choice. But no person constitutionally ineligible to the office of President shall be eligible to that of Vice-President of the United States.

AMENDMENT 13 *(RATIFIED DECEMBER 6, 1865)*

Section 1. Neither slavery nor involuntary servitude, except as a punishment for crime whereof the party shall have been duly convicted, shall exist within the United States, or any place subject to their jurisdiction.

Section 2. Congress shall have power to enforce this article by appropriate legislation.

AMENDMENT 14 *(RATIFIED JULY 9, 1868)*

Section 1. All persons born or naturalized in the United States, and subject to the jurisdiction thereof, are citizens of the United States and of the State wherein they reside. No State shall make or enforce any law which shall abridge the privileges or immunities of citizens of the United States; nor shall any State deprive any person of life, liberty, or property, without due process of law; nor deny to any person within its jurisdiction the equal protection of the laws.

Section 2. Representatives shall be apportioned among the several States according to their respective numbers, counting the whole number of persons in each State, excluding Indians not taxed. But when the right to vote at any election for the choice of electors for President and Vice President of the United States, Representatives in Congress, the Executive and judicial officers of a State, or the members of the Legislature thereof, is denied to any of the male inhabitants of such State, being twenty-one years of age, and citizens of the United States, or in any way abridged, except for participation in rebellion, or other crime, the basis of representation therein shall be reduced in the proportion which the number of such male citizens shall bear to the whole number of male citizens twenty-one years of age in such State.

Section 3. No person shall be a Senator or Representative in Congress, or elector of President and Vice President, or hold any office, civil or military, under the United States, or under any State, who, having previously taken an oath, as a member of Congress, or as an officer of the United States, or as a member of any State legislature, or as an executive or judicial officer of any State, to support the Constitution of the United States, shall have engaged in insurrection or rebellion against the same, or given aid or comfort to the enemies thereof. But Congress may by a vote of two-thirds of each House, remove such disability.

Section 4. The validity of the public debt of the United States, authorized by law, including debts incurred for payment of pensions and bounties for services in suppressing insurrection or rebellion, shall not be questioned. But neither the United States nor any State shall assume or pay any debt or obligation incurred in aid of insurrection or rebellion against the United States, or any claim for the loss or emancipation of any slave; but all such debts, obligations and claims shall be held illegal and void.

Section 5. The Congress shall have power to enforce, by appropriate legislation, the provisions of this article.

AMENDMENT 15 *(RATIFIED FEBRUARY 3, 1870)*

Section 1. The right of citizens of the United States to vote shall not be denied or abridged by the United States or by any State on account of race, color, or previous condition of servitude.

Section 2. The Congress shall have power to enforce this article by appropriate legislation.

AMENDMENT 16 *(RATIFIED FEBRUARY 3, 1913)*

The Congress shall have power to lay and collect taxes on incomes, from whatever source derived, without apportionment among the several States, and without regard to any census or enumeration.

AMENDMENT 17 *(RATIFIED APRIL 8, 1913)*

The Senate of the United States shall be composed of two Senators from each State, elected by the people thereof for six years; and each Senator shall have one vote. The electors in each State shall have the qualifications requisite for electors of the most numerous branch of the State legislatures.

When vacancies happen in the representation of any State in the Senate, the executive authority of such State shall issue writs of election to fill such vacancies: *Provided,* That the legislature of any State may empower the executive thereof to make temporary appointments until the people fill the vacancies by election as the legislature may direct.

This amendment shall not be so construed as to affect the election or term of any Senator chosen before it becomes valid as part of the Constitution.

AMENDMENT 18 *(RATIFIED JANUARY 16, 1919. REPEALED DECEMBER 5, 1933 BY AMENDMENT 21)*

Section 1. After one year from the ratification of this article the manufacture, sale, or transportation of intoxicating liquors within, the importation thereof into, or the exportation thereof from the United States and all territory subject to the jurisdiction thereof for beverage purposes is hereby prohibited.

Section 2. The Congress and the several States shall have concurrent power to enforce this article by appropriate legislation.

Section 3. This article shall be inoperative unless it shall have been ratified as an amendment to the Constitution by the legislatures of the several States as provided in the Constitution, within seven years from the date of the submission hereof to the States by the Congress.

AMENDMENT 19 *(RATIFIED AUGUST 18, 1920)*

The right of citizens of the United States to vote shall not be denied or abridged by the United States or by any State on account of sex.

Congress shall have power to enforce this article by appropriate legislation.

AMENDMENT 20 *(RATIFIED JANUARY 23, 1933)*

Section 1. The terms of the President and Vice President shall end at noon on the 20th day of January, and the terms of Senators and Representatives at noon on the 3d day of January, of the years in which such terms would have ended if this article had not been ratified; and the terms of their successors shall then begin.

Section 2. The Congress shall assemble at least once in every year, and such meeting shall begin at noon on the 3d day of January, unless they shall by law appoint a different day.

Section 3. If, at the time fixed for the beginning of the term of the President, the President elect shall have died, the Vice President elect shall become President. If a President shall not have been chosen before the time fixed for the beginning of his term, or if the President elect shall have failed to qualify, then the Vice President elect shall act as President until a President shall have qualified; and the Congress may by law provide for the case wherein neither a President elect nor a Vice President elect shall have qualified, declaring who shall then act as President, or the manner in which one who is to act shall be elected, and such person shall act accordingly until a President or Vice President shall have qualified.

Section 4. The Congress may by law provide for the case of the death of any of the persons from whom the House of Representatives may choose a President whenever the right of choice shall have devolved upon them, and for the case of the death of any of the persons from whom the Senate may choose a Vice President whenever the right of choice shall have devolved upon them.

Section 5. Sections 1 and 2 shall take effect on the 15th day of October following the ratification of this article.

Section 6. This article shall be inoperative unless it shall have been ratified as an amendment to the Constitution by the legislatures of three-fourths of the several States within seven years from the date of its submission.

AMENDMENT 21 *(RATIFIED DECEMBER 5, 1933)*

Section 1. The eighteenth article of amendment to the Constitution of the United States is hereby repealed.

Section 2. The transportation or importation into any State, Territory, or possession of the United States for delivery or use therein of intoxicating liquors, in violation of the laws thereof, is hereby prohibited.

AMENDMENT 22 *(RATIFIED FEBRUARY 27, 1951)*

Section 1. No person shall be elected to the office of the President more than twice, and no person who has held the office of President, or acted as President, for more than two years of a term to which some other person was elected President shall be elected to the office of the President more than once. But this Article shall not apply to any person holding the office of President when this Article was proposed by the Congress, and shall not prevent any person who may be holding the office of President, or acting as President, during the term within which this Article becomes operative from holding the office of President or acting as President during the remainder of such term.

Section 2. This article shall be inoperative unless it shall have been ratified as an amendment to the Constitution by the legislatures of three-fourths of the several States within seven years from the date of its submission to the States by the Congress.

AMENDMENT 23 *(RATIFIED MARCH 29, 1961)*

Section 1. The District constituting the seat of Government of the United States shall appoint in such manner as the Congress may direct:

A number of electors of President and Vice President equal to the whole number of Senators and Representatives in Congress to which the District would be entitled if it were a State, but in no event more than the least populous State; they shall be in addition to those appointed by the States, but they shall be considered, for the purposes of the election of President and Vice President, to be electors appointed by a State; and they shall meet in the District and perform such duties as provided by the twelfth article of amendment.

Section 2. The Congress shall have power to enforce this article by appropriate legislation.

AMENDMENT 24 *(RATIFIED JANUARY 23, 1964)*

Section 1. The right of citizens of the United States to vote in any primary or other election for President or Vice President, for electors for President or Vice President, or for Senator or Representative in Congress, shall not be denied or abridged by the United States or any State by reason of failure to pay any poll tax or other tax.

Section 2. The Congress shall have power to enforce this article by appropriate legislation.

AMENDMENT 25 *(RATIFIED FEBRUARY 10, 1967)*

Section 1. In case of the removal of the President from office or of his death or resignation, the Vice President shall become President.

Section 2. Whenever there is a vacancy in the office of the Vice President, the President shall nominate a Vice President who shall take office upon confirmation by a majority vote of both Houses of Congress.

Section 3. Whenever the President transmits to the President pro tempore of the Senate and the Speaker of the House of Representatives his written declaration that he is unable to discharge the powers and duties of his office, and until he transmits to them a written declaration to the contrary, such powers and duties shall be discharged by the Vice President as Acting President.

Section 4. Whenever the Vice President and a majority of either the principal officers of the executive departments or of such other body as Congress may by law provide, transmit to the President pro tempore of the Senate and the Speaker of the House of Representatives their written declaration that the President is unable to discharge the powers and duties of his office, the Vice President shall immediately assume the powers and duties of the office as Acting President.

Thereafter, when the President transmits to the President pro tempore of the Senate and the Speaker of the House of Representatives his written declaration that no inability exists, he shall resume the powers and duties of his office unless the Vice President and a majority of either the principal officers of the executive department or of such other body as Congress may by law provide, transmit within four days to the President pro tempore of the Senate and the Speaker of the House of Representatives their written declaration that the President is unable to discharge the powers and duties of his office. Thereupon Congress shall decide the issue, assembling within forty-eight hours for that purpose if not in session. If the Congress, within twenty-one days after receipt of the latter written declaration, or, if Congress is not in session, within twenty-one days after Congress is required to assemble, determines by two-thirds vote of both Houses that the President is unable to discharge the powers and duties of his office, the Vice President shall continue to discharge the same as Acting President; otherwise, the President shall resume the powers and duties of his office.

AMENDMENT 26 *(RATIFIED JULY 1, 1971)*

Section 1. The right of citizens of the United States, who are eighteen years of age or older, to vote shall not be denied or abridged by the United States or by any State on account of age.

Section 2. The Congress shall have the power to enforce this article by appropriate legislation.

AMENDMENT 27 *(RATIFIED MAY 7, 1992)*

No law, varying the compensation for the services of the Senators and Representatives, shall take effect, until an election of Representatives shall have intervened.

References

ABADINSKY, H. 1995. *Law and Justice: An Introduction to the American Legal System*, 3rd ed. Chicago: Nelson-Hall.

———. 1991. *Law and Justice: An Introduction to the American Legal System*, 2nd ed. Chicago: Nelson-Hall.

AICHELLE, G. J. 1989. *Oliver Wendell Holmes, Jr.* Old Tappan, NJ: Scribner.

ALTSCHULER, B. E., and C. A. SGROI. 1996. *Understanding Law in a Changing Society*, 2nd ed. Upper Saddle River, NJ: Prentice Hall.

ANDERSON, J. E., D. W. BRADY, and C. BULLOCK III. 1978. *Public Policy and Politics in America*. North Scituate, MA: Duxbury Press.

BECCARIA, C. 1963. *Essays on Crimes and Punishments*. Translated, with an introduction by Henry Paolucci. Indianapolis, IN: Bobbs-Merrill.

BEDAU, H. A., ed. 1997. *The Death Penalty in America: Current Controversies*. New York: Oxford University Press.

BENTHAM, J. 1789. *An Introduction to the Principles of Morals and Legislation*. New York: Oxford University Press.

BERMAN, H. J., and W. R. GREINER. 1972. *The Nature and Functions of Law*. Mineola, NY: Foundations Press.

BLACK, D. J. 1983, February. "Crime as Social Control." *American Sociological Review* 48, 34–42.

———. *The Behavior of Law*. 1976. New York: Academic Press.

———. 1970, August. "Production of Crime Rates." *American Sociological Review*, pp. 1–16.

BLACK, H. C., and J. NOLAN, 1990. *Black's Law Dictionary: Definitions of the Terms and Phrases of American and English Jurisprudence, Ancient and Modern*, 6th ed. St. Paul: West Publishing.

BLACKSTONE, W. 1993. "Commentaries on the Laws of England, 1765–1769." In *The Law of Sex Discrimination*, 2nd ed. Eds. J. R. Lindgren and N. Taub. Eagan, MN: West Publishing.

BODENHEIMER, E. 1974. *Jurisprudence, the Philosophy and Method of the Law*. Cambridge, MA: Harvard University Press.

BORRICAND, J. 1997. "France." In *World Factbook of Criminal Justice Systems*. Eds. G. Newman, A. C. Bouloukos, and D. Cohen. http://www.ojp.usdoj.gov/pub/bjs/ascii/ufbcjfra.txt.

BRINKERHOFF, D., L. WHITE, and S. ORTEGA. 1995. *Essentials of Sociology*, 3rd ed. Minneapolis/St. Paul: West Publishing.

———. 1992. *Essentials of Sociology*, 2nd ed. St. Paul: West Publishing.

BURGER, CHIEF JUSTICE W. E. (Chairman). 1976. *Foreward to [a special printing of] The United States Constitution*. Washington, DC: Commission on the Bicentennial of the United States Constitution.

BURTON, S. 1985. *An Introduction to Law and Legal Reasoning*. Boston: Little, Brown.

CHARON, J. 1996. *The Meaning of Sociology*, 5th ed. Upper Saddle River, NJ: Prentice Hall.

DAHL, D. 1995. "The Gamble that Paid Off." *ABA Journal*. May: 86–89.

DELORIA, V., ed. 1985. *American Indian Policy in the Twentieth Century*. Norman: University of Oklahoma Press.

Dictionary of Occupational Titles, 4th ed. 1989. Washington, DC: U.S. Department of Labor.

DOAN, B. 1997, Spring. "Death Penalty Policy, Statistics, and Public Opinion." *Focus on Law Studies* 12(2), 3.

DUBOIS, W. E. B. 1988. "The Black Codes." In *Racism and Sexism: An Integrated Study*. Ed. P. S. Rothenberg. New York: St. Martin's Press.

DURKHEIM, E. [1897] 1951. *Suicide*. Glencoe, IL: Free Press.

———. [1893] 1947. *The Division of Labor in Society*. Glencoe, IL: Free Press.

DUSKY, L. 1996. *Still Unequal: The Shameful Truth about Women and Justice in America*. New York: Crown Publishers.

EHRLICH, E. 1936/1975. *Fundamental Principles of the Sociology of Law*. New York: Arno Press.

EISENBERG, M. S. 1995. "The Nature of the Common Law." In H. Abadinsky, *Law and Justice: An Introduction to the American Legal System*, 3rd ed. Chicago: Nelson-Hall.

EISENSTEIN, J., and H. JACOB. 1977. *Felony Justice: An Organizational Analysis of Criminal Courts*. Boston: Little, Brown.

EVAN, W. 1965. "Law as an Instrument of Social Change." In *Applied Sociology: Opportunities and Problems*. Eds. A. W. Gouldner and S. M. Miller. New York: Free Press. Pp. 285–293.

FAIRCHILD, E. 1993. *Comparative Criminal Justice Systems*. Belmont, CA: Wadsworth.

FRIEDMAN, L. M. 1977. *Law and Society: An Introduction*. Upper Saddle River, NJ: Prentice Hall.

FULLER, L. 1969. *The Morality of Law*. New Haven, CT: Yale University Press.

———. 1968. *The Anatomy of Law*. New York: Praeger.

GARDNER, T. J. 1989. *Criminal Law: Principles and Cases*, 4th ed. St. Paul: West Publishing.

GIFIS, S. H. 1975. *Law Dictionary*. Woodbury, NY: Barron's Educational Series.

GLOVER, J. 1990. *Utilitarianism and Its Critics*. Old Tappan, NJ: Macmillan.

GOEHLERT, R. 1979. *Congress and Law Making: Researching the Legislative Process*. Santa Barbara, CA: Clio Books.

GOLDING, M. P. 1975. *Philosophy of Law*. Upper Saddle River, NJ: Prentice Hall.

GOLDMAN, S., and A. SARAT, eds. 1989. *American Court Systems: Readings in Judicial Process and Behavior*, 2nd ed. New York: Longman.

HARRING, S. L. 1994. *Crow Dog's Case: American Indian Sovereignty, Tribal Law, and the United States Law in the Nineteenth Century*. Cambridge: Cambridge University Press.

HARRIS, L. 1997. "The ABA Calls for a Moratorium on the Death Penalty: The Task Ahead—Reconciling Justice With Politics." *Focus on Law Studies*, 12(2) (Spring), p. 2.

HARRISON, R. 1983. *Bentham*. London: Routledge and Kegan Paul.

Hearings on Senate 1214. 1977. Senate Select Committee on Indian Affairs, 95th Congress, 1st Session.

———. 1978. Subcommittee on Indian Affairs and Public Lands of the House Committee on Interior and Insular Affairs, 95th Congress, 2nd Session.

HEINZ, J. P., and E. O. LAUMANN. 1994. *Chicago Lawyers: The Social Structure of the Bar*, rev. ed. Evanston, IL, and Chicago: Northwestern University Press and American Bar Association.

HEMMENS, C. 1997. "Entries for the Historical Dictionary of American Indian Civil Rights." Unpublished paper submitted to the Historical Dictionary of American Indian Civil Rights.

HOLMES, O. W., Jr. 1897. "The Path of the Law." *Harvard Law Review* 10(1), 457–478.

———. 1961. *The Concept of Law*. Oxford: Clarendon Press.

———. 1881/1963. *The Common Law*. Boston: Little, Brown.

Indian Child Welfare Program. 1974. Hearings before the Subcommittee on Indian Affairs of the Senate Committee on Interior and Insular Affairs, 93rd Congress, 2nd Session, 3.

JACKSON, C. E., and M. J. GALLI. 1998. "A History of the Bureau of Indian Affairs and Its Activities Among Indians." In *Racial and Ethnic Relations in America*, 5th ed. Eds. S. D. McLemore and H. D. Romo. Boston: Allyn and Bacon.

JONES, A. [1980] 1996. *Women Who Kill.* Boston: Beacon Press.
KATSCH, M. E. 1995. *Taking Sides: Clashing Views on Controversial Legal Issues,* 6th ed. Guilford, CT: Dushkin Publishing.
KELSEN, H. 1970. *The Pure Theory of Law.* Berkeley: University of California Press.
KROHN, M., J. CURRY, and S. NELSON-KILGER. 1983. "Is Chivalry Dead? An Analysis of Changes in Police Dispositions of Males and Females." *Criminology,* pp. 417–437.
LEWIS, A. 1964. *Gideon's Trumpet.* Birmingham, AL: Legal Classics Library.
LLOYD, D. 1976. *The Idea of Law.* Baltimore: Penguin.
MACIONIS, J. J. 1996. *Sociology: The Basics,* 3rd ed. Upper Saddle River, NJ: Prentice Hall.
MACKINNON, K. 1993. "Toward Feminist Jurisprudence." In *Feminist Jurisprudence.* Ed. P. Smith. New York: Oxford University Press.
MAGUIRE, K., and A. L. PASTORE, eds. 1999. *Sourcebook of Criminal Justice Statistics 1998.* U.S. Department of Justice, Bureau of Justice Statistics. Washington, DC: USGPO.
———. 1997. *Sourcebook of Criminal Justice Statistics 1996.* Washington, DC: USGPO.
———. 1995. *Sourcebook of Criminal Justice Statistics 1994.* Washington, DC: USGPO.
———. 1994. *Sourcebook of Criminal Justice Statistics 1993.* U.S. Department of Justice, Bureau of Justice Statistics. Washington, DC: USGPO.
MAINE, SIR H. S. 1861. *Ancient Law.* London: J. Murray.
MCLEAN, E. B. 1992. *Law and Civilization: The Legal Thought of Rosco Pound.* Lanham, MD: University Press of America.
MCLEMORE, S. D., and H. D. ROMO. 1998. *Racial and Ethnic Relations in America,* 5th ed. Needham Heights, MA: Allyn and Bacon.
MCNICKLE, D. 1998. "Native American Tribalism." In *Racial and Ethnic Relations in America,* 5th ed. Eds. S. D. McLemore and H. D. Romo. Needham Heights, MA: Allyn and Bacon.
MEZEY, N. 1996. "The Distribution of Wealth, Sovereignty, and Culture through Indian Gaming." *Stanford Law Review.* Feb.: 711–737.
MILL, J. S. 1863/1971. *Utilitarianism.* Indianapolis, IN: Bobbs-Merrill.
MILOVANOVIC, D. 1988. *A Primer in the Sociology of Law.* New York: Harrow and Heston.
MIROFF, B., R. SEIDELMAN, and T. SWANSTROM. 1995. *The Democratic Debate: An Introduction to American Politics.* Boston: Houghton Mifflin.
MONTESQUIEU, BARON DE. [1748] 1886. *The Spirit of Laws.* Trans. Thomas Nugent. Cincinnati: Robert Clarke.
MOORE, R. H., JR. 1996. "Islamic Legal Systems: Traditional (Saudi Arabia), Contemporary (Bahrain), and Evolving (Pakistan)." In *Comparative Criminal Justice: Traditional and Nontraditional; Systems of Law and Control.* Eds. C. B. Fields and R. H. Moore, Jr. Prospect Heights, IL: Waveland Press.
MORIYAMA, T. 1997. "Japan." In *World Factbook of Criminal Justice Systems.* Eds. G. Newman, A. C. Bouloukos, and D. Cohen. http://www.ojp.usdoj.gov/pub/bjs/ascii/wfbcjjap.txt.
NAACP Legal Defense Fund. 1996. *Death Row U.S.A. Reporter Current Service.* Buffalo, NY: Williams Hein.
NADER, L., and H. F. TODD, JR. 1978. *Introduction in the Dispute Process—Law in Ten Societies.* New York: Columbia University Press.
NELSON, R., and J. SHELEY. 1985. "Bureau of Indian Affairs Influence on Indian Self-Determination." In *American Indian Policy in the Twentieth Century.* Ed. V. Deloria, Jr. Norman: University of Oklahoma Press, pp. 177–196.
NEUFELDT, V., ed. 1995. *Webster's New World College Dictionary.* New York: Macmillan.
OTTEN, L. A. 1993. *Women's Rights and the Law.* Westport, CT: Praeger.
PARSONS, T. [1962] 1980. "The Law and Social Control." In *The Sociology of Law: A Social-Structural Perspective.* Ed. W. M. Evan. New York: Free Press.
POLLOCK, E. J., and S. A. ADLER. 1992, May 8. "Justice for All? Legal System Struggles to Reflect Diversity, but Progress Is Slow." *Wall Street Journal.*
POUND, R. 1959. *Jurisprudence,* Volumes I–IV. St. Paul, MN: West Publishing.
PREJEAN, H. 1993. *Dead Man Walking: An Eyewitness Account of the Death Penalty in the United States.* New York: Random House.
PRYGOSKI, P. J. 1995. *From Marshall to Marshall: The Supreme Court's Changing Stance on Tribal Sovereignty.* Chicago: American Bar Association. www.abanet.org/genpractice/compleat/f95marshall.html.
REICHEL, P. L. 1994. *Comparative Criminal Justice Systems: A Topical Approach.* Upper Saddle River, NJ: Prentice Hall.

REMBAR, C. 1980. *The Law of the Land: The Evolution of Our Legal System.* New York: Simon and Schuster.

ROBINSON, P. H. 1988. *Fundamentals of Criminal Law.* Boston: Little, Brown.

ROSSIDES, D. W. 1997. *Social Stratification: The Interplay of Class, Race and Gender,* 2nd ed. Upper Saddle River, NJ: Prentice Hall.

ROTHENBERG, P. 1988. *Racism and Sexism: An Integrated Study.* New York: St. Martin's Press.

RUSH, G. E. 1994. *The Dictionary of Criminal Justice,* 4th ed. Guilford, CT: Dushkin Publishing.

RYAN, T. P. (ed.) 1997, Spring 1 and 4–11. "The Death Penalty: A Scholarly Forum." *Focus on Law Studies* 12, (2).

SCHUR, E. M. 1968. *Law and Society.* New York: Random House.

SELZNICK, P. 1968. "Law: The Sociology of Law." *International Encyclopedia of the Social Sciences* (9): 50–59.

———. 1961. "Sociology and Natural Law," *Natural Law Forum* 6: 84–108.

SIDGWICK, H. 1874. *The Methods of Ethics.* London: McMillan and Company.

SMALL, A. W. 1924/1967. *Origins of Sociology, 1854–1926.* Chicago: University of Chicago Press.

SMITH, D. A., C. A. VISHER, and L. A. DAVIDSON. 1984. "Equity and Discretionary Justice: The Influence of Race on Police Arrest Decisions." *Journal of Criminal Law and Criminology* 75, 234–249.

SOURYAL, S. S., A. I. ALOBIED, and D. W. POTTS. 1996. "The Penalty of Hand Amputation for Theft in Islamic Justice." In *Comparative Criminal Justice: Traditional and Nontraditional; Systems of Law and Control.* Eds. C. B. Fields and R. H. Moore, Jr. Prospect Heights, IL: Waveland Press.

SPICER, E. H. 1983. *A Short History of the Indians of the United States.* Malabar, FL: Krieger Publishing Company.

STIMPSON, J., and A. STIMPSON. 1987. *Sociology: Contemporary Readings,* 2nd ed. Itasca, MN: F. E. Peacock.

SUMNER, W. G. 1906. *Folkways.* Boston: Ginn.

SUTHERLAND, E. 1939. *Principles of Criminology,* 3rd ed. Philadelphia: Lippincott.

TERRILL, R. J. 1997. *World Criminal Justice Systems: A Survey,* 3rd ed. Cincinnati, OH: Anderson Publishing.

TRUBEK, D. M. 1989, January. "Where the Action Is: CLS and Empiricism." *Stanford Law Review* 37, (1&2), 575–622.

———, and J. ESSER. 1989. "Critical Empiricism in American Legal Studies: Paradox, Program or Pandora's Box?" *Law and Social Inquiry* 14 (1), 3–52.

UNGER, R. M. 1986. *The Critical Legal Studies Movement.* Cambridge, MA: Harvard University Press.

U.S. Department of Justice, Bureau of Justice Statistics. 1994. *Pretrial Release of Felony Defendants, 1992.* Bulletin NCJ-148818, p. 4, Table 18. Washington, DC: U.S. Department of Justice.

U.S. Department of Justice, Bureau of Justice Statistics. 1990. *The Prosecution of Felony Arrests.* Washington, DC: U.S. Government Printing Office.

U.S. Judge Advocate General. 2000. *The Uniform Code of Military Justice.* 10 Dec: http://jaglink.jaj.af.mil.

VAGO, S. 2000. *Law and Society,* 6th ed. Upper Saddle River, NJ: Prentice Hall.

———. 1997. *Law and Society,* 5th ed. Upper Saddle River, NJ: Prentice Hall.

———. 1994. *Law and Society,* 4th ed. Upper Saddle River, NJ: Prentice Hall.

VINJE, D. L. 1985. "Cultural Values and Economic Development on Reservations." In *American Indian Policy in the Twentieth Century.* Ed. V. Deloria, Jr. Norman: University of Oklahoma Press, pp. 155–175.

WEBER, M. 1992. *Essays in Sociology.* New York: Oxford University Press.

———. [1914] 1954. *Law in Economy and Society.* Ed. M. Rheinstein. Trans. E. Shels and M. Rheinstein. Cambridge, MA: Harvard University Press.

WEINBERG, L. S., and J. W. WEINBERG. 1980. *Law and Society: An Interdisciplinary Introduction.* Washington, DC: University Press of America.

WELTER, B. 1966. "The Cult of True Womanhood, 1820–1860." *American Quarterly* 18, 151–174.

WINCHESTER, S. 1999. *The Professor and the Madman.* New York: Harper Perennial.

WOLFSON, H. 2000. "Tribe Pushes for Nuclear Dump Despite Opposition." *Los Angeles Times.* 10 December: A44+.

Index